CASEBOOK SERIES

PUBLISHED

Jane Austen: *Emma* DAVID LODGE
Jane Austen: *'Northanger Abbey' and 'Persuasion'* B. C. SOUTHAM
Jane Austen: *'Sense and Sensibility', 'Pride and Prejudice' and 'Mansfield Park'*
B. C. SOUTHAM
William Blake: *Songs of Innocence and Experience* MARGARET BOTTRALL
Charlotte Brontë: *'Jane Eyre' and 'Villette'* MIRIAM ALLOTT
Emily Brontë: *Wuthering Heights* MIRIAM ALLOTT
Browning: *'Men and Women' and Other Poems* J. R. WATSON
Bunyan: *The Pilgrim's Progress* ROGER SHARROCK
Byron: *'Childe Harold's Pilgrimage' and 'Don Juan'* JOHN JUMP
Chaucer: *Canterbury Tales* J. J. ANDERSON
Coleridge: *'The Ancient Mariner' and Other Poems* ALUN R. JONES AND
WILLIAM TYDEMAN
Conrad: *The Secret Agent* IAN WATT
Dickens: *Bleak House* A. E. DYSON
Dickens: *'Hard Times', 'Great Expectations' and 'Our Mutual Friend'* NORMAN
PAGE
Donne: *Songs and Sonets* JULIAN LOVELOCK
George Eliot: *Middlemarch* PATRICK SWINDEN
George Eliot: *'The Mill on the Floss' and 'Silas Marner'* R. P. DRAPER
T. S. Eliot: *Four Quartets* BERNARD BERGONZI
T. S. Eliot: *'Prufrock', 'Gerontion', 'Ash Wednesday' and Other Shorter Poems* B. C.
SOUTHAM
T. S. Eliot: *The Waste Land* C. B. COX AND ARNOLD P. HINCHLIFFE
Farquhar: *'The Recruiting Officer' and 'The Beaux' Stratagem'* RAYMOND A.
ANSELMENT
Henry Fielding: *Tom Jones* NEIL COMPTON
E. M. Forster: *A Passage to India* MALCOLM BRADBURY
Hardy: *The Tragic Novels* R. P. DRAPER
Hardy: *Poems* JAMES GIBSON AND TREVOR JOHNSON
Gerard Manley Hopkins: *Poems* MARGARET BOTTRALL
Jonson: *Volpone* JONAS A. BARISH
Jonson: *'Every Man in His Humour' and 'The Alchemist'* R. V. HOLDSWORTH
James Joyce: *'Dubliners' and 'A Portrait of the Artist as a Young Man'* MORRIS
BEJA
John Keats: *Odes* G. S. FRASER
D. H. Lawrence: *Sons and Lovers* GĀMINI SALGĀDO
D. H. Lawrence: *'The Rainbow' and 'Women in Love'* COLIN CLARKE
Marlowe: *Doctor Faustus* JOHN JUMP
The Metaphysical Poets GERALD HAMMOND
Milton: *'Comus' and 'Samson Agonistes'* JULIAN LOVELOCK
Milton: *Paradise Lost* A. E. DYSON AND JULIAN LOVELOCK
John Osborne: *Look Back in Anger* JOHN RUSSELL TAYLOR
Peacock: *The Satirical Novels* LORNA SAGE
Pope: *The Rape of the Lock* JOHN DIXON HUNT
Shakespeare: *Antony and Cleopatra* JOHN RUSSELL BROWN
Shakespeare: *Coriolanus* B. A. BROCKMAN
Shakespeare: *Hamlet* JOHN JUMP
Shakespeare: *Henry IV Parts I and II* (

D1322391

Shakespeare

Much Ado About Nothing
and
As You Like It

A CASEBOOK

EDITED BY

JOHN RUSSELL BROWN

First published 1979 by
THE MACMILLAN PRESS LTD
London and Basingstoke
Associated companies in Delhi Dublin
Hong Kong Johannesburg Lagos Melbourne
New York Singapore and Tokyo

Printed in Great Britain by
J. W. Arrowsmith Ltd., Bristol

British Library Cataloguing in Publication Data

Shakespeare 'Much ado about nothing' and
  'As you like it'. – (Casebook series).
  1. Shakespeare, William. As you like it
  2. Shakespeare, William. Much ado about nothing
  I. Brown, John Russell   II. Series
  822.3′3   PR2803

  ISBN 0–333–19420–9
       0–333–19421–7

CONTENTS

ACKNOWLEDGEMENTS

The editor and publisher wish to thank the following, who have kindly given permission for the use of copyright material: Anonymous review ('H.G.') of Nigel Playfair's production of *As You Like It* at the Shakespeare Memorial Theatre, *Manchester Guardian*, 23rd April 1919, by permission of Guardian Newspapers Limited; Anonymous review of a production of *As You Like It* at the Old Vic, *Sunday Pictorial*, 15th November 1936, by permission of International Publishing Corporation; Anonymous review of a production of *As You Like It* at the New Theatre, *The Times*, 12th February 1937, by permission of Times Newspapers Limited; Anonymous review of an All-Male *As You Like It*, *Sunday Telegraph*, 8th October 1967, by permission of the Daily Telegraph Limited; James Agate, extract from a review of *Much Ado About Nothing* at the Old Vic Theatre from the *Sunday Times*, 21st March 1931, by permission of George G. Harrap & Company Limited; John Barber, review 'A Young Company at the Royal Shakespeare Theatre' from the *Daily Telegraph*, 15th October 1968, by permission of the Daily Telegraph Ltd.; Sylvan Barnet, an essay 'Strange Events' from *Shakespeare Studies*, vol. 4 (1968), by permission of Burt Franklin & Company Inc.; Michael Billington, a review of John Barton's production at the Aldwych Theatre from the *Guardian*, 1st July 1977, by permission of Guardian Newspapers Limited; John Russell Brown, extracts from essay 'The Presentation of Comedy' from *Shakespearean Comedy*, by permission of Edward Arnold (Publishers) Ltd.; Ruth Ellis, review of *Much Ado About Nothing* John Gielgud's production at the Shakespeare Memorial Theatre from *Stratford-upon-Avon Herald* by permission of the proprietors; Barbara Everett, an essay 'Much Ado About Nothing' from *Critical Quarterly*, vol. III (1961) by permission of the author; Helen Gardner, essay on *As You Like It* from *More Talking of Shakespeare*, ed. John Garrett (1959), by permission of Longman Group Limited; Sherman Hawkins, extract from an essay 'The Two Worlds of Shakespearean Comedy' from *Shakespeare Studies*, vol. 3 (1967), by permission of Burt Franklin & Company Inc.; J. W. Lambert, review of Royal Shakespeare production of *As You Like It* from the *Sunday Times*, 9th July 1961, by permission of Times Newspapers Ltd.; Agnes Latham, extract from the Introduction to *As You Like It* in the *Arden Shakespeare Series*, published by Methuen & Company Limited; Paul and Miriam Mueschke, an essay 'Illusion and Metamorphosis' from *Shakespeare Quarterly*, 1967, by permission of the Folger Shakespeare Library; J. R. Mulryne, extract from his *Shakespeare: Much Ado About Nothing* (Studies in English Literature) by permission of Edward Arnold (Publishers) Ltd.; D. J. Palmer, essay on ' "As You Like It" and the Idea of Play' from *Critical Quarterly*, vol. XIII (1971), by permission of the author; Rosemary Anne Sisson, extract from review of Glen Byam Shaw's production of *As You Like It* from *Stratford-upon-Avon Herald*, 5th April 1957, by permission of the proprietors; Donald A. Stauffer, extract from *Shakespeare's World of Images: The Development of His Moral Ideas*, reprinted by permission of W. W. Norton & Company, Inc., Copyright 1949, and renewed 1977 by Ruth Stauffer; Peter Thompson, extract from article in *Shakespeare Survey*, XXVII (1974), by permission of Cambridge University Press; B. A. Young, extracts from reviews of Trevor Nunn's musical production of *As You Like It* at the Royal Shakespeare Theatre from *Financial Times*, 8 September 1977, and 'The National Theatre's Italianate "Much Ado About Nothing" ' from *Financial Times*, 17th February 1965, by permission of the Financial Times Ltd.; David Young, extract from *The Heart's Forest: A Study of Shakespeare's Pastoral Plays*, by permission of Yale University Press.

GENERAL EDITOR'S PREFACE

The Casebook series, launched in 1968, has become a well-regarded library of critical studies. The central concern of the series remains the 'single-author' volume, but suggestions from the academic community have led to an extension of the original plan, to include occasional volumes on such general themes as literary 'schools' and genres.

Each volume in the central category deals either with one well-known and influential work by an individual author, or with closely related works by one writer. The main section consists of critical readings, mostly modern, collected from books and journals. A selection of reviews and comments by the author's contemporaries is also included, and sometimes comment from the author himself. The Editor's introduction charts the reputation of the work or works from the first appearance to the present time.

Volumes in the 'general themes' category are variable in structure but follow the basic purpose of the series in presenting an integrated selection of readings, with an Introduction which explores the theme and discusses the literary and critical issues involved.

A single volume can represent no more than a small selection of critical opinions. Some critics are excluded for reasons of space, and it is hoped that readers will pursue the suggestions for further reading in the Select Bibliography. Other contributions are severed from their original context, to which some readers may wish to turn. Indeed, if they take a hint from the critics represented here, they certainly will.

A. E. DYSON

INTRODUCTION

Shakespeare's most memorable and most penetrating plays are the great tragedies, but his comedies have always been able to fill theatres with delighted audiences. In a poem written for the posthumous edition of his fellow–dramatist's plays, Ben Jonson reserved his last praise for the comedies and dismissed all rivals in excellence, both ancient and modern. In 1765, in the Preface to his edition of the complete plays, Samuel Johnson affirmed that Shakespeare's imagination enjoyed its fullest freedom in comedy:

In tragedy he often writes, with great appearance of toil and study, what is written at last with little felicity; but, in his comic scenes, he seems to produce, without labour, what no labour can improve. In tragedy he is always struggling after some occasion to be comic; but in comedy he seems to repose, or to luxuriate, as in a mode of thinking congenial to his nature. In his tragic scenes there is always something wanting, but his comedy often surpasses expectation or desire.

Not everyone would agree with this humane and original critic, but his judgement, quoted at greater length in Part One of this selection, repays close attention, and so does the enconium of the other Jonson, Shakespeare's contemporary, which is also reprinted.

The achievement of Shakespeare's comedies is unquestionable, even while the satisfaction that they give is difficult to explain and hard to capture in apt phrases or comprehensive critical categories. These are plays that show their true natures most freely in performance. They were written to be heard and seen. The value of a joke, the lyric beauty of a phrase, the evocation of strange, fabulous worlds, the sense of mutual celebration, the transformation of everyday affairs so that they are heightened and quickened by unusual sensibility and glancing brilliance of wit, the intimacy of understanding and the unveiling of deep, instinctive feelings—can all, in performance, come alive in the mind with the greatest ease and seem like the fulfillment of the audience's own various and private dreams.

Such instinctive pleasures are the liveliest gift of the comedies, but we cannot always see performances and there are further pleasures to be gained by more methodical and careful study. A bird on the wing gives a quick delight but it will hold more fascination for us if we know its genus and variety, its habitat and habits, its physical details and differing cries, and so the comedies, that are designed to be free in the air of performance, can also be studied with advantage, and our enjoyment of them thus extended and sharpened.

This Casebook is a collection of writings that will help the reader to appreciate the mercurial comedies. It focuses especially on two plays, *Much Ado About Nothing* and *As You Like It*, which represent Shakespeare at the height of his comic powers. His very first play was probably *The Comedy of Errors* and certainly he continued in this vein until, between 1595 and 1600, comedies outnumbered all his other products. *Much Ado* was written and first performed between 1598 and 1600, and *As You Like It* between 1599 and 1600. Together they encompass a wide range of Shakespeare's comic imagination at its most fruitful period.

Much Ado, the earlier play, presents a family and its dependents at a time when ordinary affairs are enlivened by the return of soldiers who have defeated a civil uprising with an absolute minimum of bloodshed. This comedy is busy with a sense of occasion and much domestic activity. Preparations for a 'great supper' are put in hand at once, and there are two masquerades, several practical jokes (and some unintentional ones) that involve pretence and over-hearing, a trial of two 'suspicious persons', a wedding ceremony, a challenge to a duel and a memorial service for a young girl believed to be recently 'slain' by slander.

In contrast, *As You Like It* is fantastic, set in a pastoral world of fanciful shepherds and shepherdesses where a Duke who has lost all his possessions spends the time 'carelessly' and lives 'like the old Robin Hood of England'. This comedy is enlivened by sex-disguise and idle fun; its last scene is visited by the god Hymen who materialises without explanation.

Yet the two comedies, one grounded in realistic behaviour and business and the other almost free of such restrictions, illuminate each other in sharing certain sentiments, theatrical devices and ideas, and a concern with youthful love. Both end, not in speech-making or individual action, but in a dance for the whole company that remains on stage.

For many, many years these two plays and others like them were praised in general terms, rather than criticised with helpful precision. They were said to be 'gay', 'happy', 'merry', 'improbable', 'wild and fantastic', 'lyrical', 'ridiculous', 'elegant', 'exquisite'. Those critics who considered them at any length in the eighteenth and nineteenth centuries were content to elucidate the plots and notice the subtlety of a few characters whose soliloquies, set-speeches or sustained debates cause them to stand out in crowded and quick-moving comedy. So the character of Jaques in *As You Like It*, who self-consciously delivers his judgements on other characters and on the 'seven ages of man', was the subject of a philosophising essay by William Richardson, Professor of Humanity in the University of Glasgow. This is one of a collection of similar studies in his *Shakespeare's Dramatic Characters* which was first published in 1774 and reprinted several times. In the nineteenth century, Benedick and Beatrice were similarly plucked out from *Much Ado About Nothing* so that their psychological and moral natures could be fully discussed. These were 'problem characters' whose aggressive speeches and rapid changes of mood invited debate and whose verbal energy could be appraised out of context as 'conceited' wit. They were said to be in the same tradition as the characters of Molière, and Shakespeare's achievement was compared with his and with the work of later writers of English 'comedies of manners'. Shortly afterwards Hero and Claudio, the other pair of lovers in *Much Ado*, raised more critical debate, not because their words demand attention but because their motives are not entirely clear and their actions raise moral issues. At the end of the nineteenth century, Georg Brandes's account of their contribution to the comedy exposed further problems of structure, style, irony, theme and corporate effect which were to become the chief subjects of critical debate from the 1930s onwards.

The structure of the comedies, the interactions of their various stories and the shifts of mood and understanding, have for the last fifty years been the chief subject of critical investigation. John Palmer's *Comic Characters of Shakespeare* (1946) was one of the last of a long line of individual character studies, and most critics thereafter concentrated upon dramatic form. H. B. Charlton's *Shakespearian Comedy* (1938) did most to establish the new approach. Other writers had dissociated Shakespeare's practice from 'Aristotelian' comedy that was supposed to show the comic enormities of vicious and foolish characters, but Professor Charlton offered the most thorough examination of how individual comedies were indebted to classical, Italian and English predecessors and so was able to formulate Shakespeare's intentions with greater sensitivity. Several more broadly based studies had been influential and they exemplify the range of the new research: W. W. Greg's *Pastoral Poetry and Pastoral Drama* (1906), Kathleen Lea's *Italian Popular Comedy* (1934), Enid Welsford's *The Fool: His Social and Literary History* (1935) and, for folk rituals and dramas, Janet Spens's *Essay on Shakespeare's Relation to Tradition* (1916). A narrower search for those books which Shakespeare had consulted as sources for individual comedies also contributed to an understanding of their origins and the expectations of Elizabethan audiences. It soon became an established fact that, despite a considerable and affectionate knowledge of earlier comedies, Shakespeare had written a series for which no single model had served or curtailed his own invention. M. T. Herrick's *Comic Theory in the Sixteenth Century* (1950) and Madeleine Doran's *Endeavors of Art: A Study of Form in Elizabethan Drama* (1954) both offered renaissance critical concepts with which to appraise Shakespeare's highly individual experiments.

Structural criticism is still pursued very actively today. Romantic and mythological origins have been most stressed in recent years following the lead of Northrop Frye's 'The Argument of Comedy', published in *The English Institute Essays* of 1948. Professor Frye proceeded to further and more elaborate studies of which *A Natural Perspective: The Development of Shakespearean Comedy and Romance* (1965) has been the most influential. Chapter-headings in this book indicate his handling of the comedies to stress their magical, irrational, celebratory, optimistic and folk elements: 'Mouldy Tales', 'Making Nature Afraid', 'The Triumph of Time', 'The Return from the Sea'. C. L. Barber's *Shakespeare's Festive Comedy: A Study of Dramatic Form and its Relation to Social Custom* (1959) is in the same line as Frye's work but also develops the sociological aspects of Enid Welsford's earlier book on the Fool. Professor Barber restricted his attention to only five comedies, *As You Like It* being among them but not *Much Ado*. David Young's *The Heart's Forest: A Study of Shakespeare's Pastoral Plays* (1972) is also especially valuable for *As You Like It*, while C. T. Prouty's *The Sources of 'Much Ado'* (1950) is an excellent introduction to the origins of that play. Further accounts of the sources of both plays are by Kenneth Muir and Geoffrey Bullough who take note of all the latest discoveries. The widest and most thorough of recent structural studies is Leo Salingar's *Shakespeare and the Traditions of Comedy* (1974).

Almost every writer on the comedies has been influenced by this main line of research and criticism, but some other approaches are distinguishable. The editor of this anthology published *Shakespeare and His Comedies* in 1957 which applied to these plays that close analysis of visual and verbal imagery and of reiterated words that had proved its usefulness in earlier considerations of the tragedies by L. C. Knights, Wilson Knight, D. A. Traversi and many others. This was the first book on the comedies to seek out their general 'themes' and, in the absence of an explicit judgement in the texts on their characters and actions, to attempt to define their implicit judgements. Some critics maintained that this was too solemn a method for plays whose end is mirth and pleasure, and Alexander Leggatt's *Shakespeare's Comedy of Love* (1974) was written in conscious reaction to what he dubs 'theme-hunting'. Professor Leggatt is content to notice the craftsmanship and cunning with which the plays have been written. Such a book is in the tradition of Bertrand Evans's *Shakespeare's Comedies* (1960) that had painstakingly enumerated the differing 'awareness' that Shakespeare had given to each of his characters as a play progressed. This sounds over serious, in another way, but a close encounter with one aspect of Shakespeare's technical cunning provided a means of illuminating his humane and subtle understanding of characters in action. Brian Vickers's *The Artistry of Shakespeare's Prose* (1968) and the present editor's *Shakespeare's Dramatic Style* (1970) also function in much the same way, leading to a fuller appreciation of the active minds that motivate the individual characters. M. C. Bradbrook's *Shakespeare and Elizabethan Poetry* (1951) is an important revaluation of the wit and courtliness of the comedies, a book in some respects complemented by D. L. Stevenson's *The Love-Game Comedy* (1946).

Perhaps these technical studies are the more welcome because they are concerned with the moment-to-moment of life of the plays and so off-set the more general and comprehensive appreciation that is derived from structural analysis and the tracing of sources and influences.

Certainly in the theatre, in performance, as far as press criticism can witness, it is an impression of lively, fascinating and, sometimes, bewildering individual characters that stays in the mind and continues to draw delighted audiences. The extraordinary hospitality of these plays to the varying talents of each generation of actors and actresses—and more recently to the personal interests of directors—has been proved again and again. For this reason, this anthology of criticism closes with a collection of reviews relating to productions that have caught more than usual attention. They are direct reminders of the spark and enchantment of these plays which may be missed while following the discourse of scholar or critic. By describing the settings which are used for modern staging, the reviews also indicate tones, rhythms and social references which actors have found helpful to their enactment of the texts.

The main section (Part Two) of this Casebook reprints extended critical studies written since 1939. First are two structural studies on Shakespearean comedy in general. Sherman Hawkins reviews the findings of earlier scholars and offers his own elaboration of Northrop Frye's account of the underlying pattern of the comedies. This is followed by a study of variations in the plays' appeal to audiences which argues that one structural principle of their composition is the provision of a changing presentation of its characters in action.

The first of four studies of *Much Ado About Nothing* is a passage from Donald Stauffer's *Shakespeare's World of Images: The Development of His Moral Ideas* (1949), a book which deduces from recurrent words and ideas the themes which informed Shakespeare's writing. A similar attention is brought by both Barbara Everett and J. R. Mulryne but modified by a further concern for dramatic structure and the effect of the play in performance. Miss Everett considers changing impressions and meanings, changing roles and the changing power and security of each partner in the two pairs of lovers. She concludes with an account of the sense of resolution that the play gives in its last scene. Professor Mulryne gives special attention to the Watchmen, Don John, Don Pedro, Leonato and Antonio, characters that have much to say but do not enter the intimacies of the two love-stories that provide the main plots of the play. He notes also how music, costumes and stage-business contribute to the total effect and how Shakespeare has engineered moments of surprise, near farcical madness or sustained and deliberate verbal elaboration to modify the audience's reception of the play and its main characters.

The concluding study of *Much Ado* addresses itself to a very old problem that arises whenever Shakespeare's purposes are debated: the reason why he yoked together in one play two pairs of lovers who are so very different from each other, as much in the course of their wooing as in their abilities to respond to each other and to voice their thoughts and feelings. This question has attracted attention because the balance of our emotional and imaginative responses is challenged by Shakespeare's choice in this matter. Paul and Miriam Mueschke advance a highly detailed argument which has to be followed slowly and carefully with close reference to the text of the play if its full strength is to be appreciated. It recommends an unambiguous answer to the problem, but its chief merit is not the advocacy of one solution. It is an important essay because it demonstrates the very fine, subtle and deep thought that has gone into the writing of this comedy which sparkles with such apparently spontaneous ease.

The section on *As You Like It* is headed by Dame Helen Gardner's masterly account of the interaction of all its many strands of action. The essay is justly famous and demonstrates how well our understanding of Shakespeare's comedies can be enriched by a study of its origins and structure when such research is accompanied by a ready response to the creation of character. Dame Helen also touches lightly on the main themes of the play and in doing so notes a likeness to some central scenes in *The Tragedy of King Lear*.

Two contributions consider special aspects of the play's background. David Young's account of pastoral conventions sets

its scene and helps to identify mood and tone; it also illustrates
Shakespeare's highly individual approach to theatrical convention. A passage from Agnes Latham's introduction to her new
Arden Edition of the play (1975) considers four characters that
are especially indebted to dramatic conventions: they are
satirists, clowns and fools, each with long and distinct pedigrees
and possibly some real-life progenitors.

Two further studies of *As You Like It* are thematic, but not in
the narrow way that pursues the verbal statements of certain
ideas or the repetition of key images. David Palmer examines the
playfulness of the comedy, how it exploits a freedom from usual
behaviour and ordinary order, together with the release of
hidden psychological truth through fantasy and excitement.
Sylvan Barnet is concerned with Shakespeare's handling of plot
and incident. After Act ii Scene iii, *As You Like It* has little in the
way of narrative, being more a sequence of incidents than a story
or concerted intrigue; but the whole play is cramful of improbabilities, strange twists of intention and odd coincidences, and it is
Shakespeare's handling of these that Professor Barnet examines.
He shows how this is in accord with his treatment of some
recurring ideas.

The articles and chapters from books chosen for inclusion in this
anthology represent the most prominent forms of criticism that
are now current. They also afford a basis for further exploration
by providing relevant facts, critical concepts and opinions, by
showing how to analyse language and stage action, by raising
suggestive questions and by making apt comparisons. None of the
critics writes with Shakespeare's wit and authority but sometimes
the most sober critic can lighten our laughter or the most
ingenious deepen our sense of romantic feeling. The very variety
of engagement in this book may encourage the reader to be more
free in his own pursuit of enjoyment in the comedies. Rosaline
reminds Berowne at the end of *Love's Labour's Lost* that

> A jest's prosperity lies in the ear
> Of him that hears it, never in the tongue
> Of him that makes it.

This is equally true of Shakespeare's comedies. An active, varied and exploratory response pays rich dividends in the increase of pleasure.

NOTE ON TEXTS

Much Ado About Nothing was first published in 1600 in a Quarto edition. Scholars believe that this was printed from a manuscript in Shakespeare's own handwriting. The play was included in the 1623 Folio edition of the complete plays, printed from a copy of the Quarto with some minor editorial changes. All modern texts derive from the Quarto.

As You Like It was first published in the Folio of 1623. This was probably printed from a carefully prepared prompt-book, or transcription of one. This is the sole authority for all modern editions.

In this Casebook all references to Shakespeare are to the edition of the complete plays by Peter Alexander, first published in 1951.

PART ONE

Comments and Critical Reactions before 1900

Ben Jonson (1623)

          . . . when thy socks were on,[1]
Leave thee alone for the comparison
Of all that insolent Greece or haughty Rome
Sent forth, or since did from their ashes come.
Triumph, my Britain, thou hast one to show,
To whom all scenes of Europe homage owe.
He was not of an age, but for all time!
And all the Muses still were in their prime,
When like Apollo he came forth to warm
Our ears, or like a Mercury to charm.
Nature herself was proud of his designs,
And joyed to wear the dressing of his lines,
Which were so richly spun, and woven so fit,
As since, she will vouchsafe no other wit.
The merry Greek, tart Aristophanes,
Neat Terence, witty Plautus now not please,
But antiquated and deserted lie,
As they were not of Nature's family.
Yet must I not give Nature all: thy art,
My gentle Shakespeare, must enjoy a part;
For though the poet's matter nature be,
His art doth give the fashion; and that he
Who casts to write a living line must sweat—
Such as thine are—and strike the second heat
Upon the Muses' anvil; turn the same,
And himself with it, that he thinks to frame;
Or, for the laurel, he may gain a scorn,
For a good poet's made, as well as born;
And such wert thou. Look how the father's face
Lives in his issue; even so, the race
Of Shakespeare's mind and manners brightly shines
In his well-turned and true-filed lines;
In each of which he seems to shake a lance,
As brandished at the eyes of ignorance.

          SOURCE: lines from 'To the memory of my beloved, the

author, Mr William Shakespeare, and what he hath left us', prefixed to *Mr William Shakespeare's Comedies, Histories and Tragedies* (1623).

NOTE

1. That is, when writing comedies. The *sock* was a light shoe or sandal worn by comic actors on the Greek and Roman stages. The *buskin* was worn in tragedies. [Ed.]

Leonard Digges (1640)

... let but Beatrice
And Benedick be seen, lo in a trice
The Cockpit, galleries, boxes, all are full. ...

SOURCE: lines for a prefatory poem to Shakespeare's *Poems* (1640).

David Erskine Baker (1764)

1 On *Much Ado About Nothing*

... This comedy, tho' not free from faults, has nevertheless numberless beauties in it, nor is there perhaps in any play so pleasing a match of wit and lively repartee as is supported between Benedict [sic] and Beatrice in this, and the contrivance of making them fall in love with one another, who had both equally forsworn that passion, is very ingeniously conducted. . . .

II On *As You Like It*

. . . It is, perhaps, the truest pastoral drama that ever was written; nor is it ever seen without pleasure to all present. In the closet it gives equal delight, from the beauty and simplicity of the poetry. In this play, amongst numberless other beauties, is the celebrated speech on the stages of human life, beginning with, 'All the world's a stage'. . . .

> SOURCE : extracts from *The Companion to the Playhouse* (1764), vol. I, pp. PI and c2.

Samuel Johnson (1765)

. . . Shakespeare's plays are not in the rigorous and critical sense either tragedies or comedies, but compositions of a distinct kind; exhibiting the real state of sublunary nature, which partakes of good and evil, joy and sorrow, mingled with endless variety of proportion and innumerable modes of combination; and expressing the course of the world, in which the loss of one is the gain of another; in which, at the same time, the reveller is hasting to his wine, and the mourner burying his friend; in which the malignity of one is sometimes defeated by the frolic of another; and many mischiefs and many benefits are done and hindered without design.

Out of this chaos of mingled purposes and casualties the ancient poets, according to the laws which custom had prescribed, selected some the crimes of men, and some their absurdities; some the momentous vicissitudes of life, and some the lighter occurrences; some the terrors of distress, and some the gaieties of prosperity. Thus rose the two modes of imitation, known by the names of *tragedy* and *comedy*, compositions intended to promote different ends by contrary means, and considered as so little allied that I do not recollect among the Greeks or Romans a single writer who attempted both.

Shakespeare has united the powers of exciting laughter and sorrow not only in one mind but in one composition. Almost all his plays are divided between serious and ludicrous characters, and, in the successive evolutions of the design, sometimes produce seriousness and sorrow, and sometimes levity and laughter.

That this is a practice contrary to the rules of criticism will be readily allowed; but there is always an appeal open from criticism to nature. The end of writing is to instruct; the end of poetry is to instruct by pleasing. That the mingled drama may convey all the instruction of tragedy or comedy cannot be denied, because it includes both in its alternations of exhibition and approaches nearer than either to the appearance of life, by showing how great machinations and slender designs may promote or obviate one another, and the high and the low cooperate in the general system by unavoidable concatenation.

It is objected that by this change of scenes the passions are interrupted in their progression, and that the principal event, being not advanced by a due gradation of preparatory incidents, wants at last the power to move, which constitutes the perfection of dramatic poetry. This reasoning is so specious that it is received as true even by those who in daily experience feel it to be false. The interchanges of mingled scenes seldom fail to produce the intended vicissitudes of passion. Fiction cannot move so much but that the attention may be easily transferred; and though it must be allowed that pleasing melancholy be sometimes interrupted by unwelcome levity, yet let it be considered likewise that melancholy is often not pleasing, and that the disturbance of one man may be the relief of another; that different auditors have different habitudes; and that, upon the whole, all pleasure consists in variety.

The players, who in their edition divided our author's works into comedies, histories, and tragedies, seem not to have distinguished the three kinds by any very exact or definite ideas.

An action which ended happily to the principal persons,

however serious or distressful through its intermediate incidents, in their opinion constituted a comedy. This idea of a comedy continued long amongst us; and plays were written which, by changing the catastrophe, were tragedies today and comedies tomorrow. . . .

Shakespeare engaged in dramatic poetry with the world open before him; the rules of the ancients were yet known to few; the public judgement was unformed; he had no example of such fame as might force him upon imitation, nor critics of such authority as might restrain his extravagance; he therefore indulged his natural disposition; and his disposition, as Rymer has remarked, led him to comedy. In tragedy he often writes, with great appearance of toil and study, what is written at last with little felicity; but, in his comic scenes, he seems to produce, without labour, what no labour can improve. In tragedy he is always struggling after some occasion to be comic; but in comedy he seems to repose, or to luxuriate, as in a mode of thinking congenial to his nature. In his tragic scenes there is always something wanting, but his comedy often surpasses expectation or desire. His comedy pleases by the thoughts and the language, and his tragedy for the greater part by incident and action. His tragedy seems to be skill, his comedy to be instinct.

The force of his comic scenes has suffered little diminution, from the changes made by a century and a half, in manners or in words. As his personages act upon principles arising from genuine passion, very little modified by particular forms, their pleasures and vexations are communicable to all times and to all places; they are natural, and therefore durable. The adventitious peculiarities of personal habits are only superficial dyes, bright and pleasing for a little while, yet soon fading to a dim tinct, without any remains of former lustre; but the discriminations of true passion are the colours of nature; they pervade the whole mass and can only perish with the body that exhibits them. The accidental compositions of heterogeneous modes are dissolved by the chance which combined them; but the uniform simplicity of primitive qualities neither admits increase nor suffers decay. The sand heaped by one flood is scattered by another, but the rock always continues in its place. The stream of time, which is continually washing the dissoluble fabrics of other poets, passes without injury by the adamant of Shakespeare.

If there be, what I believe there is, in every nation a style which never becomes obsolete, a certain mode of phraseology so consonant and congenial to the analogy and principles of its respective language as to remain settled and unaltered; this style is probably to be sought in the common intercourse of life, among those who speak only to be understood, without ambition of elegance. The polite are always catching modish innovations, and the learned depart from established forms of speech in hope of finding or making better; those who wish for distinction forsake the vulgar, when the vulgar is right; but there is a conversation above grossness and below refinement, where propriety resides, and where this poet seems to have gathered his comic dialogue. He is therefore more agreeable to the ears of the present age than any other author equally remote and among his other excellencies deserves to be studied as one of the original masters of our language. . . .

On *As You Like It*

. . . Of this play the fable is wild and pleasing. I know not how the ladies will approve the facility with which both Rosalind and Celia give away their hearts. To Celia much may be forgiven for the heroism of her friendship. The character of Jaques is natural and well preserved. The comic dialogue is very sprightly, with less mixture of low buffoonery than in some other plays; and the graver part is elegant and harmonious. By hastening to the end of his work, Shakespeare suppressed the dialogue between the usurper and the hermit and lost an opportunity of exhibiting a moral lesson in which he might have found matter worthy of his highest powers.

SOURCE: extract from the Preface and extract from the Notes to Johnson's edition of Shakespeare's *Works* (1765).

William Richardson (1774)

. . . Social disposition produces all those amiable and endearing connections that alleviate the sorrows of human life, adorn our nature, and render us happy. Now Jaques, avoiding society, and burying himself in the lonely forest, seems to act inconsistently with his constitution. He possesses sensibility; sensibility begets affection; and affection begets the love of society. But Jaques is unsocial. Can these inconsistent qualities be reconciled? or has Shakespeare exhibited a character of which the parts are incongruous and discordant? In other words, how happens it that a temper disposed to beneficence, and addicted to social enjoyment, becomes solitary and morose? Changes of this kind are not unfrequent: and, if researches into the origin or cause of a distemper can direct us in the discovery of an antidote, or of a remedy, our present inquiry is of importance. Perhaps, the excess and luxuriancy of benevolent dispositions, blighted by unkindness or ingratitude, is the cause that, instead of yielding us fruits of complacency and friendship, they shed bitter drops of misanthropy . . . .

On comparing the sorrow excited by repulsed and languishing affection, with that arising from the disappointment of selfish appetites, melancholy appears to be the temper produced by the one, misanthropy by the other. Both render us unsocial; but melancholy disposes us to complain, misanthropy to inveigh. The one remonstrates and retires: the other abuses, retires, and still abuses. The one is softened with regret: the other virulent and fierce with rancour. Melancholy is amiable and benevolent, and wishes mankind would reform: misanthropy is malignant, and breathes revenge. The one is an object of compassion; the other of pity.

Though melancholy rules the mind of Jaques, he partakes of the leaven of human nature, and, moved by a sense of injury and disappointment,

> Most invectively he pierceth through
> The body of the country, city, court.

Instigated by sentiments of self-respect, if not of pride, he treats the condition of humanity, and the pursuits of mankind, as insignificant and uncertain. His invectives, therefore, are mingled with contempt, and expressed with humour. At the same time, he shows evident symptoms of a benevolent nature: he is interested in the improvement of mankind, and inveighs, not entirely to indulge resentment, but with a desire to correct their depravity. [Quotes II vii 12–16.]

This mixture of melancholy and misanthropy in the character of Jaques is more agreeable to human nature than the representation of either of the extremes; for a complete misanthrope is as uncommon an object as a man who suffers injury without resentment. Mankind hold a sort of middle rank, and are in general too good for the one, and too bad for the other. As benevolence and sensibility are manifest in the temper of Jaques, we are not offended with his severity. By the oddity of his manner, by the keenness of his remarks, and shrewdness of his observations, while we are instructed, we are also amused. He is precisely what he himself tells us, often wrapped 'in a most humorous sadness.' His sadness, of a mild and gentle nature, recommends him to our regard; his humour amuses. . . .

SOURCE: extracts from *Essays on Some of Shakespeare's Dramatic Characters* (1774; 1798 edition cited), pp. 144–5, 152–5.

William Hazlitt (1817)

1 On *Much Ado About Nothing*

This admirable comedy used to be frequently acted till of late years. Mr Garrick's Benedick was one of his most celebrated characters: and Mrs Jordan, we have understood, played Beatrice very delightfully. The serious part is still the most prominent here, as in other instances that we have noticed. Hero is the principal figure in the piece, and leaves an indelible impression on the mind by her beauty, her tenderness, and the hard trial of her love. The passage in which Claudio first makes a confession of his affection towards her conveys as pleasing an image of the entrance of love into a youthful bosom as can well be imagined. . . . In the scene at the altar, when Claudio, urged on by the villain Don John, brings the charge of incontinence against her, and as it were divorces her in the very marriage-ceremony, her appeals to her own conscious innocence and honour are made with the most affecting simplicity. . . .

The justification of Hero in the end, and her restoration to the confidence and arms of her lover, is brought about by one of those temporary consignments to the grave of which Shakspeare seems to have been fond. He has perhaps explained the theory of this predilection in the following lines:

> FRIAR . . .
>   She dying, as it must be so maintain'd,
>   Upon the instant that she was accus'd,
>   Shall be lamented, pitied, and excus'd
>   Of every hearer: for it so falls out
>   That what we have we prize not to the worth
>   Whiles we enjoy it; but being lack'd and lost,
>   Why, then we rack the value; then we find
>   The virtue that possession would not show us
>   Whiles it was ours. So will it fare with Claudio:
>   When he shall hear she died upon his words,
>   The idea of her life shall sweetly creep
>   Into his study of imagination;
>   And every lovely organ of her life
>   Shall come apparell'd in more precious habit,
>   More moving, delicate, and full of life,
>   Into the eye and prospect of his soul,
>   Than when she liv'd indeed . . .   [IV i 214–30]

The principal comic characters . . . , Benedick and Beatrice, are both essences in their kind. His character as a woman-hater is admirably supported, and his conversion to matrimony is no less happily effected by the pretended story of Beatrice's love for him. It is hard to say which of the two scenes is the best, that of the trick which is thus practised on Benedick, or that in which Beatrice is prevailed on to take pity on him by overhearing her cousin and her maid declare (which they do on purpose) that he is dying of love for her. There is something delightfully picturesque in the manner in which Beatrice is described as coming to hear the plot which is contrived against herself:

> For look where Beatrice, like a lapwing, runs
> Close by the ground, to hear our conference. [III i 24–5]

In consequence of what she hears (not a word of which is true) she exclaims, when these good-natured informants are gone:

> What fire is in mine ears? Can this be true?
>   Stand I condemn'd for pride and scorn so much?
> Contempt, farewell! and maiden pride, adieu!
>   No glory lives behind the back of such.
> And, Benedick, love on, I will requite thee;
>   Taming my wild heart to thy loving hand;
> If thou dost love, my kindness shall incite thee
>   To bind our loves up in a holy band:
> For others say thou dost deserve, and I
>   Believe it better than reportingly. [III i 107–16]

And Benedick, on his part, is equally sincere in his repentance, with equal reason, after he has heard the grey-beard, Leonato, and his friend, 'Monsieur Love', discourse of the desperate state of his supposed inamorata. [II iii] . . .

The beauty of all this arises from the characters of the persons so entrapped. Benedick is a professed and staunch enemy to marriage, and gives very plausible reasons for the faith that is in him. And as to Beatrice, she persecutes him all day with her jests (so that he could hardly think of being troubled with them at night), she turns him and all other things into ridicule, and is proof against everything serious. . . . These were happy materials for Shakspeare to work on, and he has made a happy use of them. Perhaps that middle point of comedy was never more nicely hit in which the ludicrous blends with the tender, and our follies, turning round against themselves in support of our affections, retain nothing but their humanity.

Dogberry and Verges in this play are inimitable specimens of quaint blundering and misprisions of meaning; and are a standing record of that formal gravity of pretension and total want of common understanding, which Shakspeare no doubt copied from real life, and which in the course of two hundred years appear to have ascended from the lowest to the highest offices in the state.

11 On *As You Like It*

Shakspeare has here converted the forest of Arden into another Arcadia, where they 'fleet the time carelessly, as they did in the golden world'. It is the most ideal of any of this author's plays. It is a pastoral drama, in which the interest arises more out of the sentiments and characters than out of the actions or situations. It is not what is done, but what is said, that claims our attention. Nursed in solitude, 'under the shade of melancholy boughs', the imagination grows soft and delicate, and the wit runs riot in idleness, like a spoiled child, that is never sent to school. Caprice and fancy reign and revel here, and stern necessity is banished to the court. The mild sentiments of humanity are strengthened with thought and leisure; the echo of the cares and noise of the world strikes upon the ear of those 'who have felt them knowingly', softened by time and distance. 'They hear the tumult, and are still.' The very air of the place seems to breathe a spirit of philosophical poetry; to stir the thoughts, to touch the heart with pity, as the drowsy forest rustles to the sighing gale. Never was there such beautiful moralising, equally free from pedantry or petulance.

> And this our life, exempt from public haunt,
> Finds tongues in trees, books in the running brooks,
> Sermons in stones, and good in everything. [II i 15–17]

Jaques is the only purely contemplative character in Shakspeare. He thinks, and does nothing. His whole occupation is to amuse his mind, and he is totally regardless of his body and his fortunes. He is the prince of philosophical idlers; his only passion is thought; he sets no value upon anything, but as it serves as food for reflection. He can 'suck melancholy out of a song, as a weasel sucks eggs'; the motley fool, 'who morals on the time', is the greatest prize he meets with in the forest. He resents Orlando's passion for Rosalind as some disparagement of his own passion for abstract truth; and leaves the Duke, as soon as he is restored to his sovereignty, to seek his brother out who has quitted it, and turned hermit.

> . . . Out of these convertites
> There is much matter to be heard and learn'd.
>   [v iv 178–9]

Within the sequestered and romantic glades of the forest of Arden, they find leisure to be good and wise, or to play the fool and fall in love. Rosalind's character is made up of sportive gaiety and natural tenderness; her tongue runs the faster to conceal the pressure at her heart. She talks herself out of breath, only to get deeper in love. The coquetry with which she plays with her lover in the double character which she has to support is managed with the nicest address. How full of voluble, laughing grace is all her conversation with Orlando:

> . . . In heedless mazes running
> With wanton haste and giddy cunning.

How full of real fondness and pretended cruelty is her answer to him when he promises to love her 'For ever and a day!' . . .
   The silent and retired character of Celia is a necessary relief to the provoking loquacity of Rosalind, nor can anything be better conceived or more beautifully described than the mutual affection between the two cousins.

> . . . We still have slept together,
> Rose at an instant, learn'd, play'd, eat together;
> And wheresoe'er we went, like Juno's swans,
> Still we went coupled and inseparable. [1 iii 69–72]

The unrequited love of Silvius for Phebe shows the perversity of this passion in the commonest scenes of life, and the rubs and stops which nature throws in its way, where fortune has placed

none. Touchstone is not in love, but he will have a mistress as a
subject for the exercise of his grotesque humour, and to show his
contempt for the passion, by his indifference about the person. He
is a rare fellow. He is a mixture of the ancient cynic philosopher
with the modern buffoon, and turns folly into wit, and wit into
folly, just as the fit takes him. His courtship of Audrey not only
throws a degree of ridicule upon the state of wedlock itself, but he
is equally an enemy to the prejudices of opinion in other respects.
The lofty tone of enthusiasm, which the Duke and his companions in exile spread over the stillness and solitude of a country
life, receives a pleasant shock from Touchstone's sceptical determination of the question:

> CORIN And how like you this shepherd's life, Master
> Touchstone?
> TOUCH. Truly, shepherd, in respect of itself, it is a good
> life; but in respect that it is a shepherd's life, it is
> naught. In respect that it is solitary, I like it very
> well; but in respect that it is private, it is a very vile
> life. Now in respect it is in the fields, it pleaseth me
> well; but in respect it is not in the court, it is tedious.
> As it is a spare life, look you, it fits my humour well;
> but as there is no more plenty in it, it goes much
> against my stomach. . . . [III i 11–21] . . . .

SOURCE: extracts from *Characters of Shakspeare's Plays*
(1817; third edition, 1838, cited), pp. 274–9, 280–3.

Edward Dowden (1875)

On *As You Like It*

Shakspere[1], when he had completed his English historical plays,
needed rest for his imagination; and in such a mood, craving

refreshment and recreation, he wrote his play of *As You Like It*. To understand the spirit of this play, we must bear in mind that it was written immediately after his great series of histories, ending with *Henry V* (1599), and before he began the great series of tragedies. Shakspere turned with a sense of relief, and a long easeful sigh, from the oppressive subjects of history, so grave, so real, so massive, and found rest and freedom and pleasure in escape from courts and camps to the Forest of Arden:

> Who doth ambition shun,
> And loves to lie i' the sun,
>   . . .
> Come hither, come hither, come hither. [II iv 34–8]

In somewhat the same spirit needing relief for an overstrained imagination he wrote his other pastoral drama, *The Winter's Tale*, immediately or almost immediately after *Timon of Athens*. In each case he chose a graceful story in great part made ready to his hand, from among the prose writings of his contemporaries, Thomas Lodge and Robert Greene. Like the banished Duke, Shakspere himself found the forest life of Arden more sweet than that of painted pomp; a life 'exempt from public haunt', in a quiet retreat, where for turbulent citizens, the deer, 'poor dappled fools', are the only native burghers.

The play has been represented by one of its recent editors as an early attempt made by the poet to control the dark spirit of melancholy in himself 'by thinking it away'. The characters of the banished Duke, of Orlando, of Rosalind, are described as three gradations of cheerfulness in adversity, with Jaques placed over against them in designed contrast.[2] But no real adversity has come to any one of them. Shakspere, when he put into the Duke's mouth the words, 'Sweet are the uses of adversity', knew something of deeper affliction than a life in the golden leisure of Arden. Of real melancholy there is none in the play; for the melancholy of Jaques is not grave and earnest, but sentimental, a self-indulgent humour, a petted foible of character, melancholy prepense and cultivated; 'it is a melancholy of mine own, compounded of many simples, extracted from many objects; and indeed the sundry contemplation of my travels, in which my often rumination wraps me in a most humorous sadness'. The

Duke declares that Jaques has been 'a libertine, as sensual as the brutish sting itself'; but the Duke is unable to understand such a character as that of Jaques. Jaques has been no more than a curious experimenter in libertinism, for the sake of adding an experience of madness and folly to the store of various superficial experiences which constitute his unpractical foolery of wisdom. The haunts of sin have been visited as a part of his travel. By and by he will go to the usurping Duke who has put on a religious life, because

> . . . . Out of these convertites
> There is much matter to be heard and learned.

Jaques died, we know not how, or when, or where; but he came to life again a century later, and appeared in the world as an English clergyman; we need stand in no doubt as to his character, for we all know him under his later name of Lawrence Sterne. Mr Yorick made a mistake about his family tree; he came not out of the play of Hamlet, but out of *As You Like It*. In Arden he wept and moralised over the wounded deer; and at Namport his tears and sentiment gushed forth for the dead donkey. Jaques knows no bonds that unite him to any living thing. He lives upon novel, curious, and delicate sensations. He seeks the delicious *imprévu* so loved and studiously sought for by that perfected French egoist, Henri Beyle. 'A fool! a fool! I met a fool i' the forest!'—and in the delight of coming upon this exquisite surprise, Jaques laughs like chanticleer,

> Sans intermission
> An hour by his dial.

His whole life is unsubstantial and unreal; a curiosity of dainty mockery. To him 'all the world's a stage, and all the men and women merely players'; to him sentiment stands in place of passion; an æsthetic, amateurish experience of various modes of life stands in place of practical wisdom; and words, in place of deeds.

'He fatigues me', wrote our earnest and sensitive Thackeray of the Jaques of English literature, 'with his perpetual disquiet and his uneasy appeals to my risible or sentimental faculties. He is always looking in my face, watching his effect, uncertain whether I think him an impostor or not; posture-making, coaxing, and imploring me. "See what sensibility I have—own now that I'm very clever—do cry now, you can't resist this." ' Yes; for Jaques was at his best in the Forest of Arden, and was a little spoiled by preaching weekly sermons, and by writing so long a caprice as his *Tristram Shandy*. Shakspere has given us just enough of Jaques; and not too much; and in his undogmatic, artistic, tender, playful, and yet earnest manner upon Jaques Shakspere has pronounced judgement. Falstaff supposed that by infinite play of wit, and inexhaustible resource of a genius creative of splendid mendacity, he could coruscate away the facts of life, and always remain master of the situation by giving it a clever turn in the idea, or by playing over it with an arabesque of arch waggery.

> I know thee not, old man; fall to thy prayers;
> How ill white hairs become a fool and jester!
>> [2 *Henry IV*, v v 43–9]

That was the terrible incursion of fact; such words as these, coming from the lips of a man who had an unerring perception, and an unfaltering grasp of the fact, were more than words,— they were a deed, which Falstaff the unsubduable, with all his wit, could not coruscate away. 'By my troth, he'll yield the crow a pudding one of these days; the king has kill'd his heart.' Jaques in his own way supposes that he can dispense with realities. The world, not as it is, but as it mirrors itself in his own mind, which gives to each object a humorous distortion; this is what alone interests Jaques. Shakspere would say to us, 'This egoistic, contemplative, unreal manner of treating life is only a delicate kind of foolery. Real knowledge of life can never be acquired by the curious seeker for experiences.' But this Shakspere says in his non-hortatory, undogmatic way.

Upon the whole, *As You Like It* is the sweetest and happiest of all Shakspere's comedies. No one suffers; no one lives an eager intense life; there is no tragic interest in it as there is in *The Merchant of Venice*, as there is in *Much Ado About Nothing*. It is mirthful, but the mirth is sprightly, graceful, exquisite; there is none of the rollicking fun of a Sir Toby here; the songs are not 'coziers' catches' shouted in the night time, 'without any mitigation or remorse of voice', but the solos and duets of pages in the wild-wood, or the noisier chorus of foresters. The wit of Touchstone is not mere clownage, nor has it any indirect serious significances; it is a dainty kind of absurdity worthy to hold comparison with the melancholy of Jaques. And Orlando in the beauty and strength of early manhood, and Rosalind,

> A gallant curtle-axe upon her thigh,
> A boar-spear in her hand,

and the bright, tender, loyal womanhood within—are figures which quicken and restore our spirits, as music does, which is neither noisy nor superficial, and yet which knows little of the deep passion and sorrow of the world.

Shakspere, when he wrote this idyllic play, was himself in his Forest of Arden. He had ended one great ambition—the historical plays—and not yet commenced his tragedies. It was a resting-place. He sends his imagination into the woods to find repose. Instead of the court and camps of England, and the embattled plains of France, here was this woodland scene, where the palmtree, the lioness, and the serpent are to be found; possessed of a flora and fauna that flourish in spite of physical geographers. There is an open-air feeling throughout the play. The dialogue, as has been observed, catches freedom and freshness from the atmosphere. 'Never is the scene within-doors, except when something discordant is introduced to heighten as it were the harmony.'[3] After the trumpet-tones of *Henry V*, comes the sweet pastoral strain, so bright, so tender. Must it not be all in keeping? Shakspere was not trying to control his melancholy. When he needed to do that, Shakspere confronted his melancholy very passionately, and looked it full in the face. Here he needed refreshment, a sunlight tempered by forest-boughs, a breeze upon his forehead, a stream murmuring in his ears. . . .

SOURCE: extract from *Shakspere: A Critical Study of His Mind and Art* (1875), pp. 76–81.

NOTES

1. Dowden's spelling, Shakspere, is retained here, but his

spelling of Jaques as 'Jacques' has been corrected throughout. [Ed.]
    2. *As You Like It*, edited by the Rev. C. E. Moberly (1872),
pp. 7–9.
    3. C. A. Brown, *Shakespeare's Autobiographical Poems* (1838),
p. 283.

Algernon Charles Swinburne (1880)

On *Much Ado About Nothing*

If it is proverbially impossible to determine by selection the greatest work of Shakespeare, it is easy enough to decide on the date and name of his most perfect comic masterpiece. For absolute power of composition, for faultless balance and blameless rectitude of design, there is unquestionably no creation of his hand that will bear comparison with *Much Ado About Nothing*. The ultimate marriage of Hero and Claudio . . . in itself a doubtfully desirable consummation, makes no flaw in the dramatic perfection of a piece which could not otherwise have been wound up at all. This was its one inevitable conclusion, if the action were not to come to a tragic end; and a tragic end would here have been as painfully and grossly out of place as is any but a tragic end to the action of *Measure for Measure*. As for Beatrice, she is as perfect a lady, though of a far different age and breeding, as Célimène or Millamant; and a decidedly more perfect woman than could properly have trod the stage of Congreve or Molière. She would have disarranged all the dramatic proprieties and harmonies of the one great school of pure comedy. The good fierce outbreak of her high true heart in two swift words—'Kill Claudio'[1]—would have fluttered the dovecotes of fashionable drama to some purpose. But Alceste would have taken her to his own. . . .

SOURCE: *A Study of Shakespeare* (1880), pp. 153–4.

NOTE

1. I remember to have somewhere at some time fallen in with some remark by some commentator to some such effect as this: that it would be somewhat difficult to excuse the unwomanly violence of this demand. Doubtless it would. And doubtless it would be somewhat more than difficult to extenuate the unmaidenly delicacy of Jeanne Darc.

Georg Brandes (1895)

On *Much Ado About Nothing*

Shakespeare has taken the details of his plot from several Italian comedies. . . . Only for a much cruder habit of mind than that which prevails among people of culture in our days can this story provide the motive for a comedy. The very title indicates a point of view quite foreign to us. The implication is that since Hero was innocent, and the accusation a mere slander; since she was not really dead, and the sorrow for her loss was therefore groundless; and since she and Claudio are at last married, as they might have been at first—therefore the whole thing has been much ado about nothing, and resolves itself in a harmony which leaves no discord behind.

The ear of the modern reader is otherwise attuned. He recognises, indeed, that Shakespeare has taken no small pains to make this fable dramatically acceptable. He appreciates the fact that here again, in the person of Don John, the poet has depicted mere unmixed evil, and has disdained to supply a motive for his vile action in any single injury received, or desire unsatisfied. Don John is one of the sour, envious natures which suck poison from all sources, because they suffer from the perpetual sense of being unvalued and despised. He is, for the moment, constrained by the forbearance with which his victorious brother has treated him, but 'if he had his mouth he would bite.' And he does bite,

like the cur and coward he is, and makes himself scarce when his
villainy is about to be discovered. He is an ill-conditioned, base,
and tiresome scoundrel; and, although he conscientiously does
evil for evil's sake, we miss in him all the defiant and brilliantly
sinister qualities which appear later on in Iago and in Edmund.
There is little to object to in Don John's repulsive scoundrelism;
at most we may say that it is a strange motive-power for a
comedy. But to Claudio we cannot reconcile ourselves. He allows
himself to be convinced, by the clumsiest stratagem, that his
young bride, in reality as pure and tender as a flower, is a faithless
creature, who deceives him the very day before her marriage.
Instead of withdrawing in silence, he prefers, like the blockhead
he is, to confront her in the church, before the altar, and in the
hearing of every one overwhelm her with coarse speeches and low
accusations; and he induces his patron, the Prince Don Pedro,
and even the lady's own father, Leonato, to join him in heaping
upon the unhappy bride their idiotic accusations. When, by the
advice of the priest, her relatives have given her out as dead, and
the worthy old Leonato has lied up hill and down dale about her
hapless end, Claudio, who now learns too late that he has been
duped, is at once taken into favour again. Leonato only demands
of him—in accordance with the mediæval fable—that he shall
declare himself willing to marry whatever woman he (Leonato)
shall assign to him. This he promises, without a word or thought
about Hero; whereupon she is placed in his arms. The original
spectators, no doubt, found this solution satisfactory; a modern
audience is exasperated by it, very much as Nora, in [Ibsen's] *A
Doll's House*, is exasperated on finding that Helmer, after the
danger has passed away, regards all that has happened in their
souls as though it had never been, merely because the sky is clear
again. If ever man was unworthy a woman's love, that man is
Claudio. If ever marriage was odious and ill-omened, this is it.
The old taleteller's invention has been too much even for
Shakespeare's art.

When we moderns, however, think of *Much Ado about Nothing*,
it is not this distasteful story that rises before our mind's eye. It is
Benedick and Beatrice, and the intrigue in which they are
involved. The light from these figures, and especially from that
of Beatrice, irradiates the play, and we understand that
Shakespeare was forced to make Claudio so contemptible,

because by that means alone could the enchanting personality of Beatrice shine forth in its fullest splendour.

Beatrice is a great lady of the Renaissance in her early youth, overflowing with spirits and energy, brightly, defiantly virginal, inclined, in the wealth of her daring wit, to a somewhat aggressive raillery, and capable of unabashed freedom of speech, astounding to our modern taste, but permitted by their education to the foremost women of that age. Her behaviour to Benedick, whom she cannot help perpetually twitting and teasing, is as headstrong and refractory as Katharine's treatment of Petruchio. Her diction is marvellous, glittering with unrestrained fantasy. . . . In her battles with Benedick she outdoes him in fantasy, both congruous and incongruous, or burlesque. Here, again, Shakespeare has evidently taken Lyly [1554–1606] as his model, and has tried to reproduce the polished facets of his dialogue, while at the same time correcting its unnaturalness, and giving it fresh life. And Beatrice follows up her victory over Benedick, even when he is no longer her interlocutor, with a freedom which is now-a-days unthinkable in a young girl:

> D. PED. You have put him down, lady; you have put him down.
> BEAT. So I would not he should do me, my lord, lest I should prove the mother of fools. [II i 252–5]

But this unbridled whimsicality conceals the energetic virtues of a firm and noble character. When her poor cousin is falsely accused and cruelly put to shame; when those who should have been her natural protectors fall away from her, and even outside spectators like Benedick waver and lean to the accuser's side; then it is Beatrice alone who, unaffected even for an instant by the slander, indignantly and passionately takes up her cause, and shows herself faithful, high-minded, right-thinking, far-seeing, superior to them all—a pearl of a woman.

By her side Shakespeare has placed Benedick, a Mercutio redivivus; a youth who is the reverse of amatory, opposed to a maiden who is the reverse of tender. He abhors betrothal and marriage quite as vehemently as she, and is, from the man's point of view, no less scornful of all sentimentality than she, from the woman's; so that he and she, from the first, stand on a warlike footing with each other. In virtue of a profound and masterly psychological observation, Shakespeare presently makes these two fall suddenly in love with each other, over head and heels. . . .

SOURCE: extract from Brandes's study of Shakespeare (Copenhagen, 1895), translated by W. Archer *et. al.* as *William Shakespeare: A Critical Study* (1898), pp. 252–6.

PART TWO

Modern Studies

1. SHAKESPEAREAN COMEDY

Sherman Hawkins   The Two Worlds of
Shakespearean Comedy (1967)

The New Criticism has now grown old. Paradoxically, the
criticism that now seems new, with its stress on archetype and
genre, is really older still. It represents a badly needed modern
revision—an archetypal critic might say 'resurrection'—of the
traditional doctrines of imitation and the kinds. The New
Criticism taught us to analyse each literary work in isolation; it
made little distinction between a novel or a play or a poem, and it
was ill equipped to deal with the total corpus of an individual
author, much less with any wider range of works. Generic
criticism, in contrast, analyses individual works as members of
a class: epic, tragedy, lyric, and so on. Archetypal criticism
explores narrative and thematic patterns which unite even these
major divisions, recurring in various genres and different authors. In this essay, I shall outline two basic patterns which seem
to shape Shakespearean comedy; then, more briefly, I shall try to
suggest their archetypal connections with Shakespeare's other
plays and a spectrum of non-Shakespearean works. So described,
the undertaking sounds dry and flat—another exercise in critical
method. I can only attest that the patterns to be described are to
me inherently fascinating and evocative, and that the possibilities
for further application seem real and exciting.

As everyone knows, the choice of genre was a primary and
definitive factor in the Renaissance poet's intention. The Elizabethan concept of genres was flexible and often imprecise, but it
was universally accepted, and grounded in an equally universal
conception of reality. Indeed, I prefer the native and Elizabethan 'kind' to the French 'genre' precisely because the word
points to the naturalness of such formal divisions. Art, we are
assured on good authority, holds the mirror up to 'Kind', to

Nature. God creates in genera and species; so does the poet. As
the natural creation is ordered by the supreme Maker in
hierarchical classes and categories, so the poetic microcosm, the
golden world of art, has its analogous 'chain of being', ranging
from the lofty forms of epic and tragedy down to the lowly farce
and humble epigram, each in its proper style: the high, the
middle, or the low, Decorum, the canon of appropriateness, is the
literary equivalent of natural law, which assigns to every creature
the mode of working proper to its form and end. Distinctions of
genre, then, are natural, not arbitrary. The dictates of decorum
are 'artificial' only in the good Elizabethan sense of artful and
elegant—decorum being, as Milton declares, the grand masterpiece to observe. There is always the danger, of course, that form
may harden into stereotype and decorum may stiffen into rules.
We observe this petrifaction in neoclassic criticism, as the organic
universe of *Paradise Lost* gives way to the cosmic clock, and man
the microcosm becomes *l'homme machine*. But Elizabethan poetic
is still biology rather than physics. Its lively conception of the
kinds is shown by those experiments in grafting and cross
breeding that produce the hybrids listed by Polonius. It demands
a strong and profound understanding of genre, not a weak or
superficial one, to produce the tragical-comical-historical-
pastoral that is *King Lear*. On the other hand, Shakespeare
repeats certain motifs in plays of a given kind with as little
embarrassment as great creating Nature endows man after man
with nose and eyes and mouth, always in the same approximate
relation. Shakespeare, like Nature, is creating one member of a
species; with plays as with men, we need to recognise the general
pattern as well as the individual variations. To know that man is
a featherless biped, omnivorous, rational, and sociable, capable
of laughter, speech, and prayer, helps us distinguish him from a
fish, but it does more than that: these preliminary distinctions are
also final and definitive. So too the basic and recurring patterns
in Shakespeare's plays form part of our final understanding of
them.

    The generic method seems especially promising as an ap-
proach to comedy. For comedy is—next to tragedy and epic—
the most distinctive and conservative of literary kinds. But
Aristotle's treatise on the subject has been lost, and comic theory
remains largely unformulated, leaving the kind of vacuum that

nature and critics both abhor. It is one of Northrop Frye's major
achievements that his investigations of comic form help to
develop a poetics for comedy, and for Shakespearean comedy in
particular.[1] Shakespeare's comedy is seen as a variant of the
comic formula which the English Renaissance inherited from the
New Comedy of Menander, Plautus, and Terence. This traditional comedy dramatises the victory of young lovers over the
opposition of parents and rivals. The hero's opponents, the *senex*
and his allies, are slaves to some form of mental bondage: a ruling
passion or humor, the rigidity of social codes or the tyranny of
wilfulness and personal eccentricity. These figures dominate the
comic society at the beginning of the play, but in the end a new
society forms itself around the hero and his bride. The movement,
then, is from bondage to liberty: 'The normal individual is freed
from the bonds of a humorous society, and a normal society is
freed from the bonds imposed on it by humorous individuals.'
But we should notice (and Frye does not) that, at least in
Shakespearean comedy, this new freedom expresses itself in the
voluntary 'bond' of wedlock.[2] The conflict between the sexual
desires of the individual and the conventions of society is
resolved: society needs the energy of youth for its own renewal
and continuance; the individual seeks the assent of age, which
gives his private wishes the public sanction and stability of social
institution. Comedy is thus a dramatic *rite de passage*, in which the
young assume their proper place in the adult world and society
renews itself through the cycle of the human seasons. The
marriage in which comedy ends is both freedom and bond, the
fulfillment of the individual will and the nexus of a new social
order.

Shakespeare adapts this traditional pattern to what Frye calls
the drama of the green world. The action begins in a 'normal'
world, moves into a 'green' world where the comic resolution is
achieved, and then returns to the normal world (though this
return is often indicated without being acted out). The drama
thus turns on the contrast between two worlds, two orders of
experience, two perspectives on reality. Even the primary,
'normal' world is a heightened and romantic version of the world
we know. The initial action is set in a court or city which is real
but long ago or far away. The ruler of the city is a duke, placing
this romantic comedy midway between the royalty proper to

tragedy and the bourgeoisie proper to satiric comedy like that of
Jonson. The city is conceived as a close-knit community of
families where marriage is a matter of social and even civic
import, where parental will has the force of law, where the duke
himself may be called upon to discipline a rebellious son or
daughter. The hero and heroine are usually of different social or
financial standing. They find themselves opposed by an older
figure who is parent or prince or both, and sometimes by a law
against lovers, as in *A Midsummer Night's Dream*. This opposition,
like the law which embodies it, is felt to be foolish or tyrannical,
but the only way to escape its threat is to leave the old world
altogether. For beyond the walls of cities known at least by name
to the Elizabethans stretches another and magical world: forests
where fairies dance by moonlight, the pastoral landscape where
shepherds woo their loves, the beautiful mountain where is a lady
richly left, awaiting the right hero. This green world takes on
different meanings in the thematic dialectic of each play: it is the
order of grace opposed to the old order of law in *The Merchant of
Venice*, the moonlit world of fancy (in its Elizabethan double
meaning of imagination and desire) opposed to Athens, city of
reason, in *A Midsummer Night's Dream*. But always it is the world
as we wish it were instead of as it is, reality refashioned 'as you like
it'. The hero or heroine must sometimes undergo hardships to
enter the green world, and there he faces ritual trials or tests, but
these serve only to reveal or perfect his essential good nature.
Orlando worries about his lack of gentle breeding, but the tests of
court and forest confirm the strength and kindness that are his by
nature; Bassanio appears to Shylock a younker and a prodigal,
but the casket test reveals the true inner sense of values his
extravagance concealed. In the green world identities are
frequently changed or disguised: Rosalind as Ganymede surren-
ders the gifts of nature, Celia as Aliena those of fortune. Yet in
the end all that was lost is more than restored. The very defects
and dangers of the green world permit us to enjoy its dream-like
reality without losing our intellectual self-respect: we believe in
Arden, as we do not in more perfect Arcadias, because it is winter
there. Our assent is important, for the green world incarnates the
essential optimism of comedy, which makes the happy ending the
only right one. The realism of romantic comedy is a matter of
perspective: it is a 'vision in the form of youth', whose pattern of

trials leading to a happy ending is a myth which all of us believe—so long as we are young.

Frye's green world theory seems to me both true and useful; it isolates a recurring psychological and mythic pattern in Shakespeare's comedies which is clearly deliberate and which helps to account for the perennial fascination of these plays. There is one obvious limitation to the theory, however. It fits only four of the comedies: *Two Gentlemen of Verona*, *A Midsummer Night's Dream*, *The Merchant of Venice*, *As You Like It*. Frye also claims *The Merry Wives of Windsor*, but I hope to show that *Merry Wives* is written in a mixed mode. If we include the late romances, we can add *The Winter's Tale* and *Cymbeline* to our list. But what about the rest of Shakespeare's comedies? Frye has suggested a group of 'sea' comedies, including *The Comedy of Errors*, *Twelfth Night*, *Pericles*, and *The Tempest*, but I do not find this classification helpful or convincing. Is there no other pattern which accounts for all or most of the remaining plays?

Critics ask such questions only when the answer is affirmative. And indeed, it would be surprising if Shakespeare, having constructed half his comedies as variations on a basic pattern, had written all the rest at random. If, on the contrary, he employed another recurring pattern, we might expect it to bear some significant relation of analogy or contrast to the green world motif. What is the essence of that pattern, the basic dramaturgical device? Clearly, the double setting: the whole convention depends on the juxtaposition of two strongly contrasted locales, representing two different orders of reality, and the movement of the action from one to the other. What, then, do we find when we examine the use of setting in the remaining comedies? It strikes us at once that the majority are limited to a single basic locale. The court of Navarre, the streets and homes of Ephesus or Messina, the mansions of Illyria are all essentially single settings. The action may move from one street or dwelling to another, and there may even be significant contrasts between them, as between the court where Navarre and his scholars shut themselves up and the open fields were the Princess of France is lodged. But these places are closely related imaginatively and physically: they belong to the same order of reality, the same 'world'. So in *As You Like It*, there is a contrast between the orchard where we meet Orlando and the palace where we first

see Rosalind. But the usurpation of tyrant brothers in both places
makes us aware of the likeness between court and country: both
exhibit the disorder of an age of iron, contrasted to the magic
forest where courtiers and rustics together fleet the time carelessly
in a golden age. But for Navarre and the Princess, there is no
forest, no green world, no different reality. So too in most of the
remaining comedies. Against the four comedies of the green
world, we can set *The Comedy of Errors, Love's Labours Lost, Much
Ado About Nothing*, and *Twelfth Night*. These belong to what for
the present I shall call the 'alternate pattern', whose distinctive
mark is unity of place. *The Tempest* is a late variation of this
pattern, as *Cymbeline* and *The Winter's Tale* are variations of the
green world formula. The two remaining comedies, *The Merry
Wives* and *The Taming of the Shrew*, are mixed, combining features
of both patterns in their double plots; and I shall use them only
for purposes of illustration.

The unity of place in comedies of the alternate pattern
produces a striking difference in their plot and action. In green
world comedies, the hero and heroine begin by leaving the old
world behind them: whether they are exiled or elope or set off to
seek their fortune, the first phase of the action is an exodus. In the
comedies we are now describing, the characters stay put, but they
are visited by outsiders, who upset the routine of the community
into which they come. These plays begin not with expulsion but
intrusion, not exodus but advent. Thus the King of Navarre at
the beginning of *Love's Labours Lost* receives an untimely visit from
the Princess of France, and *Much Ado* opens with the arrival of
Don Pedro in Messina. The Prince himself is Spanish; Claudio is
Florentine and Benedick a Paduan: all three young men are
aliens, foreigners; and in impact their entrance is more like an
invasion than a homecoming. So in *Twelfth Night*, Viola and
Sebastian, shipwrecked in Illyria, turn Orsino's dukedom upside
down; and Dromio and Antipholus create as great a stir in *Comedy
of Errors* when they land at Ephesus. The mixed comedies,
Taming of the Shrew and *Merry Wives*, employ the same motif.
Falstaff, staying (appropriately) at the Garter Inn, is very much a
fish out of water in the quiet village: 'What tempest, I trow, threw
this whale, with so many tuns of oil in his belly, ashore at
Windsor?'' Petruchio's motives resemble Sir John's: he comes to
wive it wealthily in Padua. Contrasted to these unlikely wooers,

the heroes of the subplots are conventionally romantic, but they too are aliens: Lucentio is Florentine, and Fenton is a courtier, a companion of the wild Prince and Poins: 'He is of too high a region; he knows too much', says Master Page.

In the subplots of these 'mixed' comedies, as in the green world plays, we find the conflict of amorous youth and oppressive age: Fenton and Lucentio must each win his bride against her father's will. There is even an echo of the law against lovers in Baptista's resolution to marry off his elder daughter first. But this is not the source of conflict in the main plot, and in the other comedies no conflict of generations occurs. Fathers, when they appear at all, are sympathetic or even pathetic figures, like Leonato and Aegeon. Indeed, the unreasonable law which normally threatens young lovers is, in *The Comedy of Errors*, turned àgainst their father. But the twins do not even discover their parents till the last scene; they are independent agents, free from all constraint. So Navarre in *Love's Labours Lost* rules his own kingdom, and the Princess' father is an off-stage character whose main function is to die. In Illyria, the young are wholly in control: Orsino is a duke and Olivia a countess; she governs her household as firmly as he his dukedom; Sir Toby and Malvolio are subjects merely.[3] Her dead brother and father have not even (like Portia's cautious parent) left a.will to direct her fancies. In these plays, the young have it all their own way.

In any case, there is little social disparity between the lovers to which a tyrannic father might object. Leonato would gladly marry Hero to a prince, but he is contented with a count; and Beatrice and Benedick, as their friends realise, are destined for each other even by alliteration. The dynastic logic which matches the King of Navarre and the Princess of France is as obvious as the family link which attracts the brother of Antipholus to the sister of Adriana. The social status of Sebastian of Messaline is left ambiguous; his blood is 'right noble', but we do not know whether his son is a fit husband for a countess or his daughter the proper partner for a duke. Though Olivia has resolved not to marry above her station, there seems to be a romantic mingling of classes when Olivia falls in love with a servant and Viola becomes her master's mistress. But the traditional New Comedy *cognito* proves, as usual, that these apparent misalliances are socially acceptable. In these plays generally, the union of the lovers is socially desirable; and age, when it appears at all, acts as the benevolent ally of youth.

The obstacles to love in comedies of this alternate pattern are not external—social convention, favored rivals, disapproving parents. Resistance comes from the lovers themselves. The premise from which the green world comedies begin is sexual attraction: whoever loved that loved not at first sight? The answer is, of course, Benedick and Beatrice. They belong to a different type of comedy, whose premise is sexual antagonism. Instead of the conflict of generations, we watch the war between the sexes. Instead of age versus youth, the dramatic patterning pits male against female. Thus in *Love's Labours Lost* and *Much Ado*, the 'intruders' belong to one sex, the 'natives' to the other; men visit women or women visit men. In *Love's Labours Lost*, as we have seen, this sexual opposition is further emphasised by setting: Navarre has his court, the Princess her tents, and the action consists of raids, sorties, and ambushes between these hostile camps. In *Much Ado*, Don Pedro and his courtiers break in upon the quiet seclusion of Messina, where young women joke and gossip with old men. The aged Leonato, like the effete Boyet, is a being of a middle state, free of both sides, but the advent of a Benedick or Claudio among the ladies produces instant effervescence. The developing action of *Much Ado* sets scenes involving women in contrast and parallel with scenes involving men; attempts to bring the sexes together in a masque or marriage produce comic mistakes or tragic mishaps almost to the end of the play. So in *Twelfth Night*, Orsino's household is set against Olivia's in a kind of amatory stalemate, with a girl in boy's clothing as ambassador and go-between.

Such contrasts of place and character-groupings emphasise sexual oppositions which may take the form of marital conflict, as in *Comedy of Errors* and *Merry Wives*, or of warring lovers, as in *Much Ado*. In the marital comedies, husband and wife attack each other, directly or through a surrogate. Thus Ford incites Falstaff to prove his wife's infidelity and beats him in a woman's form, while Mistress Ford punishes his masculine lust by having him cleansed and beaten and frighted with fairies and hobgoblins. *The Taming of the Shrew* stands midway between these plays about marriage, comedies of experience, where conflict springs from the sexual distaste and disillusionment of middle age, and plays about wooing, comedies of innocence, where the conflict springs from the shyness or hostility of adolescence. Boys go off in one corner, girls in another; the sexes shun or plot against each other. The reluctant bachelor confronts the shrewish spinster, and their witty skirmishes are both flirtation and aggression. Petruchio and Katherina, Berowne and Rosaline, Benedick and Beatrice face each other in a courtship which is part dance, part duel. In *Twelfth Night*, Orsino and Olivia seem as hard to bring together as Cesario and Sir Andrew: they do not even meet till the last scene. One loves, the other mourns, and love and grief are counterpointed throughout the play. But the alliteration of their names points to the likeness in these apparent opposites: the grief of love and love of grief alike betray a certain self-involvement, an emotional solipsism: both Orsino and Olivia are withdrawn into the self-centered privacy of melancholy. These plays reveal a spectrum of sexual hostility and inhibition; in none of them is the force opposed to love social convention or parental tyranny. Love is denied by lovers; husband turns upon wife; youth is divided against itself.

We have seen that in the green world comedies, the social opposition that thwarts young love is sometimes dramatised as an actual law or threat of punishment. In plays of the alternate pattern, the lovers, free from external frustrations and restrictions, proceed to bind themselves with their own wilful bonds. In *Comedy of Errors*, marriage itself has become such a bond: for Antipholus, the ornamental 'chain' which he promises first to his wife and then to a courtesan; for Adriana, the literal bonds in which she binds her errant husband and imprisons him at home. In the comedies of wooing, the bonds are psychological, but they are sometimes objectified as an oath or vow: the law against lovers is replaced by a law against love. So Navarre and his bookmen swear not to see a woman for three long years: Olivia has 'abjured the company and sight of men' to live like a 'cloistress' for seven. Less formally articulated but just as binding is Benedick's determination to die a bachelor. In these vows, as in the attitude that begets them, there is inhibition as well as exclusion, 'shutting in' as well as 'shutting out'. The scholars plan to deny themselves food and sleep; Olivia will 'water once a day her chamber round/With eye-offending brine'. It is as if society's distrust of sexual love and all the energies of appetite and emotion had here become internalised: young men and women turn ascetic, warring against each other, their own affections, the 'huge army of the world's desires'. The father's jealous hostility towards his daughter's wooer has likewise been internalised, transferred to the heroine herself. So Beatrice scoffs at Benedick and Katherina rages against the whole race of men. It needs no Bradley to detect the real interest Beatrice feels for Benedick; no Freud to see that Katherina, jealous of Baptista's fondness for her sister, yearns for someone who will combine the dominating authority of a father with the exclusive absorption of a lover. Their surface aggressions are 'humors', forms of compulsive and irrational behavior which deny and thwart their deepest wishes, their natural selves. In the green world comedies—as in New Comedy generally—the humor characters are the opponents of the hero. In comedies of the alternate pattern, the heroes and heroines themselves sometimes resemble humor characters, imprisoned in their inhibitions and aggressions, isolated by fear or repugnance from the general life, cut off not merely from others whom they ought to love but even from themselves. Their 'laws' are only whims, but to the compulsive personality whims are law: there is no bondage stricter than bondage to the self.

By now it should be clear why these comedies begin with an intrusion into what is in some sense a closed world. The public and social equivalent of the attitudes we have discussed is the law which in *Comedy of Errors* makes it death for anyone from Syracuse to enter Ephesus (or vice versa). A law which thus blocks traffic between these 'adverse towns' is cruel and unnatural, for they are mercantile communities, whose life depends upon the intercourse of trade. Such a law punishes its agents and victims: the Duke of Ephesus, who 'Excludes all pity' to enforce it, must resist a natural and growing sympathy for old Aegeon's suffering and search. But life keeps breaking in: not only Aegeon but Antipholus and Dromio come to Ephesus from Syracuse. And within the city itself, we see the other Antipholus hammering at the doors his wife has shut against him, and Adriana in her turn preparing to storm the abbey and regain her husband. Something there is that does not love a wall, that seeks to break down the laws that divide city from city, the barriers that 'separate the husband and the wife'. And we recall how Navarre, true to his vow, denies the Princess admission to his court, how Olivia, who 'will admit no kind of suit', refuses to receive Orsino's messengers till Viola threatens to remain forever at her doors. So Bianca's lovers disguise themselves to gain admission to her father's house, and Falstaff insinuates himself in Master Ford's. The motif of gaining entrance to a closed house or dwelling repeats in miniature the major pattern of these comedies, in which intruders force their way into a closed world and draw its thwarted or random emotional forces to themselves. In green world comedies where houses are shut up, like Shylock's, they are places to escape from, not to break into; so Orlando is warned to flee from Duke Frederick's court and his own home. *The Merry Wives* stands between the two conventions: Falstaff's problem is to escape from Ford's house, but he is an intruder in a home which should be shut against him. In general the distinction seems clear: one pattern turns on escape, the other on invasion. And as one group are comedies of the green world, so we may call these others comedies of the closed world.

The closed world is a metaphor, a symbol for the human heart. The force which knocks at its closed door is love. And in these comedies, love finally gains admittance: Navarre and Olivia renounce their vows: Katherina and Beatrice fall in love with men they thought they despised. The happy ending comes about not by perseverance through trials and changes of fortune, as in the green world comedies, but by a reversal, by conversion, by a change of heart. This is the work of love: one of these plays is named *Love's Labours Lost*, and almost any of the others could be called *Love's Labours Won*. For Cupid here becomes a Hercules, performing the seemingly impossible task of changing negative to positive, hostility and inhibition to normal human affection. This is not accomplished by supernatural intervention, by a Cupid from a machine. Love enters the closed world wearing a human face, the face of Viola or Benedick, of Rosaline or Petruchio. And there is nothing sentimental about the way these unconscious agents of love set to work. They come speaking the language of judgement: 'I see you what you are—you are too proud. . . .' The beginning of regeneration is the conviction of sin:

> What fire is in mine ears? Can this be true?
> Stand I condemn'd for pride and scorn so much?
> Contempt, farewell! And maiden pride, adieu!
> [*Much Ado*, III i 107–9]

In contrast to such self-recognition, Navarre and his friends undergo a *peripeteia* without an *anagnorisis*. They resolve to conquer 'these girls of France' as confidently as they formerly resolved to war against their own affections: 'Saint Cupid then! and, soldiers, to the field!' Hence when these 'brave conquerors' mock a pedant in the role of Judas Maccabaeus or a braggart soldier playing Hector, they do not realise that they are indirectly making fun of themselves. There has been no real conversion, no change of heart: the same comic hybris inspires their studies and their wooing; the owls have turned to cuckoos, that is all. Thus at the end, they must hear the words of judgement: 'Your Grace is perjur'd much, / Full of dear guiltiness.'

Love's labors are not really lost. Berowne and his fellow 'Worthies' are saved by grace, not merit; the ladies love them despite their guiltiness. Still, penance is necessary to bring about the happy ending and turn 'sport' into 'comedy'. The usual penance comedy imposes is the ridicule involved in a drastic reversal of behavior or attitude. Olivia, the cruel fair who refuses a duke, must humble herself to woo a servingman; she who shut her doors against all men now rushes forth into the street and almost carries off the bewildered Sebastian. So Benedick, the cynical woman-hater, must pose as champion of feminine virtue and challenge Claudio in defense of Hero's honor.

Sometimes, however, the penalty is more drastic. In a 'demonic' inversion of the green world motif, Katherina is dragged off to what editors call 'Petruchio's country house', a place of hunger, cold, and wrath; a purgatory where Katherina is punished, with Dantesque justice, by suffering Petruchio's caricature of her own shrewishness. But Katherina throughout is in the hands of love: this topsy-turvy world, where old men become maidens and the sun becomes the moon, is the point of reversal and unbeing on the path to a rebirth. Petruchio insists that Katherina really is what Bianca pretends to be: gentle, submissive, lovable. Thus 'Kate the curst' is freed from a role which was always a form of protest, freed to become her true self—if by 'true' we understand not what she is 'underneath', but what she and (according to the play) all women are meant to be. Her metamorphosis is parodied in Christopher Sly, who is never truly himself whether 'disguised' in drink or as a lord.

What happens to Kate is less a catharsis than an exorcism. She is freed from the spirit of shrewishness which was her curse. Beatrice too is 'cursed', despite her name: she is 'possessed by a fury', and the 'infernal Ate' must be driven out of her if she and Benedick are ever to be blessed. So Rosaline rebukes Berowne's gibing and bids him to

> throw away that spirit,
> And I shall find you empty of that fault,
> Right joyful of your reformation. [*L.L.L.*, v ii 855–7]

Metaphor becomes dramatic action in *The Comedy of Errors*, where Doctor Pinch conjures Antipholus:

> I charge thee, Sathan, hous'd within this man,
> To yield possession to my holy prayers,
> And to thy state of darkness hie thee straight.
>
> [*C.E.*, iv iv 51–3]

The scriptural symbolism of demons 'hous'd' within a madman fits well in plays where a closed house or dwelling is often the emblem of the mind or heart. Thus Ford in *Merry Wives* hunts through his house for his wife's lover but is told he exists 'nowhere but in your brain'. Ford is 'possessed' by his jealousy: it is a demonic self, projected in 'Master Brook', who 'wrongs' the true Ford. But it is not enough to exorcise Ford's jealousy and scare the 'spirit of wantonness' out of Falstaff. These are manifestations of a larger madness, a spirit of discord that possesses the closed world as a whole and expresses itself in the quarrels and humors of the different characters.

The dramatic exorcism necessary to subdue or expel the anticomic spirit seems to proceed on two principles. One is 'acting out' its latent impulses: Ford is encouraged to act out his jealousy and Falstaff his lust—up to a point. So in *Much Ado*, the pervasive suspicion of women which exploits Claudio's gullibility as well as Benedick's cynicism must be acted out in the accusation of Hero. So in *Twelfth Night* Malvolio is tricked into acting out his egotistic fantasies, and the device of twins in *Comedy of Errors* permits Adriana to act out her ambivalence towards her husband: one brother she welcomes and feasts; the other she alternately locks out and locks up.

The second principle is 'fixing the blame'. 'Acting out' is expansive and cathartic: it allows the anticomic spirit its full and often violent expression. Only after sexual antagonism has expressed and spent itself in the cruel verbal assault which 'kills' Hero can Benedick be detached from the masculine party or declare his love for Beatrice. Fixing the blame, on the other hand, is a focusing; it locates the general lunacy or evil in a criminal or a scapegoat in whom it can be overpowered or driven out. So the blame which attaches itself to Hero is finally traced to Don John; and Antipholus, escaping from his madman's bonds and darkness, binds and manhandles Doctor Pinch. The conjurer is fit scapegoat for a society which an outsider like Antipholus of Syracuse sees as bewitched, and we observe a similar thematic decorum with Malvolio and Falstaff. Malvolio's 'madness' and imprisonment is an intensification of the isolating melancholy that afflicts Olivia and Orsino. Like them, but far more fatally, he is 'sick of self-love', a spirit Feste cannot exorcise either as clown or curate. 'Let me enjoy my private', cries Malvolio, and his wish is granted; the loneliness and darkness of his prison only dramatise what has been his spiritual condition from the start. Falstaff is not imprisoned but expelled—twice from Ford's house, finally from the village to the forest in animal disguise. The first time his bodily grossness merges with the smell and grease of foul linen in a disgusting and undifferentiated 'first matter', a cumulative image for all the stench and soilure of the flesh. His second metamorphosis is as a monstrous woman—hag, witch, polecat, runnion—and his last as a yet more monstrous man, bestial in lust and crowned with cuckold's horns. In his feminine role of Mother Prat he is beaten and vilified by Ford; in his masculine role as Herne the Hunter he is scolded and pinched by the Queen of Fairies and her following. *Merry Wives*, as its title suggests, is much concerned with marriage; there is more discussion than is usual in comedy about which wooer will make the best husband, and the main plot deals with conflicts among those already wed. What is driven out in Falstaff, then, is all that makes for dissension in marriage, the physical distaste, the sexual antagonism that sometimes grow up within an outwardly respectable and happy union.

Reversal, recognition, penance, exorcism: the form of these plays seems closer to the conventions of tragedy or the punitive logic of satire than to romance. This is not to deny that similar motifs occur in both green and closed world comedy. But their function, tone, and meaning differ in ways appropriate to each kind. Consider, for example, the 'anticomic' figures, those antagonists of love who refuse or are refused the happy ending. Malvolio and Jaques are both anticomic in their melancholy; Shylock and Don John are both branded by their very lineage as villains. But Jaques and Shylock in the green world plays are figures of parental opposition to love.[4] Malvolio and Don John in the closed world plays represent extreme forms of the self-love or skepticism that afflicts the lovers themselves. Thus Jaques contrasts with the lovers but Malvolio mimics them. Jaques stands outside and over against the lovers' world, criticising and commenting objectively upon it. Malvolio, inside the household of love, embodies—as his name implies—a subjective distortion in 'what you will', a misdirection of love itself. Characteristically, the anticomedians are let off more easily in green world comedy. *As You Like It* suggests by its title that the dramatic conflict within the Forest of Arden is a dialectic of tastes and attitudes. The melancholy wisdom of Jaques is refuted, but he is allowed to withdraw with dignity intact, while the narcissism of Malvolio must be exposed and exorcised by ritual humiliations. In the great trial scenes of *Merchant of Venice* and *Much Ado*, the villainies of Shylock and Don John bring green and closed world comedy to the verge of tragedy and death. But Shylock's feeling for his dead wife and his daughter allies him—however distantly—to the community of love; whereas Don John loves nobody, not even himself. Hence Shylock can be baptised, while Don John can only be punished. The new law offers to fulfill and liberate the old, a promise we see prefigured in Jessica. But the lonely malice of Don John must be expelled or imprisoned; it is the eternal adversary of love. Or again, compare the amatory confusions caused by the heroine's disguise in *Twelfth Night* and *As You Like It*. In each play, both a man and woman fall in love with a girl in boy's attire. In both, the attraction felt by the man grows and deepens till it is confirmed when the seeming boy is revealed as the heroine. In both, the sudden passion of the woman can have no natural fruition: it serves to reverse and punish her initial refusal to love. The green world comedy typically emphasises the positive and evolving love of Orlando for the disguised Rosalind;

the conversion of Phebe is only a subplot. The closed world comedy stresses the abrupt and humiliating conquest of Olivia by the aptly named Cesario, while Orsino's growing affection for Viola is more lightly sketched. It is characteristic that the mock wooing of Orlando and Ganymede is a delightful game, a form of erotic play, whereas the erroneous wooing of Viola by Olivia is one of Cupid's practical jokes, parallel at a higher level with the trick that converts Malvolio from puritanism to love. Both practical joke and play are native to the comic spirit, but one is 'funny' while the other is 'fun': they tend, like closed and green world comedy, towards the opposed poles of corrective satire and romantic idyl. Hence the lyricism of Olivia and the witticisms of Rosalind may seem indecorous. But the more impassioned Olivia is, the more nearly ridiculous she becomes, whereas Rosalind's 'cure' for love actually nourishes and fosters it: she can make even satire promote romance.

The theme of love itself is handled less romantically in closed than green world comedy. Orlando and Rosalind in the springtime of their passion are ourselves as we wish we were; Benedick and Beatrice are wittier versions of what we actually are, and their problems are ones we know too well: to be humble, to trust and forgive, to learn at last to love. Yet for these very reasons, the happy ending in these comedies remains an act of faith in life—the life which comedy teaches should be grasped. Nor is this faith blind. The fact of sexual antagonism did not dismay Shakespeare or Spenser. The progression from conflict to reconciliation is not a distortion of love but its essential pattern, the *discordia concors* or harmony of opposites. In *Faerie Queen* IV, we find that the sons of Concord are Hate and Love; Hate is the elder, but he is constantly mastered by his younger brother. They are contrary but kindred principles, and the overcoming of hate by love is the way order is brought from chaos. Creation is an act of reconciliation, atoning the warring qualities of hot and cold and wet and dry in a harmonious cosmos; and the agent of creation is Love. Without discord, there can be no concord; without hatred, the instinctive opposition of things different in kind, there can be no love to atone them. So Arthegall and Britomart fight before they woo.[5] The sexes, like the elements, are at war; and in marriage, which unites woman (according to Renaissance physiology, cold and moist) to man (who is hot and dry), there is always a sense of creation. It is the making of a new world or—as Frye puts it—a new identity: the true self of the individual, the union of lovers, a society made one in charity. This new creation is the labor of Love, a task too large for any hero—or even for the Shakespearean heroine. The felt presence of a power working through semitragic errors and comic confusions is at the center of the comic faith in life, the intuition that apparent catastrophe, instinctive hostilities, and seeming chance alike direct us to our happiness. The secret meaning of Shakespeare's comedy is joy.

It only remains to see whether we can fit the two patterns of Shakespearean comedy together. Two possible ways suggest themselves: the closed world may correspond to either the first or second phase of the green world pattern, the 'real' or 'normal' world or the green world itself. And we observe that the primary, 'real' world in green world comedies is often in some sense closed. The lovers are divided; the hero must overcome barriers which separate him from his mistress. But these obstacles are not internal: they are barriers of social convention or parental prejudice. The heroine is shut up in her father's house, and we find the familiar motif of the closed dwelling as her lover comes to her window by night to woo and win her. So Egeus complains that Lysander has 'bewitched' his child: 'Thou hast by moonlight at her window sung/With feigning voice verses of feigning love.' So Proteus serenades Sylvia, and Valentine carries the motif one step further in his plan to scale her window with his rope ladder. The penetration of the lady's chamber has its obvious sexual analogy: in that play upon words, *Much Ado About Nothing*, it is enough for Hero to talk with a man at her chamber window to be proved unchaste. But in green world comedies, as we have seen, escape rather than intrusion is the lover's aim: Valentine intends to use his ladder to 'enfranchise' Sylvia. Lorenzo does not climb to Jessica's window; she comes down to him. He is drawing her out of Shylock's house, the closed world of the old law, its 'ears' locked shut against the music of Christianity and comedy, which Lorenzo can teach her to hear and understand only in the gracious world of Belmont.

When no such escape is possible, tragedy results. Romeo overcomes the hatred that divides Montague and Capulet, makes his way into his enemies' feast, surmounts the 'stony limits'

of their orchard walls, and discovers—in the greatest of such
wooing scenes—that he is already in Juliet's heart. The sexual
analogue is completed when he later climbs to her chamber to
consummate their love. But for these star-crossed lovers there is
no green world. Mantua is another Verona to which Romeo is
'banished'; Juliet remains behind in the over-protective confines
of her family and home, a womb that turns into a tomb, that
ultimate closed world which Romeo invades only to die. Yet the
sexual parallel persists: it makes the grave a wedding bed, the
vault a feasting presence full of light. *Romeo and Juliet* is thus a
closed world tragedy which corresponds to the primary phase of
the green world pattern, a reality which in tragedy can only be
escaped or transcended through death. But as we find in *A
Midsummer Night's Dream*, even the green world itself, the second
phase, has its tragic possibilities. Pyramus and Thisbe also find
ways to communicate through the wall that parts their fathers—
a psychological division materialised in loam and plaster much as
the sexual analogies materialise in jokes on 'hole' and 'chink'.
Like Hermia and Lysander, these lovers run away to meet by
moonlight. But it needs only the substitution of Lion for Puck to
turn dream into nightmare, the lucky accidents and confusions of
comedy into the fated misfortunes of tragedy. Pyramus and
Thisbe, like Romeo and Juliet, are united in death, but this time
the tomb is appropriately Ninny's.

 If the primary phase of green world plays resembles a closed
world, the setting of closed world plays resembles the courts and
cities of the primary phase. The crucial difference remains: there
is no need to escape Messina or Illyria or the court of Navarre.
They suggest a world potentially green or golden, but somehow
at odds with its own happiness. Romeo and Juliet declare their
love in an orchard where moonlight tips with silver all the fruit
tree tops: within the city walls of Verona, Capulet's garden
creates an 'internalised' green world. And there are other
orchards in Leonato's house and in Olivia's, where Benedick and
Beatrice, Olivia and even Malvolio can fall in love. These
gardens with their 'arbor' or 'box tree' are certainly tamer, more
domesticated than the forest of Arden; nevertheless, they stand
for the latent fertility, the source of potential life, at the heart of
the closed world. And while the settings of these comedies are
less romantic than the green world, that is partly a matter of

perspective: they present a green world seen, as it were, from inside. To those who enter this world, it often seems a place of romantic wonder or romantic peril: Antipholus, landing in Ephesus, like Sebastian in Illyria, assumes that the people are bewitched, that he is dreaming. But for Olivia or Adriana, who live there, Illyria or Ephesus is about as magical as Boston. Rosalind is enchanted by the pastoral world of Arden; for Corin, Arden is a place to tend sheep, where one's present master is stingier than the last. The natives of the green world, like those of the closed world, seem unable to love: Silvius woos Phebe, who scorns him; Titania and Oberon quarrel over a changeling; Portia is besieged by suitors she detests. But into this world of discord comes a stranger—Rosalind or Bassanio or the egregious Bottom—and soon we have a happy ending. To turn the pattern into tragedy, however, we need only substitute for the invading power of love the coming of retribution or the encroachments of demonic evil.

Audience perspective finally determines which is a green world and which is closed. Whatever Corin thinks of Arden, we see it as Rosalind does; for us Ephesus is a closed world, since we see the humdrum causes for the bewitchment of Antipholus. But, of course, we are dealing with the continuum of a creative imagination, not the rigid oppositions of a system. Illyria, though closed, is nearly a green world, while Hermia, Helena, Lysander, and Demetrius in their alternating attraction and repulsion are not unlike the lovers of a closed world comedy. The patterns interlock in *Merry Wives* and *Taming of the Shrew*, and in the 'problem' comedies Shakespeare went on to experiment with sophisticated and ironic versions. *All's Well* is a green world comedy but deals with sexual antagonism; *Measure for Measure* is a closed world comedy in which a law against lovers is averted by an intruder who turns out to be the lover, the father, and the ruler of us all. The two patterns merge in *The Tempest*, where the green world and the closed world are definitively one, as reality becomes indistinguishable from dream. . . .

SOURCE: extract from 'The Two Worlds of Shakespearean Comedy', *Shakespeare Studies*, III (1967), pp. 62–75.

NOTES

[Modified and renumbered from the original Notes to this essay—Ed.]

1. These investigations extend from 'The Argument of Comedy' in *English Institute Essays* for 1948 through The *Anatomy of Criticism* (1957) to *A Natural Perspective* (1965). My debt to Frye, both in substance and method, is very great and very obvious. My remarks on *Twelfth Night* are indebted to Robert Speaight's interpretation of the play as a comedy of privacy, in a lecture delivered some years ago at Princeton. The notion of an 'internalised' green world . . . I have stolen from two of my students, Stephen Nathan and Bruce Hardy. The concept of the 'closed heart' is taken from *The Sense of Shakespeare's Sonnets* (Princeton, 1952) by Edward Hubler, to whose memory this essay is dedicated.

2. This fact suggests a parallel modification of Frye's thesis that tragedy moves from liberty to bondage: in 'redemptive' tragedy, the hero's doom becomes a liberation of the spirit.

3. I am indebted for this point to Joseph H. Summers, 'The Masks of Twelfth Night', in Leonard F. Dean (ed.), *Shakespeare: Modern Essays in Criticism* (New York, 1957), p. 128. . . .

4. This may not seem true of Jaques. But Jaques and the Duke are clearly intended as doublets or complementaries: *il penseroso* and *l'allegro*, the weeping and the laughing philosopher. Jaques's melancholy is a plausible attitude for an exiled Duke (compare the choler of Prospero). But the old Duke, finding 'good in everything', aligns philosophic age with the youthful optimism of the lovers. Psychologically, then, Jaques stands for an attitude, a role, a potential self the Duke repudiates. Generically and archetypally, he expresses the opposition to love such a father would present (compare Prospero's deliberate adoption of the role of wrathful senex to test Ferdinand). In Arden, such opposition is only philosophic: there is no final resolution of the debate between the wisdom of experience and the wisdom of love; Signior Love and Monsieur Melancholy agree only to become better strangers. This archetypal role may explain why, if Shakespeare ever intended Jaques to be Orlando's brother, he changed his mind; why Duke Senior so loves to 'cope' his opposite and counterpart; why Jaques confronts both hero and heroine while the benevolent Duke is kept in the background; and why, at the happy ending, he shares with the Duke in the benediction on the lovers.

5. For a fuller discussion of love and *concordia discors* in Spenser, see Thomas P. Roche, *The Kindly Flame* (Princeton, 1964), passim.

John Russell Brown   The Presentation
of Comedy (1972)

I

The dominant focus of Shakespeare's comedies is wide. Their very titles proclaim it, for these plays are not named after their main characters like the tragedies. *The Merchant of Venice* sounds like an exception: but who is the 'Merchant'? Antonio, Shylock, the venturer Bassanio, Lorenzo and Jessica who exchange a turquoise for a money, or Portia who tries to buy Antonio's life and encounters Shylock's bond?

The audience of a Shakespearean comedy is not led towards an intimate knowledge of a single character, but towards a wide view of the whole stage. It will sympathise with several of the characters in turn; it will be excited, charmed, interested, enlivened, surprised, but when all has been experienced in the due sequence of performance and is thus truly summed up, then the audience must sit back and be aware of the whole effect, must 'take it all in', the relation of character to character, the contrasts in attitudes, words and silences. Shakespeare's comedies lead towards such a wide focus.

This accords with much that has been said about the comic spirit in general. A wide view of the stage can ensure an experience in keeping with Bergson's notion of comedy: 'Step aside, look upon life as a disinterested spectator: many a drama will turn into a comedy.'[1]

It provides the appropriate view for comic acting, as described by Athene Seyler in the light of her accomplished stage-career: 'Comedy is simply a point of view. It is comment on life *from outside*, an observation on human nature.'[2]

A wide focus permits an audience to make the comparisons or contrasts which are often held to be the source of comic pleasure. The opposite, intense focus would involve an audience too directly and minutely to allow laughter: to take an example from every-day life, the teacher of dancing does not laugh at the movements of his pupils as a disinterested person entering the room is free to do. No matter how serious a playwright's intention may be, to raise laughter from his audience he must relax each auditor so that, in one sense, he becomes 'disinterested'. Freud put this point in other terms when he said that:

> The pleasure in jokes has seemed to us to arise from an economy in expenditure upon inhibition, the pleasure in the comic from an economy in expenditure upon ideation and the pleasure in humour from an economy in expenditure upon feeling. All those are agreed in representing methods of regaining from mental activity a pleasure which has in fact been lost through the development of that activity.[3]

'Economy', in this sense, implies the opposite of intent and close involvement. Whether we explain the comic spirit in Freud's terms, or in an actor's, or by observing how we laugh in everyday life, we may believe that, if a comedy is to provoke laughter in a theatre, it must gain our interest but must also induce a width of view and ease of reception. It needs the range and relaxation of a predominantly wide dramatic focus.

A Shakespearean comedy is not, of course, 'laughs all the way'. A romantic, fantastic or ideal strain runs through each of them. Often this is quantitatively the greater part, and always it provides the dominant mood of the concluding scene. But then, for romance, a somewhat similar width of focus is required as for comedy. Numerous authors have described the kind of relaxation that is called for by their romantic fictions: so Sir Philip Sidney told his sister to read *The Arcadia* in her 'idle times' (and its style and narrative method clearly presuppose a leisured reader); and Edmund Spenser has confessed that his own delight in the 'spacious and wyde' ways of 'the land of Faery' often caused him to forget his detailed and 'tedious' work, even as he was writing *The Faerie Queene* (Book VI, Proem i). Shakespeare himself has caused Puck, in his epilogue, to liken *A Midsummer Night's Dream* to a 'weak and idle' dream; and John Lyly presented his earlier romantic and witty comedies on the same condition: 'Remember all is but a Poet's dream', advises the Prologue to *The Woman in the Moon*, and 'imagine yourself to be in a deep dream', the Prologue to *Sapho and Phao*. Such instructions were intended to excuse improbabilities to the censorious, and they do so by invoking a relaxation of precise and close concerns. Viewing a romantic comedy is like enjoying an idle dream.

Some modern critics have argued that Shakespeare encountered difficulties in linking the comic elements with the romantic, but such problems often disappear when we view the plays in the theatre, in the relaxed, wide focus which is suitable to both elements. Indeed, Shakespeare's comparison of his play to a dream may be more apt than he could have known. It may be true of both the romantic and the comic elements, for Freud has argued that the mental processes which he called 'wit-work' are very similar to those he called 'dream-work'. Both involve displacement of normal experience, illogical sequences, exaggerations, condensations, substitutions and indirections. Freud concluded that jokes and dreams alike provide a release of reactions which are normally censored by the alerted ego. Perhaps Shakespeare sensed that the relaxation of a wide focus was required both for comedy and for romance. Christopher Sly calls for relaxation from immediate concerns as the players enter:

Come, madam wife, sit by my side and let the world slip:
we shall ne'er be younger.
[*The Taming of the Shrew*, Induction ii 139–40]

II

Some of the basic decisions that Shakespeare made in planning his comedies helped to ensure a predominantly wide dramatic focus. When he chose to present, not one pair of lovers, but two, three or four, and to develop their stories simultaneously rather than successively, he was deciding for range rather than for concentration. As the intertwining actions of the plays cause solemn lovers to follow close upon lighthearted ones, hesitant upon confident, selfish upon generous, the audience is invited to compare and contrast, to remember, as one character stands pleading, how another had done so earlier, in the same place and with the same gesture. Often three or four pairs of lovers are on stage at the same time, and often all in similar predicaments. And likewise, when Shakespeare chose to present stories which involve disguise and the over-hearing of plots and counter-plots, he often provided for two or three centres of interest on the stage at one time, a dispersal of interest and a wide dramatic focus.

These effects can be illustrated abundantly from any of the comedies. In *As You Like It*, for instance, Rosalind disguised as a country youth over-hears the talk of two shepherds, one of whom is as hopelessly in love as she thinks herself. At the same time Touchstone, the clown from court, listens to the wisdom of a country clown, and Celia who is free of love-thoughts listens, with impatience, to the two shepherds and then to Rosalind and Touchstone. Later in the play, Celia talks to Oliver, not knowing he is Orlando's brother, and then Oliver speaks to Rosalind as if she were the youth she appears to be, not knowing that she is the woman his brother loves: here the audience's attention is claimed by the unlooked-for arrival of a changed Oliver, by Celia's growing concern for him, and by Rosalind's inward concern for Orlando's danger. While each centre of interest is here subtly presented, in other comedies—*The Comedy of Errors*, *The Shrew* and *The Merry Wives*—the misunderstandings have greater exaggeration and vigour, and are in the mood and tempo of farce rather than that of fine or 'high' comedy. But one effect they have in common—the view of the audience tends to encompass the whole stage: Petruchio finally wins his shrew on a crowded stage, Falstaff is discomforted as the whole *dramatis personae* assemble at Herne's Oak.

Not every scene is thus complicated, and in the more straightforward ones we may often observe how Shakespeare has used verse and prose, humour and plot-development in ways that ensure a wide focus. The opening of *A Midsummer Night's Dream*, for example, presents young Hermia strenuously defying her father and then being threatened with death by her sovereign. With a sudden action or command, a prolonged or unexpected silence, a soliloquy, or a single speech in a more spontaneous style than the others, Shakespeare could easily have focused attention closely on the Duke's predicament, or on the father's, or on the girl's. But for this comedy he did not use these devices which he had used already in other plays. Here the verse is consistently full-phrased, varied only by the simplest commands and appeals; the scene flows with but one interruption, and then all four parties in the dispute enter together, each claiming attention. Emphasis is given by repetition, not by sudden immediacy:

Therefore, fair Hermia, question your desires,
Know of your youth, examine well your blood. . .

[*M.N.D.*, 1 i 67–8]

or in young Lysander's vein:

Demetrius, I'll avouch it to his head,
Made love to Nedar's daughter, Helena,
And won her soul; and she, sweet lady, dotes,
Devoutly dotes, dotes in idolatry,
Upon this spotted and inconstant man.   [1 i 106–10]

The Duke leaves the stage among a peaceful concourse and the next movement of the play begins with Hermia and Lysander alone. But the focus remains wide: although their situation is desperate, they speak in close metrical, as well as verbal, harmony; their plight is impressed by repetition, and by images relating to 'roses' and 'tempests', and comparisons involving the 'lightning in the collied night'. As they plan to escape from Athens, Hermia's resolution is robbed of the audience's most intent interest by chiming rhymes, a jest at Lysander's expense, and the immediate entrance of Helena, the fourth in the quartet of young lovers. At the end of the scene, Lysander and Hermia depart busily and happily, and this new character bids for her full share of interest with a concluding soliloquy about herself and her love, Demetrius—and once more each line of verse is full-phrased and rhymed.

Much Ado about Nothing can provide many examples of this persistent dispersal of dramatic interest. In its first scene, Claudio's avowal of love could have afforded a poignant moment of intense focus, for he is hesitant and inexperienced, and yet entirely filled with desire. But Shakespeare has presented it in three stages: first Claudio speaks in modest prose accompanied by the mocking, dominating comments of Benedick, then more shortly as Benedick tells the secret to Don Pedro, and then, when he is alone with Pedro and his purpose already known, he speaks fully in clear and flowing verse, to be dominated now by Pedro in similar style. Claudio's shyness and passion have both been presented, and in lively manner, but he has not drawn attention wholly to himself for more than the briefest, undeveloped moment.

Shakespeare's technique in the larger problems of structure and development—matters of great importance for the comedies with multiple plots which were then in fashion—shows the same concern. A brilliant example is Act II of *The Merchant of Venice*, which speedily forwards the narrative and establishes characters, places and moods, yet without sustaining the development of any single interest or state of feeling, and without allowing any character to draw all interest to himself consistently. Shylock's grief at the loss of gold and daughter and Antonio's at parting with Bassanio are both wittily reported by others. Portia is presented in exotic and somewhat comic company. Shylock parts with Launcelot as he instructs his daughter to lock up all treasures. Jessica elopes dressed as a boy amid preparations for a masque and, possibly, accompanied with fifes and drums. Despite excitement, pathos and lyrical utterance, the dramatic focus is kept predominantly wide.

Music, song and dance can fill the stage with uniform movement or with stillness, and the air with patterned and completed sounds, and thus they are particularly useful for maintaining a wide focus. Before the last scene of *Much Ado* there are music and formal solemnities at Hero's supposed tomb, and towards the end of *As You Like It*, as the affairs of Rosalind and Orlando grow to a crisis, an anonymous forester sings at the death of a deer and others bear the burden of his bawdy song and lead the victor to the Duke, dressed as an animal in deer-skin and horns. Either of these episodes could be (and often has been) removed from its play without loss to the plot-development or characterisations. One of their main justifications is that they relax the quickening pulse of the action with the measure of their music and widen the focus visually with formal movement or celebration. Intellectually they are a reminder of the timeless or the general. They take a considerable time to perform but pay their way theatrically by their influence over tempo and focus.

Music, song, dance and processions are especially common at the very end of these comedies, when almost all the characters meet together in new or tried relationships. Each conclusion is, indeed, a general resolution, a full close which occupies the whole stage. So Benedick and Beatrice make but one pair in a dance with Hero and Claudio, and probably Margaret and Balthazar, Ursula and Antonio. Viola walks with Orsino, while Sebastian walks with Olivia. *Love's Labour's Lost* closes with two songs with no direct reference to the personages of the play but listened to by them—songs which tell of Spring and Winter, all married men and Dick, Tom, Joan and Marian.

Such general conclusions, involving the whole stage, make a great impression, for they answer lengthy preparations, the final dispositions having been suggested as soon as the lovers exchanged looks. Shakespeare's plots are often complicated—lovers are separated by distance or misunderstandings, parents at odds with children, men struggling with ill-understood duty—yet the disorder will always seem eminently tidiable. Each of the comedies is viewed within the frame of an expectation of ordered resolution so that, as the stage fills at the end of the performance, the audience observes it all gratefully, with a sense of completion and satisfaction. Even when the audience is concerned with the most precarious moments in the unfolding of the comedy, a deeper and timeless consciousness may still keep its members aware of the incipient balance, the final stability. (So in looking at a detail of a fully-balanced picture—a Poussin or a Cézanne—one may be simultaneously half-conscious of its complete reference.) Certainly, after a performance the momentary excitements are all but forgotten, being satisfied in the wider, almost static, perception of the whole consort of the comedy.

III

Any writer of comedy, and especially one who mingles several plot-interests, runs the danger of superficiality. The focus of a comedy can be so wide that it is also unsteady and indistinct. By avoiding a consistent growth in the audience's knowledge of a character, the dramatist may destroy all sense of its particular identity, by providing laughs he may introduce trivial irrelevances, and by contriving a general conclusion he may invent one that is slick and mechanical.

Of course, the enduring popularity of Shakespeare's comedies has shown beyond doubt that he avoided superficiality. In the first place, we may say that he did this by submitting the material for each play to a governing theme or idea, and by selecting, shaping and emphasising every detail of his writing in accordance with that idea. So one comedy may present generous and possessive loves, another deep and shallow loves, another the privacy and precariousness of all human idealisms. But this puts the matter in a way that sounds routine and intellectual. We might prefer to say that each comedy is an image of a world—with idealisms, wit, humour, tensions and resolutions—in which the audience can see what Shakespeare's Hamlet called the feature of virtue, the image of scorn and the form and pressure of the very age and body of the time. Or we might say that the stage-action and speech of each of the comedies is a world which Shakespeare accepted as true to his imagination. The mood of these plays is, for the most part, easy and light (Shakespeare is concerned more with the happiness of events than with their inevitable cost and seeds of sorrow), but his essential artistry ensures that they have a unifying conception as little superficial as the judgements which so obviously underlie the histories and tragedies. In short, the comedies are great and enduring because they are shaped by Shakespeare's full imagination.[4]

But such a general assertion can bring us little closer to an understanding of these plays in performance. A play which is laden with significance for its author might communicate to its audience nothing that was not disordered and trivial. More practically, we may say that Shakespeare avoided superficiality by writing dialogue that is vital, musical and varied, that attracts attention. He also imagined his characters in close detail, so that small parts, and large, have individual voices and are realised in a precise environment. This is a matter of detail, and needs to be considered in detail, by choosing one character or one passage of dialogue, and discussing that at length, rather than by engaging in a roll-call of Shakespeare's obvious successes in this kind.

Dogberry, the clown's part in *Much Ado*, will serve as an example. We know that this character was written for William Kemp to perform (we learn this from speech-prefixes in the first quarto edition of the play), and Shakespeare might have been excused if he had written it with little study, leaving the actor to embellish it with his own individualising tricks. The author and playwright Thomas Nashe called this actor, the 'most comical and conceited Cavaliere Monsieur du Kemp, Jestmonger and

Vice-gerent General to the ghost of Dick Tarleton'.[5] The role of Dogberry is marked out for such an entertainer: he makes relatively few appearances but all, effectively enough, rather late in the play; and most of the time he is obviously intended to hold the centre of the stage. He has been given a wealth of professional (and now famous) malapropisms, and he is provided with a 'stooge' or 'feed' in Verges (a part originally played by the experienced actor, Richard Cowley). Yet Shakespeare has made even these old conventions illuminate a consistent character. We can say that Dogberry has kindliness, vanity and an absurd inability to know what his words or actions mean to other people: so a malapropism—'If I were as tedious as a king, I could find it in my heart to bestow it all of your worship'—is benignly pronounced to the busied Leonato; so Dogberry treats his 'feed' with kindness, flattering him from the eminence of his own greatness while pretending not to need him. Yet Dogberry is more than a characterised clown; he is a Constable of the Watch as well, and Shakespeare has also taken care with his perform- ance of this office. About 1681, John Aubrey, the collector of gossip and facts concerning the great, reported of Shakespeare that:

The humour of the Constable in *A Midsummer Night's Dream*, he happened to take at Grendon (I think it was midsummer night that he happened to lie there) in Bucks., which is the road from London to Stratford, and there was living that Constable about 1642 when I first came to Oxon. Mr Jos. Howe is of that parish and knew him. Ben Jonson and he did gather humours of men daily wherever they came.

Even if this tale is untrue—and only the name of the play is unbelievable[6]—Shakespeare might have 'gathered' some notion of Dogberry nearer home, for his own father had been a Constable and later had been acquainted with magisterial procedures as Alderman.

Lambard's *Duties of Constables . . . and such other low Ministers of the Peace* (1583) tells how Dogberries must 'see their watches duely set and kept' and may arrest a 'suspected person and . . . carry him to a Justice of the Peace together with him that doth suspect him, . . . to the end that they both may be examined.'[7] All this Dogberry enacts, and in a way that makes

him the epitome of one kind of volunteer, unpaid, public servant
which, in Volunteer Corps of various kinds, is not unrecognisable
today. He is obviously pleased with himself and with the dignity
of his office, and he cannot help saying so:

> I knew it would be your answer . . . Five shillings to one
> on't, with any man that knows the statues . . . an there be
> any matter of weight chances, call up me.
>
> [*Much Ado*, III iii 16–19]

—Dogberry allows himself no leisure for uncertain, long words
here. But truly the Constable is little better than his watchmen:
he probably can't read or write; he takes sleep on duty as a
normal course. Characteristically he is much concerned with
those pieces of equipment that were probably chargeable to
himself, making a great fuss about trusting the head-watchman
with his lantern and charging, strictly, 'have a care that your bills
be not stolen'. The humour is further developed when Dogberry
is given a job far above his proper status, when the local JP—that
is, Leonato—tells him to take the 'examination' of the suspected
persons himself. Now the Constable's pleasure and dignity have
no bounds: he departs alone on his mission, sending Verges off on
an errand with a dramatic 'meet me at the gaol'. He starts the
enquiry [IV ii] in his own highest style—'Is our whole dissembly
appeared?'—and he attempts a superior sarcasm—'A marvellous witty fellow, I assure you'. But, really, he cannot handle his
'malefactors', and the sexton who is clerk-of-court has to guide,
and finally control, proceedings. And, then, his hour of greatness
over, the way to Dogberry's heart is still through a tip, the sign
of dependence for which he cries 'God save the foundation!'
[v i 328].

The more one knows about Elizabethan Constables and JPs,
the funnier and the livelier Dogberry appears. When he defends
his wounded dignity by asserting that he has 'two gowns and
every thing handsome about him', he may have put on the
Constable's gown (a purple one was provided by the Corporation
at Stratford-upon-Avon) and on top of that put another, to
represent his second temporary office. When he insists that he
should be 'written down an ass' he is clutching, perhaps
somewhat pathetically, to his official dignity—for Lambard

rules: 'if any such officer, . . . do take hurt, he shall have good remedy by action against him that did the hurt.'[8] Here Shakespeare may have been developing an old family story dating from 14 April 1559, when his father was Constable and the Stratford Court Leet had to deal with a case of assault, and fined a certain butcher on two counts. As the Corporation Account Book records it: 'gryffyn the bochar (ij^d) for makynge a sawt & gevynge obprobryous [words] to the constabulles'.[9]

Dogberry is watched by the audience with an unattached mind, for he does not involve them in his puzzlement. His most dominating and personal speech, which is almost a soliloquy, is an expression of what he knows ('O that I had been writ down an ass'), not of what he wants to know or is striving to understand and express. But his character is not superficial, not merely the jesting of a comedian with his 'feed'; it is individualised, and within the wide focus of the comedy a lively imitation—with exaggeration and special emphasis—of life itself, perhaps of daily life at Grendon or Stratford.

Not every character in the comedies is created with the same close study, but many are; so that, by catching such traces of their own world, the audience will watch the dreamlike mirror-world of the stage with attention, even though the predominant focus is wide and far-ranging.

IV

We may say that the audience observes Dogberry 'with an unattached mind', but this needs qualification, for when Dogberry dominates the stage with personal utterance there is a *tendency* towards a more intense focus. The audience's view is never very close or deep, and this moment, coming at the very end of a scene, can have no immediate development; yet in watching a performance the alteration of focus will surely be felt. This is, in fact, a recurrent experience in all the comedies: the wide view of the stage is maintained against a series of momentarily narrowing and intensifying elements.

Such a tension must have been consciously devised, for it accomplishes several essential tasks: it keeps the audience attentive and encourages a greater regard for detail, and it

emphasises particular points in the narrative or characterisations. This is, in short, another means whereby Shakespeare
avoided superficiality in his romantic comedies, and prevented
their predominantly wide focus from being imprecise or unsteady.

The soliloquy is an obvious device for introducing such a
tendency towards an intense focus, and Shakespeare used it
frequently. In one of his earliest comedies, *The Two Gentlemen of
Verona*, Launce, the servant of Proteus, soliloquises three times,
speaking directly to the audience. In one way these scenes serve
the overall wide focus, for Launce's talk of parting from his family
and of loving a milkmaid compares obviously with the affairs of
his master. His last tale, of how he allowed himself to be whipped
in the place of his offending dog and then offered to give that dog
away to serve his master, is a preparation for Valentine's suffering
and his generous, rapid and inadequate offer to give away 'all
that is his in Silvia' to satisfy his friend. The emphasis derived
from the more intense focus is not wasted in the larger issues of the
play, but neither is the change of focus allowed to be too strong.
Despite Launce's painstaking efforts to be correct, his utterance is
not fully immediate. He makes emendations and adds new detail
in too leisured and balanced a way for his soliloquies to represent
thought and feeling directly: his style is picturesque, not nervous
or truly sentimental. What appears at first to be a personal
utterance is really a 'turn', a 'personality' performance. Nevertheless, intimate soliloquy of any kind—especially in a play
where much of the dialogue is easily fluent—is bound to intensify
the dramatic focus to some degree, and if he wished to maintain
the predominantly wide focus, Shakespeare had good reason for
banishing Launce from the play in the fourth act.

Most of the soliloquies in the comedies stop short of full
intimacy. Those of Proteus, Valentine, Helena and others in the
earlier plays are written in sleek and, sometimes, rhyming verse
which sharpens the presentation of their dilemmas without
permitting the audience to recognise the inner movement of
thought and feeling: such, from *The Two Gentlemen*, is:

> I cannot leave to love and yet I do;
> But there I leave to love where I should love . . .
>   [II vi 17–18]

or

> I am my master's true confirmed love,
> But cannot be true servant to my master
> Unless I prove false traitor to myself. [IV iv 99–101]

At other times a soliloquy is, like Launce's, more truly a performance: such are most of Benedick's in *Much Ado*. But any of these can become immediate or revealing. So after Benedick hears that Beatrice loves him, and before he begins to enjoy his new role, he has a few abrupt, unwitty sentences that offer a deeper view. [II iii 201–10]

Among the comedies written before *Twelfth Night*, *The Merchant of Venice* has the strongest tendency towards an intense focus. Shylock's passionate and reasoned resentment against the Christians[III i]—'Hath not a Jew eyes? . . . If you prick us, do we not bleed? . . . if you wrong us, shall we not revenge?'—brings the dramatic focus to bear intensely on himself. But Shakespeare has carefully avoided soliloquy here by bringing first Salerio and Solanio, and then Tubal, to fill the stage. Moreover, if Shylock is played fully in this scene, the horror aroused by his callous talk of desiring Antonio's flesh will repulse the audience's sympathy even as the presentation of his suffering draws it. Later in the same scene, Shylock's rapid alternations between greedy hope and despair, as Tubal tells the news point by point, may even bring the relaxing—and therefore the widening—influence of humour; certainly there is no occasion for a single emotional response or identification to develop. Shylock's strongest bid for an intense focus is in his defeat, when he draws attention away from Gratiano's easily bloodthirsty gibe by a silent exit across the crowded and attentive stage. For such an important character, the absence of an 'exit-line' is a remarkable stage-trick, and very rare in Shakespeare's works (there were long distances to be negotiated on the stages of his time). In default of words, the attention of the audience is intensified on the inward feelings of the character who has just suffered a complete reversal of fortune and has spoken little of it. The least experienced actor would recognise this opportunity, while great ones have used it to powerful and still memorable effect; so Irving's audience knew that Shylock walked 'away to die in silence and alone', and

Kean's 'withering sneer, hardly concealing the crushed heart' was the 'crowning glory of his acting' in this role.[10] Such concentration of attention may well be permitted here, for Shylock is leaving the play as well as the stage; but even so, Shakespeare rapidly followed it with new business, widening the focus by a sudden transition to general talk about having dinner, and to a game of disguised identities, initiated in the most sprightly and mocking manner by Portia and Nerissa.

These moments of intense focus can continue to affect the play long after they have passed. The memory of Shylock, kept alive by Jessica's presence in the final act and by direct reference to him, is liable to influence the reception of all the succeeding action, causing the audience—or some of them—to question the fullness or security of the various joys-in-matrimony which are presented.

Not all members of the audience will experience this double view: the relaxation of a predominantly wide focus gives scope for it, but it also precludes its enforcement. And this seems to have suited Shakespeare's purposes, for in later comedies a permissive, double view of the stage became one of his most useful and distinctive means of counteracting superficiality and giving definition within the wide frame.

We have already noticed that the disguises involved in the plots of the comedies were used to provide two or more centres of interest within a single scene, and so help to maintain the general width of focus. In some scenes, however, they give rise to a further mode of double vision or double focus, for two 'persons' are then seen in a single 'figure'. Occasionally the view of the person within the disguise sharpens into a momentarily intense and precise focus on innermost thoughts and feelings. This cannot last too long or be too overwhelming in effect, because the disguise must soon be re-established in accordance with the exigencies of the plot. In *As You Like It*, the device is used freely, especially in the long, central scene [IV i] between Rosalind, disguised as Ganymede, and Orlando who believes that the seeming youth is only impersonating the Rosalind he loves. Drawing Orlando out to confess and re-confess his love, Rosalind easily assumes the role of a witty, outspoken, disinterested Ganymede pretending to be a Rosalind: but the performance is not perfect. The true Rosalind as well as the supposed Ganymede takes part in the dialogue:

'Then love me, Rosalind', says Orlando and 'Yes, faith, will I' answers Rosalind, and 'Fridays and Saturdays and all' adds 'Ganymede', turning it to laughter. 'Ganymede' draws Celia in to act as the priest at a make-believe wedding, so that the true Rosalind within him may hear Orlando's vows and make hers in return with her double voice. The interchange is like quicksilver, for 'Ganymede' has continually to redirect the conversation so that it veers away from tenderness to scorn or laughter, or to an abrupt demand that Orlando shall again affirm his love. In a later scene, Silvius, Phebe and Orlando vow faithfulness and service to their respective loves:

> PHE. Good shepherd, tell this youth what 'tis to love. . . .
> SIL. It is to be all made of faith and service;
> And so am I for Phebe.
> PHE. And I for Ganymede.
> ORL. And I for Rosalind. [v ii 76–85]

and 'Ganymede' then dares to add his voice, knowing that the true Rosalind speaking within him will not sound out of key, without ardour, even though he speaks a riddle:

> And I for no woman.

The others do not question these words; indeed Orlando finally addresses Rosalind as if she were truly present, and 'Ganymede'—or is it Rosalind?—has to change the tune abruptly, calling:

> Pray you, no more of this; 'tis like the howling of Irish wolves against the moon. [v ii 102]

In hesitation, in simply spoken words, and in the quick veering away to a new line of attack, the audience may sense the deepest thoughts and feelings of Rosalind. Within the predominantly wide focus of the comedy, a double vision gives a kind of flickering intensity, and during a few moments of avowal, for some of the audience, the dramtic focus may be still, deep and intimate.

The revelation of a different consciousness existing beneath the main comic or romantic world is used in a more settled and controlled way in the later comedies, without resort to disguise. At the height of the absurd trial-scene in *Much Ado*, the practical Sexton quietens the stage with his own sober view that Hero has 'suddenly died'. He is not answered, so there is probably a moment's silence before he resolves to tell Leonato, and then comic momentum reasserts itself and the audience is back in the world of Dogberry's ambitions. In *As You Like It* Jaques often establishes his own dispirited, experienced view of the world, to be laughed at or ignored the next instant, as other realities are asserted. He sees the absurdities of passionate conviction, and has himself lost all obvious interest; if he had licence he would rail at others, but he has not and so he sometimes finds peace by being 'sad and saying nothing'. Rosalind suggests that he has gained nothing by travelling: 'Yes, I have gained my experience', he replies, but to no effect, for Rosalind, full of the immediate sensations of love, answers brightly:

> And your experience makes you sad. I had rather have a fool to make me merry than experience to make me sad. [IV i 24ff.]

This is the reality of confident youth, and as Orlando, also free of that world, enters immediately, Jaques' isolated private world is lost to view and he leaves the stage. Such moments are summed up at the end of the play, when Jaques leaves the stage again, saying he is for 'other than for dancing measures'. Once more the audience will momentarily see his reality, lonely and barren; and they will know that impassive, unexcitable experience walks out of the conclusion of the play. This moment is elaborated by Jaques' summing up of the hopes of the Duke and the lovers, and it is prolonged by the others watching him go, forgetting to dance. The Duke has to recall them to the world of hope:

> Proceed, proceed. We will begin these rites,
> As we do trust they'll end, in true delights. [v iv 191–2]

The stage is filled with dancing, and then the comedy can conclude. By introducing another view of the stage—a different tempo, different speech and standards of judgement—

Shakespeare has reminded us of its precariousness, of how the lovers give themselves to happiness because of feelings and convictions they can justify to no-one but themselves. And Shakespeare has thereby sharpened the wide dramatic focus. One of the strangest qualities of Shakespeare's comedies is their unassertiveness. An audience will follow easily and comprehensively the interweaving threads of narrative, and so will enjoy moments of lyricism, humour, fantasy and conflict, and respond to lively speech and varying spectacle; and finally, it will rest assured in a general resolution. Beyond this the comedies make few demands, but offer many opportunities. The life-like details of characterisation are not underscored, and are not necessary to an understanding of the development of the action. The ideas, or themes, which shape each of the comedies are never stated explicitly, so that an audience may appreciate the dance-like sequences and the contrasts and reflections between the characters without being made aware of the precise words or movements which give this unity, without having to understand, in general terms, the 'meaning' of the play. The moments which tend to induce an intense focus are not followed by incidents which depend on the knowledge or sympathy given by the closer contact. The moments of double view and unsettled focus may pass unnoticed and yet the audience feel quite at ease, as if in possession of all they need to know. The action, dialogue, narrative and characterisation of the comedies are understandable and of lively interest without these elements. To further their comic and dream-like qualities, Shakespeare has used a predominantly wide focus which permits the audience to observe all in relaxed mood and with a wide and comprehensive view; and only unassertively, almost as if by stealth, are there further invitations which sharpen the definitions and reveal more depth and more variety of colour. To many of these invitations an audience can respond unknowingly, so that after a performance its members will find it hard to account for the complexity, depth and subtlety of their involvement. . . .

v

If directors and audiences are left free to respond with whatever intensity or double consciousness that is suggested to them by the play in performance, actors have a more inescapable responsibility. Their roles start with an abundance of defining words and actions, but these lead towards later moments when textually there is little to rely upon, when the audience may view them more deeply than before and when credibility and effectiveness have to come from the very centre of their impersonations. Once Viola has recognised Sebastian, she has very few words: four lines of a love-confession and four of explanation; yet the audience will watch closely. After Malvolio has been freed, Viola has only a silent approach to Orsino and this must serve to sum up all her performance. On one level this approach to Orsino completes a pattern and ends a narrative; on another, it must speak of a happiness and denote a kind of peace. How much laughter, relief, forgetfulness or understanding is expressed will depend upon the person who acts the part, and upon the entire performance up until that moment.

Again and again Shakespeare ends a role with this kind of opportunity for the actor, where the audience will accept him according to his performance as a whole. In *Twelfth Night* Malvolio and Sir Toby have notably limited final appearances, as far as words go; yet both draw from Olivia an expression of concern, as if Shakespeare felt the need to define a sympathy for their different defeats that might have been awakened in the audience. When Rosalind reappears in women's dress at the end of *As You Like It*, she has only five punning lines to speak before words tumble out again in her Epilogue, when the play is done. The audience follows Bottom through fear and happiness in the wood and is drawn towards him by soliloquies of lively immediacy, but in the last scene he speaks only in the words of his 'tedious brief' play and a few lines of prose to help his stage-audience and offer Epilogue or dance. Nevertheless, the audience will continue to follow his progress intently, imagining no worse of him than he does of himself (as Theseus has hinted). The actor's opportunities in this scene are manifold and can set the crown upon his performance. Bottom will be accepted at last, for what he is, beneath the foolish words he speaks.

Sometimes the end is a kind of riddle, capable of many interpretations; such are Malvolio's last words, or Antonio's in *The Merchant of Venice*. In *The Taming of the Shrew*, the conclusion of the main tale of wooing is accompanied by Petruchio's simple words: 'Why, there's a wench! Come on, and kiss me, Kate' [v ii 180]. But this is not a simple dramatic moment: has Kate already knelt in submission, or has Petruchio prevented her? does Petruchio kneel with her? does Petruchio embrace Kate before he speaks, or afterwards? how soon does he smile, or laugh? how quickly or slowly does Kate respond? Every pair of actors will make their own decision, and should try to find whatever is appropriate to the way they have played their entire roles; this riddle, this intently perceived moment, demands their most considered, their most truly felt and carefully created response. Even this tempestuous comedy, with a stage full of lively characters at the close, will be accepted partly through the audience's appreciation of what can be revealed only riddlingly in words. In *Much Ado About Nothing*, Benedick and Beatrice are given a run of such speeches before finishing with the explicit but brief and factual: 'Peace; I will stop your mouth'. [v iv 97]

Shakespeare wrote his comedies with prodigal invention, creating 'worlds' in which members of an audience may 'lose' themselves and view each episode for what the actors' perform-ances and their own imaginations can make of it. Intense focus upon a single character is always momentary, and never sustained for an unbroken sequence. Yet at last the 'dream' grows 'to something of great constancy' (*A Midsummer Night's Dream*, v i 26) which is grounded in the deepest, most silent element of human personality, and which is also reflected and sustained by the widest view of the stage, action, words and story.

The achievement is extremely subtle, and the degrees of intensity and double vision vary with each of the comedies. Shakespeare is never a writer at ease with a formula that works to his own and his audience's satisfaction, and it is not surprising that after *Twelfth Night* there came a radical change in his approach to comedy. . . .

SOURCE: excerpt from 'The Presentation of Comedy', in Malcolm Bradbury and David Palmer (eds), *Shakespearian Comedy*, Stratford-upon-Avon Studies, 14 (London, 1972), pp. 9–25, 28–9.

NOTES

1. Henri Bergson, *Laughter*, trans. F. Rothwell (1900); quoted in R. W. Corrigan (ed.), *Comedy: Meaning and Form* (San Francisco, 1965), p. 473.

2. Athene Seyler and S. Haggard, *The Craft of Comedy* (London, 1943), p. 8. (The italics are mine.)

3. S. Freud, *Jokes and Their Relation to the Unconscious*, trans. J. Strachey, *Works*, VIII (London, 1960), p. 236.

4. In *Shakespeare and His Comedies* (London, 1957) I have tried to trace the main ideas underlying the comedies.

5. *An Almond for a Parrott* (1590); *Works*, edited by R. B. McKerrow (Oxford, 1904–10), III, 341.

6. It would imply that Shakespeare saw Dogberry as a young, upstart Constable, rather than the old buffoon that is usually seen on the stage today; Aubrey's Constable could hardly have been above thirty years of age in 1596.

7. Lambard, *Duties of Constables* . . . (1583; 1594 edition), A7 and A8.

8. Ibid, A8.

9. R. Savage and E. I. Fripp (eds), *Minutes and Accounts of the Corporation of Stratford-upon-Avon* (Dugdale Society, Stratford-upon-Avon, 1921), p. 94.

10. Article in *Blackwood's Magazine* (Dec. 1879) and J. Doran, *Their Majesties Servants* (1897 edn), pp. 430–1. See also my 'The Realisation of Shylock', in J. R. Brown and B. Harris (eds), *Early Shakespeare*, Stratford-upon-Avon Studies, 3 (London, 1961).

2. *MUCH ADO ABOUT NOTHING*

Donald A. Stauffer   'Words and
Actions' (1949)

The spirit of the farces, *The Taming of the Shrew* and *The Merry Wives of Windsor*, most nearly parallels the approach to romantic love in *Much Ado About Nothing*. Like them, this play is written with more than a dash of prosaic common sense. Portia's real home had been in the gardens and galleries of Belmont, from which she sallies forth into the world of action like a feminine and effective Don Quixote. But in *Much Ado About Nothing* Shakespeare's sympathy from the beginning lies with the hard-headed and sharp-tongued Benedick and Beatrice. The play constitutes his severest criticism to date of the weaknesses lying in romantic love. He takes as his main plot a highly fanciful story—what could be more romantic than a crucial scene in which a lady swoons into supposed death upon hearing her honor falsely traduced by her lover at the altar? Yet the lady Hero, shadowy and almost silent, is strangely ineffective, the villain is little more than a conventional malcontent, and Shakespeare is satisfied to develop in a few fine touches the weak impulses of his smart young gentleman Claudio.

So full of tricks is fancy that Claudio, in his melodramatic scene of accusation, rails against the 'cunning sin' and 'savage sensuality' of his Hero, who is as modest, chaste and sincere in reality as he accuses her of being only in 'exterior shows'. He wilfully makes over the world to his own mistaken misogyny:

> . . . on my eyelids shall conjecture hang,
> To turn all beauty into thoughts of harm,
> And never shall it more be gracious. [IV i 105–7]

Before he is forgiven and restored to his happiness, the Friar insists that the crime must be purged and punished in the place where it was committed—Claudio's own mind. Slander must change to remorse.

> Th'idea of her life shall sweetly creep
> Into his study of imagination;
> . . .
> Into the eye and prospect of his soul,
> . . .   then shall he mourn,
> . . .
> And wish he had not so accused her. [IV i 224–32]

The reconciliation scene is as melodramatic as the denunciation. It too plays with the paradoxes of true love that transcends, or runs counter to, this world of shadows. The resurrected Hero presents the truth as a conceit:

> And when I liv'd I was your other wife;
> And when you lov'd you were my other husband.
>   [V iv 60–1]

Leonato enforces love's transcendence: 'She died, my lord, but whiles her slander liv'd.' And the Friar reaffirms the joy and the remorse before the miraculous grace of love that will not die 'Meantime let wonder seem familiar.'

The trouble is that in the main plot wonder does not seem familiar enough. The operatic situations and the ill-developed or poorly motivated characters are not convincing. Shakespeare rescues them through his favorites, Benedick and Beatrice. The denunciation scene turns from verse to prose, from melodrama to drama, when the stage is left to the two lovers and Benedick asks the question that shows again Shakespeare's dramatic use of silence: 'Lady Beatrice, have you wept all this while?' She does not weep much longer, nor does she allow Benedick to fall into conventional vows of love. When he protests: 'Bid me do anything for thee', she answers in two words: 'Kill Claudio.' As she thinks of Claudio, her bitter eloquence pronounces a moral judgment not only on his blindness but on the unnecessary cruelty of his procedure:

O that I were a man! What? bear her in hand until they
come to take hands, and then with public accusation,
uncover'd slander, unmitigated rancour—O God, that I
were a man! I would eat his heart in the market place.
[IV i 299–304]

Mere words are useless. When Benedick swears 'By this hand, I
love thee', Beatrice retorts: 'Use it for my love some other way
than swearing by it.' And Benedick replies with equal economy:
'Enough, I am engag'd; I will challenge him.' Actions will speak,
and 'As you hear of me, so think of me.' Benedick has had to
choose between loyalty to Claudio and love for Beatrice.The
greater love eclipses the smaller, and Benedick acts contrary to
the presented evidence, on the strength of his trust in Beatrice's
loyal love. Faith begets faith. He has asked but one question:
'Think you *in your soul* the Count Claudio hath wrong'd Hero?'
She answers: 'Yea, as sure as I have a thought or a soul.' And the
debate in his mind has been decided in favor of Beatrice.

This is serious matter for comedy. But Shakespeare had long
felt restive at the thought of mere manners passing for sound coin.
In the court of love, there had been too much courtliness and
courtesy, not enough love. This is evident in Berowne's renunciation of 'taffeta phrases, silken terms precise', as well as in
the portrayal of the villain Tybalt in *Romeo and Juliet* as one of
'these antic, lisping, affecting fantasticoes—these new tuners of
accent!' Portia herself waxes sarcastic against the tribe of
immature swaggerers and the 'thousand raw tricks of these
bragging Jacks'. And Beatrice showers vitriol on such courageous
captains of compliment:

But manhood is melted into courtesies, valour into
compliment, and men are only turn'd into tongue, and
trim ones too. He is now as valiant as Hercules that only
tells a lie, and swears it. [IV i 315–19]

Old Antonio, uncle to Beatrice and Hero, grieving at the younger
generation, carries on the tongue-lashing of these 'Boys, apes,
braggarts, Jacks, milksops!' 'I know them,' he says:

> . . .   I know them, yea,
> And what they weigh, even to the utmost scruple,
> Scambling, outfacing, fashion-mong'ring boys,
> That lie and cog and flout, deprave and slander,
> Go anticly, show outward hideousness,
> And speak off half a dozen dang'rous words,
> How they might hurt their enemies, if they durst;
> And this is all. [v i 92–9]

Why has Shakespeare taken such an antipathy to the vain young slanderers, the hot-headed lying Jacks of which Tybalt, and Claudio in *Much Ado*, show possible varieties? In part because he loathed particularly those evil elements that base their hostile actions on unfounded suspicion or on nothing whatever. Jealousy and slander he viewed with special aversion, for how can chastity and integrity oppose them? They mock our eyes with air. Of the two, slander may be the more sordid, since jealousy at least springs from misguided passion, whereas slander is purely malicious, destructive, and irresponsible. Who steals my purse steals trash; and outlaws are not such bad fellows, as *The Two Gentlemen of Verona* and *As You Like It* testify. But the slanderers, almost alone among Shakespeare's sinners, are nearly unforgivable; and Shakespeare, like Spenser, treats with revulsion the Blatant Beast whose myriad tongues wound for sheer spite. In the plays with political implications, of course, slander becomes even more criminal than in the dramas of personal fortune.

Partly Shakespeare is bitter against the young swaggering slanderers out of his usual contempt for pretension in any form. And partly he seems to have developed, with considerable deliberation, a distrust for the cocksureness of callow youth. He works himself into a rather curious position: the smooth, privileged young men are too young to know what they are talking about; on the other hand, old age with its wise saws is impotent in convincing anybody. There seems little left for Shakespeare to acknowledge as a principle for conduct except Poor Richard's adage, 'Experience keeps a dear school, but fools will learn in no other.' Men's passions make all of them fools, incapable of accepting any sage advice or profiting from any hard-won experience except their own. Let us take a formally developed illustration. When old Leonato is grieving for his daughter Hero's shame, his yet older brother Antonio admonishes him:

> If you go on thus, you will kill yourself,
> And 'tis not wisdom thus to second grief
> Against yourself. [v i 1–3]

Leonato answers in a thirty-line speech, 'I pray thee cease thy counsel', the gist of which is that no one can console him except a comforter 'whose wrongs do suit with mine', that no man can patch his grief with a few proverbs, that only those who do not feel grief mouth comfortable counsel, that aches cannot be charmed with air, nor agony with words. He ends with certainty:

> No, no! 'Tis all men's office to speak patience
> To those that wring under the load of sorrow,
> But no man's virtue nor sufficiency
> To be so moral when he shall endure
> The like himself. Therefore give me no counsel.
> My griefs cry louder than advertisement.

And old brother Antonio answers with too much truth: 'Therein do men from children nothing differ.' Knowledge of this lamentable fact in human behavior is not the monopoly of the old men. Benedick has said earlier in the play: 'Well, every one can master a grief but he that has it.' And Romeo had answered the Friar's soothing wisdom in some irritation: "Thou canst not speak of that thou dost not feel."

To sum it up, Shakespeare is no believer in the schoolroom. Copybook maxims, admirable as they may be, are ineffective. The only school is experience, and axioms are proved upon the pulses. Believing this, Shakespeare finds the drama a most excellent moral instrument, since in the drama characters reach conclusions by putting their various conflicting beliefs into action. Their passions and philosophies are forced to work out practicable solutions, in conflict with a larger world and with unsympathetic alien forces or personalities. The audience may profit vicariously from the display of life in action. This belief, so slowly affirmed, accounts for the greater soundness and sanity of

Shakespeare's handling of love in the Golden Comedies. Romantic love, in the characters that interest him in *Much Ado About Nothing*, is not to be a doctrine promulgated to puppet lovers and forced upon them. Benedick and Beatrice will fight it to the last gasp. They take their stand against sentimentality, and carry on the war between the sexes with gusto.

The main interest of the play, then, starts in the world of common sense. Raillery and wit will protect light hearts. 'There is measure in everything', says Beatrice, and lest that remark on moderation sound immoderately serious, she makes it into a pun and dances out her conviction. The lovers are too clear-eyed not to be self-critical. When Beatrice overhears her disdain, scornful wit, and self-endearment exaggerated, she abandons them. 'Contempt, farewell! and maiden pride, adieu!' And when Benedick also overhears a conversation on his character—that he will scorn Beatrice's love, since he 'hath a contemptible spirit'— he decides to forsake 'quips and sentences and these paper bullets of the brain', because, he says, 'I must not seem proud. Happy are they that hear their detractions and can put them to mending.' Part of this, of course, is not the result of the lovers' good resolutions but of their instinctive attraction toward each other. 'Good Lord, for alliance!' cries Beatrice, as she watches Claudio and Hero making love, and there is a touch of envy and self-pity in her jest: 'Thus goes every one to the world but I. . . . I may sit in a corner and cry "Heigh-ho for a husband!"'

'Alliance', then, catches these two independent spirits, who have too much good sense to resist nature. Leonato in his passion of grief had asserted:

> . . .   I will be flesh and blood;
> For there was never yet philosopher
> That could endure the toothache patiently.

Now Benedick feels the pangs of love, and when his friends twit him on his sadness, he replies: 'I have the toothache.' They ascribe it to love and suggest a remedy, but Benedick already knows well that 'Yet is this no charm for the toothache'.

To himself, he will not deny the effects and the power of love. Yet he will try to keep it in proportion through humor:

. . . Leander the good swimmer, Troilus the first em-
ployer of panders, and a whole book full of these
quondam carpet-mongers, whose names yet run smoothly
in the even road of a blank verse—why, they were never
so truly turn'd over and over as my poor self in love.

[v ii 27–31]

He has too much respect for his genuine feelings to transform
them into fashionable conventions; he 'cannot woo in festival
terms', and when he looks for rhymes for 'lady', 'scorn', and
'school', he can only come out with 'baby', 'horn', and 'fool'.
Sentiment—even when it is experienced directly—is to be kept in
its place by anti-sentiment.

His sincerity is best shown in that excellently conceived
dramatic scene of his challenge to Claudio. Here we have
dramatic reversal of moods, for the perpetual giber Benedick is
now in deadly earnest—'You have among you kill'd a sweet and
innocent lady'—and his friends Pedro and Claudio are uneasily
jesting against his estrangement and their own bad consciences.
In critical moments Benedick controls both his emotion and his
wit; their interaction protects him at once against the affectations
of intellect and the extreme sallies of passion.

The integrity and sincerity of his love, based so broadly, make
him in the end impervious to mockery, and it is 'Benedick, the
married man' who, after kissing Beatrice heartily, replies in all
surety: 'I'll tell thee what, Prince: a college of wit-crackers cannot
flout me out of my humour', who demands music and dancing,
and who advises Pedro: 'Prince, thou art sad. Get thee a wife!' In
the wedding of Benedick and Beatrice, humor has been married
to love on both sides of the family. Since humor presupposes a
greater consciousness of the world and of one's self, the wedding promises more stability and happiness than in any of
Shakespeare's previous imaginings. 'Man is a giddy thing', says
Benedick, 'and this is my conclusion.' Man is less giddy, surer in
his moral sense, in direct proportion to his awareness of his own
giddiness. . . .

SOURCE: extract from *Shakespeare's World of Images: The
Development of His Moral Ideas* (Bloomington, Indiana,
and London, 1949), pp. 69–76.

Barbara Everett   'Something of Great
Constancy' (1961)

Much Ado About Nothing is not, I think, among Shakespeare's most
popular comedies. It lacks many of those perpetuating devices
that we look for to give us a sense of timeless pleasure, of a
'holiday' that is at once a sportive release and also, through
lyricism, gives the faintest air of holiday blessedness and calm. It
contains no sunlit or moonlit wood where every Jack finds his Jill.
No heroine leaps happily into hose to find the sexless and timeless
liberty of intellectual sport. There is no 'play within a play' to
strengthen the artifices that surround it with the solidity of
comparative reality, and so to give their happy ending the stamp
of truth. If 'we did keep time, sir, in our snatches', it is not a
snatch of perpetuity that is given in the songs of the play—no
Journeys end in lovers meeting, nor *It was a lover and his lass*, nor *When
daisies pied and violets blue*—but an omen of change: *Men were
deceivers ever.* The play appears to present, by contrast, a world
rather for 'working-days' than for 'Sundays'; a world that is
as formal, and potentially as harsh, as the comic world that
probably preceded it, that of *The Merchant of Venice*. But the
moneyed, legalistic, and formal world of Venice resolves at last
into moonlit Belmont, from which one can see

> . . .   the floor of Heaven
> Thick inlaid with patines of bright gold.

The equally and beautifully formal Portia, in whom 'The will of
a living daughter is curbed by the will of a dead father' ceases to
be a 'Daniel come to judgement' and becomes a Diana in love,
her homecoming heralded by Lorenzo and Jessica with lyrical
myths and fables, and herself drawn into a dream from which she
'would not be awaked'.

Much Ado About Nothing is a play cut off from such pleasant
natural resources. It is essentially 'inland bred', and relies only on

the natural forms of a great house where

> Ceremony's a name for the rich horn,
> And custom for the spreading laurel tree.

'Nature lovers' are offered only the flowers of rhetoric, the pleached arbour of wit, and the 'dancing star' of human individuality. Not only the courteous, but the customary, matters in this play: not only the urbane, but the mundane: in fact, it is the unusual fusing of these into one world that is one of the individual characteristics of the play. The chief fact that makes this play unusual and individual (though there are other characteristics, which I shall discuss later, that develop straight out of earlier comedies) is the manner in which 'time and place' do *not* 'cease to matter', but matter very greatly.

It is not merely that the props of an urban or domestic existence—the window, the arras of a musty room, the church, the tomb, the wedding dress, the night-watchmen's staves, even the barber's shop—*are* important 'props' in the world of this play. Nor is it merely that 'time and place' have a crucial importance in the action:

> What man was he talked with you yesternight
> Out at your window betwixt twelve and one?
> Now if you are a maid, answer to this. [IV i 82–4]

It is rather that the play concerns itself with what can only be called the most mundane or 'local' fact in that world of love, in all its forms, that the comedies create: that is, that men and women have a notably different character, different mode of thinking, different system of loyalties, and, particularly, different social place and function. Not only this; but this is the first play, I think, in which the clash of these two worlds is treated with a degree of seriousness, and in which the woman's world dominates.

This is a rash generalisation and objections spring to mind. *All's Well That Ends Well* seems to indicate just such a victory. But not only does the style of parts of it, at least, suggest a date some time after *Much Ado About Nothing*; but also the character of Helen so dominates the play that no *meeting* of the two worlds can be said to be present: the play presents rather a deliberate reversal of a

familiar situation, such as that presented by *Venus and Adonis*, or
by another Helena's unhappy and outraged lines of midsummer
madness:

> . . .   the story shall be chang'd;
> Apollo flies, and Daphne holds the chase;
> The dove pursues the griffin; the mild hind
> Makes speed to catch the tiger . . .
>
> [*M.N.D.*, ii ii 171–4]

Similarly, the ladies in *Love's Labour's Lost* seem to hold the field at
the end of the play when they turn the expected ending by
proposing a trial of their perhaps rather complacent lovers. But
this is a conclusion in which nothing is concluded—a Pyrrhic
victory at best:

> Our wooing doth not end like an old play:
> Jack hath not Jill. These ladies' courtesy
> Might well have made our sport a comedy . . .
>
> [*L.L.L.*, v ii 862–4]

I am thinking rather of the way in which *Much Ado About Nothing*
for the first time takes up and resolves matters which are either
barely touched on or left unconcluded in earlier plays. The
ladies' awareness in *Love's Labour's Lost*—that

> We are wise girls to mock our lovers so.
>
> You'll ne'er be friends with him; 'a killed your sister.
> . . .
> He made her melancholy, sad and heavy,
> And so she died. Had she been light, like you,
> Of such a merry, nimble, stirring spirit,
> She might 'a been a grandam ere she died.
>
> [*L.L.L.*, v ii 58 & 13–7]

is present in all the earlier comedies, but the ladies, if the play is to
end rightly, never are 'light'. One remembers the mourning
Adriana, even in so light and cheerful a piece as *The Comedy of
Errors*:

Since that my beauty cannot please his eye
I'll weep what's left away, and weeping die. [*C.E.*, II i]

who stands by with Luciana while the men's doubleness is sorted
out:

Alas, poor women! Make us but believe,
Being compact of credit, that you love us:
. . .
We in your motion turn, and you may move us.
                                    [*C.E.*, III. ii 21–4]

Or that 'shallow story of deep love', the *Two Gentlemen of Verona*,
in which the women's sympathetic solidarity—'I cannot choose
But pity her'—is finally and necessarily subordinate to the men's
chivalric friendship: 'All that is mine in Silvia I give thee'. It is
hardly necessary to mention the triumphant conclusion of *The
Taming of the Shrew*; where the battered and hungry vixen
Katherina steps forward at last as the most docile and dulcet of
wives:

Thy husband is thy lord, thy life, thy keeper,
Thy head, thy sovereign; one that cares for thee.
                                    [*T.S.*, v ii 146–7]

Such suggestions are much more beautifully and subtly expanded in *A Midsummer Night's Dream*. They touch even the
heroic lovers' plot, where Theseus kindly educates Hippolyta in
dramatic criticism; but they are plainest in the two plots of the
young lovers, and of Oberon and Titania. The doped and
changeable Demetrius and Lysander at last manage, under
Oberon's charge, to sort out their amorous inclinations; while
Hermia and Helena stand by innocently throwing overboard a
childhood loyalty which takes on an ornamental, emblematic,
and Paradisiacal peacefulness in contrast to their new world,
which both at different times find 'hellish':

We, Hermia, like two artificial gods,
Have with our needles created both one flower,
Both on one sampler, sitting on one cushion,

> Both warbling of one song, both in one key;
> . . .
> And will you rent our ancient love asunder,
> To join with men in scorning your poor friend?
>
> [*M.N.D.*, III ii 203–6, 215–16]

The world of feminine loyalty that Titania clings to is even more interesting, in the rich and strange sensuousness with which it is presented. She keeps the Indian child out of loyalty to the physical world of 'spiced Indian air, by night', 'on Neptune's golden sands':

> When we have laugh'd to see the sails conceive
> And grow big-bellied with the wanton wind;
> . . .
> But she, being mortal, of that boy did die;
> And for her sake do I rear up her boy;
> And for her sake I will not part with him.
>
> [*M.N.D.*, II i 128–9, 135–7]

But she does, of course; Oberon's revenge is to give her loyalty to this mortal physical world full play. Dazed by her unseemly passion for an ass-headed Bottom, she at last hands over the child without a murmur, and is glad to get back her 'fairy kingdom' of detached and aerial magic, in which she is always subordinate to an Oberon who has no such weaknesses, because no such loyalties.

Since *The Merchant of Venice* is the first play in which there appears a comic heroine who is also a great lady, one watches with interest to see what part the dominating Portia will play, how she will handle her subjection to the 'will of a dead father', and whether she will prove to 'fit her fancies to her fathers will' better than does Hermia. She and Bassanio equally 'give and hazard all they have'; but it is, at least nominally, a man's world that they give themselves up to:

> . . .   her gentle spirit
> Commits itself to yours to be directed,
> As from her lord, her governor, her king.
> Myself and what is mine to you and yours
> Is now converted. [*M. V.*, III ii 164–8]

Portia is the salvation of the play; her wealth, her wits, and her pleading of a feminine quality of mercy—deeply Christian in its language and connotation, but allied too to that quality of compassion that is reserved for the women in the comedies— defeat the harshly logical and loveless intellectualism of Shylock. But they do so in masculine disguise, in a masculine court of law, and at the service of a chivalric friendship between men whose values Portia and Nerissa accept gaily, but seriously, at the end of the play. They lose, as women, the rings they have gained as men; the loyal and unhappily solitary friend Antonio is the peace-maker, being 'bound again, His soul upon the forfeit' for the marriage, and is still in some sense master of the play.

It is here that the world of *Much Ado About Nothing* begins. There is no symbolic Antonio to keep the balance; the situation works itself out on its own resources. It does this by the characteristic of the play which has been sometimes regarded as a most happy accident of careless genius—the displacement of Claudio and Hero by Benedick and Beatrice as the play's dominating figures, in the course of what is 'logical and necessary' in its action. This is brought about by allowing, more distinctively and fully than in any earlier comedy, a dance and battle—(a 'merry war' in which not every 'achiever brings home full numbers') of two worlds, which it is a gross, but serviceable, generalisation to call the 'masculine' and the 'feminine' worlds. And this in itself is achieved by the creation of a peculiarly social and domestic context—rarified, formal, and elegant, but still suggesting a social reality that makes the character of the sexes distinct. The sense of place, in its importance to the play, I have mentioned earlier; the sense of time has also an unusual function. One need only reflect on the obvious difference of age between Claudio and Hero, and Benedick and Beatrice—who play lightly with the idea of an obstinate, and therefore time-tried, celibacy; and ask oneself in what earlier comedy there is any differentiation other than that of Youth and Age. One can contrast, also, the references to past and future time that occur in earlier comedies with those in *Much Ado About Nothing*. ''A killed your sister', in *Love's Labour's Lost*, or Helena's memory of 'schooldays' friend-ship, childhood innocence', or Titania's memories of the sport on the Indian shore—all quoted above—have all, to varying degrees, an exquisite stylisation, an emblematic quality, that prevents their giving another temporal dimension to the play; they are an inset, not a perspective; an intensification of or contrast with the present, not an evocation of the past. But the casual, continual and colloquial harking-back in *Much Ado About Nothing* has a quite different effect.

> O, he's returned, and as pleasant as ever he was . . .

> He set up his bills here in Messina, and challenged Cupid at the flight; and my uncle's fool, reading the challenge, subscrib'd for Cupid, and challenged him at the bird-bolt . . .

> They never meet but there's a skirmish of wit between them . . .

> In our last conflict four of his five wits went halting off . . .

> Indeed, my lord, he lent it me awhile; and I gave him use for it, a double heart for his single one . . .

> I have heard my daughter say she hath often dreamt of unhappiness, and waked herself with laughing . . .

One can, if one likes, play the same game with references to the future, contrasting *Love's Labour's Lost's*

> You shall this twelvemonth term from day to day
> Visit the speechless sick, and still converse
> With groaning wretches . . . [*L.L.L.*, v ii 838–40]

with *Much Ado About Nothing's*

> O Lord, my lord, if they were but a week married, they would talk themselves mad . . .

> I will live in thy heart, die in thy lap, and be buried in thy eyes; and, moreover, I will go with thee to thy uncle's . . .

This easy, humorous, and conversational manner, that refers to a past and future governed by customary event and behaviour, and that carries a sense of habitual reality in a familiar social group, gives the play the quality that it would be certainly unwise to call 'realism'; it is an atmosphere easier to feel than to define. It is one of ennobled domesticity, aware of, touched by, and reflecting events in the outside world, but finally providing its own rules and customs: it is, in fact, a world largely feminine in character.

Into this world, at the beginning of the play, come the warriors, covered with masculine honours, cheerful with victory, and heralded importantly by a messenger. They even bring their own style of figured public rhetoric with them:

> He hath borne himself beyond the promise of his age,
> doing in the figure of a lamb the feats of a lion . . .

> The fashion of the world is to avoid cost, and you
> encounter it . . .

> I had rather be a canker in a hedge than a rose in his
> grace; and it better fits my blood to be disdained of all
> than to fashion a carriage to rob love from any . . .

The 'most exquisite Claudio', the 'proper squire', is the flower of such a world; the plot that concerns him, and that seems at first to dominate the play, can be seen as the survival of all that is most formal, and least flexible, in the earlier comedies: a masculine game of romantic love with a firm—and sensible—business basis, the whole governed by an admirable sense of priorities in duty:

> I look'd upon her with a soldier's eye,
> . . .
> But now I am return'd, and that war-thoughts
> Have left their places vacant, in their rooms
> Come thronging soft and delicate desires,
> All prompting me how fair young Hero is,
> Saying I lik'd her ere I went to wars. [1 i 260, 263–7]

If modern sentimentalism makes one dislike the foundation to Claudio's case—female good looks plus paternal income—it is as well to remember that it is an attitude embedded in all the

comedies to date, whenever they touch on realism, and shared
not only by Bassanio but—even though half-mockingly—by
Benedick: 'Rich she shall be, that's certain . . . fair, or I'll never
look on her.'

The beginning of the play, then, presents, in a social context, a
company of young bloods, headed by the noble Don Pedro, who
all hold together with a cheerful masculine solidarity. The 'sworn
brothers' are companions-in-arms, and if one deserts, there is
cause for lamentation: 'I have known when he would have
walked ten mile afoot to see a good armour, and now will he lie
ten nights awake carving the fashion of a new doublet.' If
Claudio dramatically distrusts Don Pedro at first—

> Let every eye negotiate for itself,
> And trust no agent; for beauty is a witch
> Against whose charms faith melteth into blood.
>
> [II i 157–9]

then the discovery of his mistake only strengthens his later trust
in, and solidarity with, Don Pedro; and this trust is implicit even
in the terms of his first doubt, which still postulates a male world
of 'negotiation' and 'agents', against the hypnotic and possibly
devilish enemy, Woman. Claudio's world, and Claudio's plot,
are never 'reformed'—in a dramatic, or moral sense—because
they neither can nor need be changed; the simple course of
loving, mistaking, and winning again, written from a specifically
masculine point of view (again using the word masculine in its
idiosyncratic sense here) that is half romance and half business, is
a necessary backbone to the play, and holds the comedy together:

> Look, what will serve is fit: 'tis once, thou lovest;
> And I will fit thee with the remedy.

And though Hero is in the course of it 'killed, in some senses', as
Dogberry might have said, she also gets her place in the world,
and all is well. A comedy of romance needs something stable,
limited, and circular, in which ends match beginnings, and in
Claudio it gets this:

Sweet Hero, now thy image does appear
In the rare semblance that I loved it first. [v i 237–8]

Another Hero!

Nothing certainer: . . . [v iv 62]

But if this world is not 'reformed', it is to a large extent displaced;
and the moment of that displacement is not hard to find:

D. PED. Myself, my brother, and this grieved Count
Did see her, hear her, at that hour last night
Talk with a ruffian at her chamber window; . . .

[IV i 88–90]

Exeunt D. Pedro, D. John and Claudio
BENE. How doth the lady? [IV i 112]

Left on stage we have a fainting and dishonoured girl; her wholly
doubting and wretched old father, held to her only by paternal
obligation; a wise and detached old Friar; and the dishonoured
girl's cousin, in a rage of loyal devotion that is familial, sexual,
and instinctual. One cannot help asking what the young, witty
and independent soldier Benedick is doing in that gallery. He has
broken the rules of the game, and entered upon a desertion far
more serious than Claudio's ever appeared: he is crossing the
boundaries of a world of masculine domination. How serious the
desertion is, is indicated by his comic—but only partly comic—
exchange with Beatrice, at the centre of their professions of love,
that follow immediately on the church scene:

BENE. Come, bid me do anything for thee.
BEAT. Kill Claudio.
BENE. Ha! Not for the wide world.
BEAT. You kill me to deny it. Farewell. [IV i 286–9]

'Kill Claudio' has become such a famous line that perhaps
something of its importance, underlying its comic gesture of an
unfeasible rage, has been lost. A pacific, sensible and level-
headed bachelor is being forced toward a decision of alarming
significance; and he accepts it. Beatrice's taunt "You dare easier

be friends with me than fight with mine enemy" colours the whole of the end of the play, and produces the peculiar dramatic and psychological complexity of the scene of the challenge. In it, three characters, once a joint group of young men exchanging cheerful and witty backchat, begin to speak and think in two different worlds. Don Pedro's and Claudio's return to the old game between themselves—perfectly in place an hour earlier— becomes curiously embarrassing by the degree to which it can take no account of the dramatic change in Beatrice and Benedick's status, their siding with what the audience knows to be truth, or rather, a truer game than Don Pedro's and Claudio's:

> D. PED. But when shall we set the savage bull's horns on the sensible Benedick's head?
> CLAU. Yea, and the text underneath, 'Here dwells Benedick the married man'?
> BENE. Fare well, boy: you know my mind. I will leave you now to your gossip-like humour; you break jests as braggarts do their blades, which, God be thanked, hurt not. My lord, for your many courtesies I thank you. I must discontinue your company. Your brother the bastard is fled from Messina. You have among you killed a sweet and innocent lady. For my Lord Lackbeard there, he and I shall meet; and till then, peace be with him. (*Exit*)
> D. PED. He is in earnest.
>   . . .
> What a pretty thing man is when he goes in his doublet and hose and leaves off his wit!
>   [v i 174–86, 91–2]

It is not sufficient to say simply that this effect is gained by some 'change' in Benedick's—the witty Benedick's—character. It is rather that our own attitude has changed in the course of the play, so that something developing under the agency of the 'important' characters has relieved them of their importance. Certain qualities, certain attitudes that have been found, in the earlier comedies, mainly confined to the women's and fools' parts, have here come into their own.

The plays have such artistic continuity that it is almost impossibly difficult to distinguish certain attitudes and feelings, and call *this* a specifically 'feminine' attitude, or *that*, one belonging to a 'fool' or 'clown'; and the more mature the play, the more danger of falsifying there is. Perhaps it is merely possible to indicate certain speeches of Beatrice which do cohere into an attitude that utilises a 'fool's' uncommitted wit and detached play of mind, together with a clown's grasp of earthy reality, yet committed in such a new way that they are given the effect of a female veracity against a masculine romanticism or formality.

> Yes, faith; it is my cousin's duty to make curtsy, and say 'Father, as it please you'. But yet for all that, cousin, let him be a handsome fellow, or else make another curtsy and say, 'Father, as it please me'. [II i 44–7]

The whole game of romantic passion was never glossed more conclusively than by her foreboding 'I can see a church by daylight'; nor the silliness of romantic jealousy than by her sturdy description of Claudio as 'civil as an orange, and something of that jealous complexion'; nor the game of formal, courteous and meaningless proposals—(Don Pedro's 'Will you have me, lady?') than by her: 'No, my lord, unless I might have another for working-days: your Grace is too costly to wear every day.' (Certainly, Don Pedro does prove to be a costly guest, since he all but causes the death of his host's daughter.) The beautiful and formal scene that the men have arranged for the uniting of Claudio and Hero—'his Grace hath made the match, and all Grace say amen to it!' begins to be disarranged by Beatrice's detached sense ('Speak, Count, 'tis your cue') and she hastily has to give her 'merry heart' the fool's harmless part in the play: 'I thank it, poor fool, it keeps on the windy side of care.' But the rising flight of her impertinence, which provokes Leonato to bustle her off the scene ('Niece, will you look to those things I told you of?') is not unacquainted with 'care'. Don Pedro's kindly and polite.

> out of question, you were born in a merry hour

is met by her

> No, sure, my lord, my mother cried; but then there was a
> star danced, and under that was I born. [II i 302–3]

However light the reference, one goes back to the lamenting
Adriana, out of place in a play of brisk farce; or the surprising
seriousness of the reference in *Love's Labour's Lost* to Katharine's
sister—

> He made her melancholy, sad and heavy,
> And so she died . . .

or the equally surprising seriousness of Titania's loyalty:

> But she, being mortal, of that boy did die . . .
> And for her sake I will not part with him . . .

The liaison of Claudio and Hero draws the 'fools' Benedick and
Beatrice into the play; and it is Beatrice who first here begins to
show in her apparently detached wit, only partially revealed in
her sparring with Benedick, the depth that the occasion demands. Marriage is seen here not as a witty dance of 'wooing,
wedding and repenting', but as the joining of Beatrice's 'cousins',
and her remarks have greater and more dangerous point. It is not
surprising that on her exit Don Pedro sets afoot his second piece of
matchmaking, since Beatrice patently needs a master, 'We are
the only love-gods.'
    It is only at the crisis of the play, in the church scene, that this
dogged, loyal, and irrational femininity that characterises
Beatrice comes into its own. The still hesitating and just Benedick
is swept into her degree of belief simply by her obstinate passion
of loyalty:

> Is 'a not approved in the height a villain that hath
> slandered, scorned, dishonoured my kinswoman? O that I
> were a man! What! bear her in hand until they come to
> take hands, and then with public accusation, uncovered
> slander, unmitigated rancour—O God that I were a man!
> I would eat his heart in the market-place. [IV i 298–304]

Certainly her storms are comic; nevertheless our own sense at
the end of the play of the limitations of the romantic background,
and critics' unanimous conviction that Benedick and Beatrice
'take over the play', is largely summed up by her own 'Talk with
a man out at a window! A proper saying!' and the comparative
shallowness of the romanticism of the main plot very neatly and
adequately summed up in her voluble harangue:

> Princes and Counties! Surely, a princely testimony, a
> goodly count, Count Comfect; a sweet gallant, surely! O
> that I were a man for his sake! or that I had any friend
> would be a man for my sake! But manhood is melted into
> curtsies, valour into compliment, and men are only
> turned into tongue, and trim ones too. He is now as
> valiant as Hercules that only tells a lie and swears it. I
> cannot be a man with wishing, therefore I will die a
> woman with grieving. [IV i 312 ff.]

This is simultaneously a remarkable picture of a woman in a state
of outraged temper, and an excellent piece of dramatic criticism.
For Benedick, this is 'Enough. I am engaged'. The fools of the
play have become the heroes.

To use the word 'fools' is perhaps incautious: since, for one
thing, Benedick's and Beatrice's speeches are characterised by a
degree of sophistication and self command; and for another, the
play itself has an excellent collection of clowns who do,
noticeably, help to bring about the dénouement and save the
day. But if one is attempting to explain the feeling of maturity
and development that Beatrice and Benedick bring into the play,
then it becomes apparent that a part of their strength comes from
Shakespeare's drawing on resources of feeling expressed, in
earlier comedies, as much by witty jesters and innocent clowns, as
by the kind of sophisticated commentators that one finds in
Berowne and Rosaline. The sense of wisdom that they give is best
glossed, perhaps, by Blake's 'If the fool would persist in his folly,
he would become wise'.

Folly is an almost impossibly difficult thing to define. Perhaps
one can say at least that the chief source of humour in
Shakespeare's early comedies comes from a dichotomy between
aspiration and actuality; the chief source of satisfaction, from the

final resolution of these two things. If one looks at *Love's Labour's Lost* for instance, one sees a comic pattern repeated throughout. The young men first aspire toward a noble, beautiful, and impossible sublimity of monastic ascetism—

> . . .   brave conquerors, for so you are
> That war against your own affections
> And the huge army of the world's desires . . .
>
> [*L.L.L.*, i i 8–10]

and then of course fall in love with the first females at the gate. Then again they aspire lyrically towards the heights of love—

> For valour, is not love a Hercules,
> Still climbing trees in the Hesperides?
>
> [*L.L.L.*, iv iii 336–7]

and from this height it takes the clowns (who prove that Hercules is, after all, a mere Moth) and the women to bring them down, offering a second and harsher ascetism, in 'some forlorn and naked hermitage'; or a second sphere for wit:

> To move wild laughter in the throat of death?
> It cannot be; it is impossible;
> Mirth cannot move a soul in agony.
>
> [*L.L.L.*, v ii 843–5]

If the hermitage and the hospital are not 'actuality', they are nearer to being a figure for it, in the exquisite and formalised world of the play, than are the secluded and noble park-lands. The clowns and fools of the play suffer a similar fall, in aspiring toward similar nobilities of love and learning; and the actuality of the play that they perform proves the degree of their folly. Armado, who sees himself as Hector, must play the 'Honest Troyan' by Jaquenetta; Costard's Pompey the Great finds himself merely the Big. But the fairly simple satire is transformed, in the games that both 'high' and 'low-life' characters play, in what is to prove the highly individual Shakespearian manner. Folly begins to transmute itself; out of this very discovery of the ridiculousness of aspiration, something not in itself ridiculous grows, generating a second movement upward:

> Let us once lose our oaths to find ourselves;
> Or else we lose ourselves to keep our oaths.
> It is religion to be thus forsworn;
> For charity itself fulfils the law,
> And who can sever love from charity?
>
> [*L.L.L.*, iv iii 357–61]

This statement of what might be *gained* from folly is more clearly indicated and illustrated by some of the most surprising lines in the play. Armado, who is throughout genuinely ridiculous, is never more so than when enacting Hector. Yet he turns the laughter of the audience by his famous 'The sweet war-man is dead and rotten; sweet chucks, beat not the bones of the buried; when he breathed, he was a man . . .' This is akin to Holofernes' suddenly serious rebuke to the mockery of the young lovers: 'This is not generous, not gentle, not humble.' For once more affecting than affected, Armado's plea for the dignity of the dead becomes a plea for the dignity of the fool; mortality, after all, makes equal fools of all men. 'Get you to my lady's chamber, and tell her, let her paint an inch thick, to this favour she must come; make her laugh at that.' Or—to gloss Armado from a later comedy—'as all is mortal in nature, so is all nature in love mortal in folly'.

This suggestion, brilliantly scattered throughout *Love's Labour's Lost*—that dignity comes through an acceptance of folly; and that through this self-acceptance, and even better, self-knowledge, a man is twice a fool and yet 'not altogether fool, my lord'—is present in *The Two Gentlemen of Verona* in a more solid and simple form. The noble chivalric love of the main characters transforms itself before our eyes into Launce and his dog. The dog is a bleak and simple positive in the play at the opposite end to Silvia's simple god-head; he is, so to speak, the god of love spelt backwards. 'Ask my dog. If he say ay, it will; if he say no, it will; if he shake his tail and say nothing, it will.' Launce's dog is infallible. To substitute a dog for a cold Petrarchan mistress is the simplest of comic tricks; but not so simple when done by genius.

> I think Crab my dog be the sourest-natured dog that lives: my mother weeping, my father wailing, my sister crying,

> our maid howling, our cat wringing her hands, and all
> our house in a great perplexity; yet did not this cruel-
> hearted cur shed one tear. He is a stone, a very pebble
> stone, and has no more pity in him than a dog.
>
> [*T.G.V.*, ii iii 4–9]

All the possibilities of folly in idealistic love, and in the play, are
'placed' by Launce's plaintive laments: 'How many masters
would do this for his servant? Nay, I'll be sworn, I have sat in the
stocks for puddings he hath stolen, otherwise he had been
executed . . .' And yet, as before, this is transformed satire. 'I am
but a fool, look you, and yet I have the wit to think my master is a
kind of knave.' In an idealistic world, earthy commonsense looks
foolish enough; yet there is a savoir-faire, a calm satisfaction
about Launce that makes us think again about folly. Launce gets
what he wants: his dog.

Bottom is an expanded Launce; Launce with imagination,
Launce sitting in the lap of the Gods. 'Out of doubt he is
transported.' *A Midsummer Night's Dream* is so subtle, and so
integrated in its depiction of folly, that one hesitates to coarsen it
by sketchy generalisation. The ridiculous and the beautiful grow
so much closer together in this play that it is harmful to try to
separate them: 'Man is but an ass if he go about to expound this
dream' is a good enough warning. But that one can quote this
remark of Bottom's indicates something of the growing complexity of the foolish nature. The young lovers, and the heroic
couple, know the difference between dreaming and waking only
by the common consent of their senses:

> The Duke was here . . .
> . . .
> Why then we are awake . . .
>
> And all their minds transfigur'd so together,
> More witnesseth than fancy's images,
> And grows to something of great constancy . . .
>
> [*M.N.D.*, iv i 192–5; v i 24–6]

But to Bottom 'a dream is a dream is a dream'. He is both more
rooted in a narrow, flat and earthy sense that makes nonsense of

all dreams and games—of love or of magic or of dramatics—and
more innocently capable of entering into them with easy belief,
taking them for what they are.

> Let me play the lion too. I will roar that I will do any
> man's heart good to hear me; I will roar that I will make
> the Duke say, 'Let him roar again, let him roar
> again.' [*M.N.D.*, I ii 61–5]

> . . . tell them that I Pyramus am not Pyramus but
> Bottom the weaver. This will put them out of fear.
> [III i 18–20]

Books could be written—and probably have been—on the
nature of dramatic illusion in *A Midsummer Night's Dream*; but
one remark of Bottom's neatly clarifies the nature of dramatic
belief, at least as far as the actor is concerned: 'What beard were I
best to play it in?' There may be little apparent similarity
between a Bottom and a Beatrice; but her gift, too, is to 'Find out
Moonshine', and she, like Bottom, refuses to fall back on the
evidence of the eyes and ears of noblemen to find out whether a
dream is true or not: she trusts herself.

The folly of the clowns and naturals in *A Midsummer Night's
Dream* is interesting, then, in its fertility; it lacks any nobility, but
it leaves room for development. In the folly of Bottom there are
the vestiges of wisdom, which could become self-knowledge.
Theseus, the noblest figure in the play, can only judge; he has too
much dignity to 'play'. Demetrius and the other young lovers
'play', and are made fools of; but they can only judge other men's
games, not their own. Bottom and the others have folly bred in
the bone—an innocent, ignorant, and self-loving conviction of
their own adequacy in a magical or artistic world—but they are
also given a tough common sense that makes them, like Launce,
and like the naturals in *Love's Labour's Lost*, twice fools, and not
fools. 'Sixpence a day in Pyramus, or nothing . . .' or ' . . . No, I
assure you, the wall is down that parted their fathers,' shows
something of a capacity at once to 'play', and to 'judge' the play.

Falstaff takes us far closer to Benedick and Beatrice, though his
is a different world from theirs. Like Bottom, and like Launce,
Falstaff is imperturbably at home in physical things (as Costard

says: 'It is the simplicity of man to hearken after the flesh.' 'If sack
and sugar be a fault, God help the wicked!') and Falstaff wanders
in a world of heroic values, both mocking them and mocked by
them. 'Let us be Diana's foresters, gentlemen of the shade,
minions of the moon; and let men say we be men of good
government, being governed, as the sea is, by our noble and
chaste mistress the moon, under whose countenance we steal.'
This is a revitalising of Berowne's plea:

> Sweet lords, sweet lovers, O let us embrace.
> As true we are as flesh and blood can be.
> The sea will ebb and flow, heaven show his face;
> Young blood doth not obey an old decree . . .
>
> [*L.L.L.*, IV iii 210–3]

but it is backed by the irony of self-knowledge.

Falstaff, like all clowns, elbows aside the rules of the world he
lives in: 'This chair shall be my state, this dagger my sceptre, this
cushion my crown . . . And here is my speech. Stand aside,
nobility.' But his presence is more disturbing than that of any of
the earlier clowns, by the increased degree of consciousness, and
of self-consciousness, that he is given. The physical challenge of
the 'tun of man' is enormous; much more so is the intellectual
challenge of his awareness, both of what he is, *and* of the world
which he mocks and parodies. To a far greater extent than
Bottom, Falstaff is both actor *and* critic, playing out his game, and
judging it. 'Dost thou hear me, Hal? . . . Do so, for it is worth the
listening to . . .' 'Gallants, lads, boys, hearts of gold, all the titles
of good fellowship come to you! What, shall we be merry? Shall
we have a play extempore?' Hal only barely dominates him by
two simple devices, which give him something of the superiority
of the jester over the natural. He stands, like a dwarf on a giant's
shoulders, on the grandeur of History, of historic, and not
imaginative, fact; and he is given a statement of consciousness
and self-consciousness, in the first movement of the play, that
'trumps' even Falstaff's:

> I know you all, and will awhile uphold
> The unyok'd humour of your idleness . . .
>
> [I *H.IV*, I ii 188–9]

Falstaff's magnificent usefulness only begins to wear out in Part II of *Henry IV*. The game of politics begins to turn into the game of life itself, since Hal must 'play the king' in all seriousness; that Falstaff's superlative wits detach themselves from *that* game arouses a certain sense of the need for yet another development of clowning.

> DOLL . . . Thou whoreson little tidy Bartholomew boar-pig, when wilt thou leave fighting a days and foining a nights, and begin to patch up thine old body for heaven?
>
> FALS. Peace, good Doll! Do not speak like a death's-head; do not bid me remember mine end.
>
> [2 *H.IV*, II iv 220–5]

There are games—the second part of *Henry IV* suggests—in which the comic poise, that is generated by a knowledge of human ridiculousness and limitation, must generate something else to defeat that limitation:

> BENE. . . . If a man do not erect in this age his own tomb ere he dies, he shall live no longer in monument than the bell rings and the widow weeps.
>
> BEAT. And how long is that, think you?
>
> BENE. Question: why, an hour in clamour, and a quarter in rheum. [v ii 67–71]

So, in this colloquy between Benedick and Beatrice, one returns to *Much Ado*. Benedick and Beatrice are a delightful lesson in how the fool can 'Serve God, love me, and mend'. This they do by 'persisting in their folly', in order to 'become wise'.

Their attitude at the beginning of the play is the comic stance of self-consciousness. Both gain dignity by an intellectual independence—by 'sitting in a corner and crying Heigh-ho!' while they watch 'everyone going to the world'. This intellectual independence is largely a full and mocking knowledge—especially, at first, on Beatrice's side—of the physical realities underlying romantic aspirations. 'But, for the stuffing . . . well, we are all mortal.' Over and over again, 'my uncle's fool' takes the place of Cupid. 'Lord! I could not endure a husband with a

beard on his face: I had rather lie in the woollen . . .' Mars as
well as Cupid falls: the heroic warrior, who has done good
'service' is 'a very valiant trencherman; he hath an excellent
stomach . . . (and is) a good soldier—to a lady'. Yet the very
intellectual detachment that gives a jester his dignity is the power
to see general truths; and what is true of 'mortals' must therefore
be true also of Benedick and Beatrice, who are intellectually and
dramatically joined to the hero and heroine of the main plot, by
being friend and cousin to them, and by understanding—
therefore sharing—their folly. Benedick's *ubi sunts* for bachelors
derive their humour from the steadily-increasing knowledge that
he is, like Barkis, going out with the tide: 'In faith, hath not the
world one man but he will wear his cap with suspicion? Shall I
never see a bachelor of three score again? . . . Like the old tale,
my lord: It is not so, nor 'twas not so, but indeed, God forbid it
should be so!' Like Falstaff, Benedick is comic by being both actor
and critic, and knows which way 'old tales' go; and though he
may cast himself as bachelor, 'he never could maintain his part
but in the force of his will'. Benedick and Beatrice are 'fooled' and
'framed' by the dramatist even before they are 'fooled' by the
trick played on them by Don Pedro and the others; their
detached intelligence is, by definition, an understanding of the
way their "foolish" desires will go. 'Shall quips and sentences and
the paper bullets of the brain awe a man from the career of his
humour? No: the world must be peopled.'

Thus, when Benedick and Beatrice do 'run mad', they suffer—
like Falstaff in love—a loss of dignity the more marked by
contrast with their intellectual detachment earlier. Benedick
searching for double meanings, and Beatrice nursing a sick heart,
a cold in the head, and a bad temper, are as 'placed' within the
others' play as are the clowns in *Love's Labour's Lost* or *A
Midsummer Night's Dream*, attendant on the critique of their
superiors. It is, of course, the church scene, and all that follows,
that changes this, and shows their double 'folly' coming into its
own. Beatrice is loyal to Hero simply by virtue of an acquaint-
ance with common sense physical realities—'Talk with a man
out at a window! A proper saying!'—and by a flood of intuitive,
irrational, and 'foolish' pity and love, that instinctively recognises the good when it sees it—good in Benedick, or in Hero; and
Benedick is drawn to her, here, through very similar feelings.

'Lady Beatrice, have you wept all this while?' In the professions of love that follow Benedick's opening, there are touches of great humour; but the scene is a serious one, nevertheless. Both Benedick and Beatrice gain a new and much more complex equilibrium and dignity; both pledge themselves by their 'soul' to Hero's cause, and hence to each other. To be intelligent is to be aware 'that we are all mortal'; and to be mortal is to be a fool; and therefore intelligent men are most fools; but to be a fool, in a good cause, is to be wise. This is an old paradox that echoes through and through Shakespeare's comedies, and after.

Because Beatrice and Benedick are 'too wise to woo peaceably', they continue to bicker comfortably through the rest of the play, as though enjoying the mutual death of their individuality:

> Two distincts, division none.

Like Theseus' hounds, the quarrels of all the players grow, finally, into:

> Such gallant chiding . . .
> . . .
> So musical a discord . . .
> . . .
> . . . matched in mouths like bells,
> Each under other . . . [*M.N.D.*, IV, i 112–21]

An unlyrical play grows into a new and interesting harmony, as all the forms of folly in the play find 'measure in everything, and so dance out the answer':

> BENE. Come, come, we are friends. Let's have a dance ere
> we are married, that we may lighten our own hearts
> and our wives' heels.
> LEON. We'll have dancing afterwards.
> BENE. First, of my word; therefore play, music.
>   [V iv 113–17]

Though the play can be summed up by the image of the dance, it is also a battle, in which certain things are lost. Hero's 'death' is an illusion, but other things do seem to die out of the comedies:

part of an old romantic ideal, and a sense of easy loyalty between young men. Rosalind's 'Men have died from time to time, and worms have eaten them, but not for love . . .' and Antonio's bitter, though mistaken, reflections on friendship, both represent a kind of feeling that can be seen to emerge with some clarity in *Much Ado*. Some more important things take the place of what is lost, all perhaps developing out of the sense of that loss; a wisdom, balance, and generosity of mind and feeling, largely expressed through the women's rôles.

This paper has itself probably been unwise, unbalanced and ungenerous in all that it has omitted. I have concentrated only on certain elements in *Much Ado About Nothing* that interest me, and may have distorted them in the process. My intention has not been to present Shakespeare as an earnest—though early— leader of the feminist movement, but only to suggest the development, through the comedies, of certain feelings and attitudes which are a constituent part of the plays as a whole, but which do tend to be most clearly expressed through the women in them. In Messina, Arden, and Illyria the expression of humane principle, of generous and constant feeling, comes principally from the women—whether we choose to see them as symbols merely of an area of the mind possessed by both sexes in common, or whether we see Shakespeare creating a world in which some kind of distinctively female rationale is able to have full play, and to dominate the action. When, in tragedy, the action moves on to the battlements of civilisation, and beyond, the difference of the sexes becomes of minor importance, and the rôle of the women diminishes; they become little more than functions of the hero's mind, barely aware of the area in which that mind operates. Ironically, the heroic qualities which make the woman's stature minor by comparison can be seen as developing through and out of qualities confined largely to the women in the 'mature' comedies; the values that are proved by their success in the comedies come to stand the proof of failure in the tragedies. Something of the tragic heroes' passionate constancy and painful knowledge, and something of the sane and honourable happiness that is felt most sharply in the tragedies by its absence, is first developed in the secure limitations of the 'mature' comedies, and is chiefly expressed through the talkative and intelligent women who guide events and guard principles. So *Much Ado About*

Nothing can be seen to have a certain aptness of title. The small world that it presents with such gaiety, wit, and pleasurable expertise, is perhaps relatively a 'nothing' in itself; but a certain amount of the interest and delight it produces comes from the awareness that much can be held in little, and that in 'nothing' can 'grow . . . something of great constancy'.

SOURCE: paper read at the Shakespeare Summer School, Stratford-upon-Avon (September 1961); published, with minor alterations, in *Critical Quarterly*, III (1961), 319–35.

J. R. Mulryne (1965)　　　The Large Design

If we were challenged to state, in general terms, the 'subject' of Shakespeare's early and mature comedies, we could properly reply 'love'. Or more precisely, 'love in courtship'. Their plots centre round the initial or consequent difficulties that stand in the way of love, and end with love's eventual triumph in marriage. They share the assumption that true intersexual love represents the highest good (male friendship, so highly valued by the Elizabethans, is barely dealt with) and make such love at once the standard of moral judgement and the subject of a delighted exploratory study. Each of the five most rewarding comedies— *The Merchant of Venice, A Midsummer Night's Dream, Much Ado, As You Like It, Twelfth Night*—concerns itself importantly with the nature of a lover's experience: its social and personal implications, its strength and its precariousness, its delusions, contradictions, exaltations and humiliations, and (before the debasement of the word) its enchantments. When we attempt for the first time, therefore, to explore the essential meaning of *Much Ado*, it will be useful to consider the fortunes of love-in-courtship as primary guide.

The overall design of *Much Ado* is not difficult to grasp. Basically the play is composed of three movements, the first (and longest) establishing the love-relationship between Benedick and Beatrice and between Claudio and Hero; the second portraying a crisis (when Don John's treachery causes the repudiation of Hero and her 'death'); and the third providing a resolution, as the deceit is exposed and a 'new' Hero marries a remorseful Claudio, and Beatrice Benedick. The comic thesis of the play in other words takes the form of love begun, love challenged and love confirmed: we are first made sympathetically aware of the love of two young couples (one pair willingly acknowledging love's claims, the other reluctantly); next, a malicious intrigue threatens to wreck all thoughts of joy and love; and finally life sails out into the clear once more, with a new strength and promise of endurance.

Each of Shakespeare's mature comedies holds in some measure a threat to the happiness of the figures for whom our sympathy is invited; in *Much Ado* our sense of comic triumph, of 'pleasurable reassurance' that 'all shall be well', is strong in proportion to the prominence given to the possibility of disaster. Only *The Merchant of Venice* gives equal weight to the threat that faces the protagonists. And so, when the play ends in double marriage (or rather in the dance that symbolises the concord of marriage) we enjoy vicariously a sense of good now established all the more firmly and valuably by virtue of the testing adversity to which it has been subjected. Characteristically, Shakespeare has anticipated the nature of this experience by figuring it in miniature in the first few lines of the play:

> MESS. . . . . He [Claudio] hath borne himself beyond the promise of his age, doing, in the figure of a lamb, the feats of a lion. He hath indeed better better'd expectation than you must expect of me to tell you how.
>
> LEON. He hath an uncle here in Messina will be very much glad of it.
>
> MESS. I have already delivered him letters, and there appears much joy in him; even so much that joy could not show itself modest enough without a badge of bitterness.

LEON. Did he break out into tears?
MESS. In great measure.
LEON. A kind overflow of kindness. There are no faces
truer than those that are so washed. How much
better is it to weep at joy than to joy at weeping!

[I i 11–24]

It is an experience of this nature, joy tempered by (modified and rendered more valid by) 'weeping', that the play will offer us. To speak in these terms, while a useful guide to the basic 'shape' of the play, is very far from precise enough. We must take the feel of the various episodes much more carefully if we are to appreciate, even on this initial, very general, level, the individual experience offered by *Much Ado*. Critics have never been in doubt as to the dominant figures of the play's first movement; some of the earliest references to *Much Ado* actually name the play 'Beatrice and Benedick'. Nor is there dispute about the type of experience these two figures convey. 'The mirth of Beatrice (and no less that of Benedick) is an outbreak of the joyous energy of life' (Dowden); '. . . the exuberant quality of lively minds which strike fire by scoring off each other . . . *competitive* vitality' (Rossiter); 'gay, light-hearted critics of every illusion' (J. R. Brown). These are phrases typical of the agreed response: abundant vitality, gaiety, self-confidence, a brilliantly witty command of language, are the qualities all of us respond to, and which bulk large in our experience of the play's initial movement. We have our first taste of their 'competitive vitality' very early. Shakespeare allows the messenger and Leonato to make the thematic point about joy and weeping, and then a distinctive voice cuts across the rather formal, even awkward and halting exchange—a capable actress can make much of this opportunity—to pose a question in a quite different idiom:

BEAT. I pray you, is Signior Mountanto returned from the wars or no?

The voice is distinctive partly because, as Hero immediately explains, it is unwilling to espouse even the most ordinary conventions; the irrepressible mockery that burgeons as the scene goes on here refuses to Benedick even the courtesy of his own name. And a few moments later there is another voice in concert with this one, each vying with the other to weave the more fanciful, witty and outrageous tracery of words, endlessly inventive and endlessly reckless of convention and simple truth. The first set of wit they play is typical of many to follow:

> BENE. What, my dear Lady Disdain! Are you yet living?
> BEAT. Is it possible Disdain should die while she hath such meet food to feed it as Signior Benedick? Courtesy itself must convert to Disdain if you come in her presence.
> BENE. Then is courtesy a turncoat. But it is certain I am loved of all ladies, only you excepted; and I would I could find in my heart that I had not a hard heart; for truly I love none. [I i 101–8]

And so on, almost inexhaustibly. We take delight in their carefree self-reliance, their refusal to acknowledge any claims but those of their own wit. Even as we recognise that they are engaged (whether conscious of it or not) in a common form of preliminary flirtation. And when their friends ease them, in parallel scenes rich in opportunities for comic by-play (as we have noted), into a hesitant recognition of their mutual affection, the play's dominant mood does not alter. Our experience is still one very largely of non-responsible gaiety. So all-pervasive, indeed, is this mood, that when we look back on the first movement, we scarcely remember the bethrothal of Claudio and Hero, nor Don John's sideline villainy. These characters and their affairs seem no more than necessary episodes in a plot whose main purpose is to give life to Beatrice and Benedick, and the emotional and intellectual experience they convey. And this, on an overall view, is to see them in proper perspective. For the moment, gaiety and non-responsibility dominate. . . .

The point of turn comes in Act III scene ii. As Benedick exits with Leonato to 'break' about his love for Beatrice (that situation, we think, is happily concluded; now 'the two bears will not bite one another when they meet'), Don John enters to initiate his malicious plot against Hero—an instance this of the fine dovetailing of event that characterises the whole *Much Ado* narrative. We move at once from a world of carefree gaiety, where the characteristic activity of language was a free and zestful elaboration, into a world that is cold and purposeful, a world of economic, even staccato utterance. Don John's careful qualification of 'disloyal' exemplifies the new temper:

> D. JOH. The word is too good to paint out her wickedness. I could say she were worse. Think you of a worse title, and I will fit her to it. Wonder not till further warrant. [III ii 97–9]

Where a single word had been, on Beatrice's lips or Benedick's, the impetus to an exuberant, fertile inventiveness, it is now the occasion for meticulous adjustment; language has grown unfruitful, open only to grudging dissection. Don John's accusation of Hero shows the same withholding brevity:

> D. JOH. I came hither to tell you, and, circumstances shorten'd (for she has been too long a-talking of), the lady is disloyal. [III ii 91–2]

An audience or reader cannot but respond to this altogether different emotional climate; the exhilaration of a few moments ago modulates into a sense of cold malice, a malice far more formidable than Don John had hitherto seemed to represent. In a moment the entire positive and reassuring drive of the play towards marriage has been halted, and we are plunged into a world where the obstacles to successful courtship may be substantial. We must allow ourselves to visualise a new gravity on the face of Claudio and Don Pedro, a new and colder tone in their voices, a new stiffness in their posture and movements. Sensitive production could convey the new temper very forcefully.

Shakespeare exercises a nice control over the extent of an audience's or a reader's involvement in this threatening new world; the next scene introduces for the first time Dogberry, Verges and the Watch, figures of sufficient humorous weight to counterbalance the villainies of Don John and his henchmen. We enter unaffectedly into the world of official bumbledom to which Dogberry introduces us; we delight in his selfimportance, his garrulous inconsequence, his huge and magnificent absurdity. And yet the Dogberry world merely *balances* that of Don John, it does not cancel it; it relieves tension sufficiently to preserve the comic hypothesis of 'all shall be well'—the mould would crack otherwise—but without in any way preventing us from responding with appropriate gravity to other and contrary scenes in this movement. . . .

It is in this connection that comment on the play, whether in print or verbal, often seems least adequate. Critics, unanimous and vocal in discussing Beatrice and Benedick, are equally unanimous and vocal in their treatment of the Watch. But lengthy and appreciative discussion of the 'Church' scene [IV i] and of some other, grave, episodes at this point in the play, is indeed rare. Despite this, an appeal to any serious remembered performance, or to a sensitive, visually-receptive reading, will confirm that these dark scenes bulk large in our experience; it is only through the distortion that non-imagining reading gives that they appear inconsiderable. Let us see what a critically alert, visually-conscious reading will make of at least the more obvious features of these episodes.

It is worth noticing, to begin with, that they are consciously and overtly 'theatrical': the setting and the properties suggested, as well as the language, help to press our experience right up to the frontiers of melodrama. In the 'Church' scene itself, we must see with the mind's eye the lighted candles and the monk's garb, the altar and the other church-like 'props', and take in the sense of formal decorum the grouping and gestures would imply. This is a solemn occasion, invoking for reader or audience sacred associations, and a heightened sense of convention, of propriety in behaviour and language. The Friar strengthens these responses by quoting from the Marriage Service itself:

> If either of you know any inward impediment why you should not be conjoined, I charge you on your souls to utter it. [IV i 11–12]

It is in such a context as this that Claudio's accusation is uttered, and in which it makes such a powerful impact. Our sense of occasion, of propriety and decorum is outraged; the violence of Claudio's language, in this hushed setting, causes horrified shock:

. . .

> But you are more intemperate in your blood
> Than Venus, or those pamper'd animals
> That rage in savage sensuality.   [IV i 58–60]

It is not so much that we feel for Hero as an individual—we know very little about her—but we respond with acute pain to this abrupt and even savage denial of marriage; here, on the very brink of the ceremony itself, in church. The whole play has been gathering towards the goal of wedlock—Claudio and Hero betrothed in the opening act, Benedick just gone off-stage to ask Beatrice's father for her hand—and now the whole edifice lies apparently wrecked. We have been conditioned to thinking of the comedy as working towards the confirmation of happiness in marriage (Don John's machinations have seemed idle threats) so that we respond to this crisis with an appropriate degree of shock. The shock, certainly, that the crises of melodrama bring; the contrived setting, the exaggeration of the language, the incredible promptitude with which Hero 'dies' all advise us of the appropriate provisional, half-detached response. But for the moment it takes our breath away.

After the accusation itself, attention is directed towards Hero's father and her uncle. If we rarely find adequate discussion of the early part of the scene, discussion of the two old men's grief is even more infrequent. And yet the central part of the 'Church' scene and the opening of Act v are concerned at some considerable length with Leonato's grief and Antonio's. Nor is it a matter of length only; the language employed is under a pressure of emotion and displays a metaphorical suggestiveness that marks it off from the common run of verse in this play. A critical reading of the text cannot afford to ignore lines such as these, to take a single example:

> LEON. . . .
>> Why ever wast thou lovely in my eyes?
>> Why had I not with charitable hand
>> Took up a beggar's issue at my gates,
>> Who smirchèd thus and mir'd with infamy,
>> I might have said, 'No part of it is mine;
>> This shame derives itself from unknown loins'?

But mine, and mine I lov'd, and mine I prais'd,
And mine that I was proud on, mine so much
That I myself was to myself not mine,
Valuing of her—why she, O, she is is fall'n
Into a pit of ink, that the wide sea
Hath drops too few to wash her clean again,
And salt too little which may season give
To her foul tainted flesh! [IV i 130–43]

This is, certainly, transitional verse; the lines that play with
'mine' are reminiscent of the early sonnets or of parts of *Richard II*
rather than the verse of Shakespeare's maturity. But the
rhetorical drive, the economy of means in the early lines are
unmistakably the work of a poet in full command of his medium;
and of one who would wish the subject treated given due weight
in performance or reading. Even the 'mine' sequence of thought
has in its iteration an appropriateness to the distraught re-
petitiveness of deep grief. And the metaphors of 'tainted
flesh', 'the wide sea' and 'cleansing' do not recall several of
Shakespeare's greatest plays (notably of course *Macbeth* and
Hamlet) merely by chance. For Shakespeare is here allowing this
play to ride as close as he dare to the borders of tragedy; and his
purpose evokes the appropriate language. If we are to appreciate
the full richness of the *Much Ado* experience we must be prepared
to give due emphasis to this 'tragic' aspect; no other comedy
embraces anything like such a range of emotional states, from the
wholly carefree to the desperately grieved.

At the risk of causing an imbalance in our response, we ought
to notice in a little detail the other scene in which Leonato's grief
and Antonio's is conveyed. Act V scene i confronts us with a
problem of response: is the opening sequence of this scene written
to extend the experience of deep dismay in which the Church
scene deals, and to hint at further possibilities of evil as Don Pedro
and Claudio are challenged to a duel by Antonio and Leonato; or
is it intended to provide local comic effect as two old dotards,
unhinged by grief, utter they know not what? The scene is often
played as though the second were Shakespeare's (or perhaps one
should say the play's) intention; and the opening scene of Act II
would seem to support this attitude. For there Antonio is very
evidently characterised, during the masked dance, as an inept

old man, a conventional portrait of old age, provocative of laughter only (see II i 111–23). Is the actor to present, then, a consistent portrait, and behave here in Act V with parallel absurdity? If he does so, the strong possibility arises that this whole portion of the scene will slide into farce, making the challenge to Don Pedro and Claudio ludicrous, and reflecting back undermining laughter on Leonato's protestations of grief at his daughter's disgrace. Carefully critical reading is necessary to determine which way performance ought to turn.

Some of Antonio's lines clearly suggest that he loses self-control; his utterance at lines 8off. is that of an over-excited, incompetent old man, quite unfitted to challenge the confident, reserved Don Pedro (the physical contrast between the two men, on the stage or in the mind's eye, will enforce the contrast):

> ANT. He shall kill two of us, and men indeed.
> But that's no matter; let him kill one first.
> Win me and wear me! Let him answer me.
> Come, follow me, boy; come, sir boy; come, follow me.
> Sir boy, I'll whip you from your foining fence!
> Nay, as I am a gentleman, I will. [V i 80–5]

These are the accents of an ultra-Polonius. And yet we ought to hesitate before we play them for laughter. Because they may equally well be evidence of a mind near the borders of sanity, uncomprehending of the probabilities understood by a mind less disturbed, since a single grief has occupied and controlled all its faculties. That this is a more fitting interpretation is suggested by the verse Shakespeare gives Leonato, Antonio's partner in grief. His opening speeches contain some of the play's most forceful dramatic poetry:

> I pray thee cease thy counsel,
> Which falls into mine ears as profitless
> As water in a sieve. Give not me counsel,
> Nor let no comforter delight mine ear
> But such a one whose wrongs do suit with mine.
> Bring me a father that so loved his child,
> Whose joy of her is overwhelmed like mine,
> And bid him speak of patience;

. . .
I pray thee peace. I will be flesh and blood;
For there was never yet philosopher
That could endure the toothache patiently,
However they have writ the style of gods
And made a push at chance and sufferance.

[v i 3–10, 34–8]

We have here a sorrow that is intended to strike us as pitiably
real; the language of these and the omitted speeches testifies
eloquently to that. The mixture of unaffected simplicity and
metaphoric (here almost allegoric) strength, together with
the lithe aphorism that caps the argument, bespeak a perfectly
serious intention, one realised with all the verbal means at the
author's command. It would seem mere wilfulness to risk diluting
the reality of Leonato's grief by placing it side-by-side with
absurdity. With pathetic incomprehension, perhaps. We cannot
on a sensitive reading agree to a laughter-provoking rôle for
Antonio: the full gravity of the opening section of Act v must be
appreciated.

   As we have seen, then, the first two movements take us through
gaiety and sorrow—'joy could not show itself modest [moderate,
fitting] enough without a badge of bitterness.' The non-
responsible light-heartedness associated with Benedick and
Beatrice, careless of 'chance and sufferance', has modulated into the grave emotions of the Church scene and after. Thus
Shakespeare has contoured the affective 'shape' of the play, and
set up conflicting emotions. Now he proposes what we have
called a 'resolution'. Again, to a visually unreceptive reading,
this resolution may seem peculiarly lightweight and incon-
sequential, a forced and hurried ending. But in the theatre, or on
visualised reading, it can have the effect of a real conclusion, the
establishment of a new and more permanent happiness; much as
a full close in music, with every discord resolved.

   The final movement begins (though it has important links
stretching backwards) with the action at 'Hero's tomb' (v
iii). . . . [An] impressive emotional experience [arises from] the
action before the tomb . . ., the sense of an exhausted darkness,
as the black-dressed mourners and musicians sing and chant. But
in the following lines a contrary impulse manifests itself; there

supervenes a passage that brings with it opposite ideas, the springing of new life and new purposes:

> D. PED. Good morrow, masters; put your torches out.
> The wolves have preyed, and look, the gentle day,
> Before the wheels of Phoebus, round about
> Dapples the drowsy east with spots of gray.
> Thanks to you all, and leave us. Fare you well. [v ii 24–8]

The delicate lyric grace of these lines sets them apart from everything else in the play; spoken by a gifted actor, their cadence alone sufficiently informs us that an important turning-point in the action has arrived. The lyric note hints that less burdensome experience will follow, and this the language used confirms. The emphasis falls on images of sunrise and morning; the darkness in which evil thrived (the wolf-image) is over, and morning comes with its new life and freedom. The famous lines that follow the departure of the Ghost in *Hamlet* ('But, look, the morn in russet mantle clad . .') carry the same message of assurance after the terror of the night (though in that play the day's purposes may seem clearer than they are). Here Shakespeare goes on to underline the promise of the new day by referring specifically to the fresh and brighter clothes his actors will wear when they next appear:

> D. PED. Come, let us hence and put on other weeds,
> And then to Leonato's we will go. [v iii 30–1]

In the theatre, the visual contrast between the 'tomb' scene and the final scene at Leonato's house (v iv.) would be very marked. Already, on the modern stage, intensifying light would imitate the dawning of a new day, a new day of theatrical experience as well as in the play's time-scheme; on both Elizabethan and modern stages gesture and movement would give the effect of new freedom—the play has shaken off the grave restraints of its second movement. Altogether, the change-over is an impressive theatrical experience; assuring us, despite what has occurred, of the confirmed happiness in which the comedy will end.

The, as yet, muted promise of the 'tomb' scene bears fruit in the full morning that succeeds it. Amid the chatter and

movement of Leonato's house, (note that 'good morrow' is
repeated four times between ll. 34 and 40), Shakespeare invokes
an even more powerful symbolism than the morning-and-new-
clothes we have just been discussing. The 'rebirth' or 'resurrection' of Hero carries further, in terms familiar to the
Elizabethans, and not entirely obscure to a modern reader,
themes of new life and innocence:

> CLAU. Give me your hand; before this holy friar
> I am your husband if you like of me.
> HERO And when I lived I was your other wife; (*unmasking*)
> And when you loved you were my other husband.
> CLAU. Another Hero!
> HERO   Nothing certainer.
> One Hero died defiled; but I do live,
> And surely as I live, I am a maid.
> D. PED. The former Hero! Hero that is dead!
> LEON. She died, my lord, but whiles her slander lived.
>
> [v iv 58–66]

This is the final confirmation of the comic experience the play
exists to communicate. The 'death' that Don John's slander
brought with it—the grievous experience of the second
movement—has been cancelled by the re-birth of happiness, a
happiness the comic form bids us take as permanent.

Much Ado closes with a dance. It is devised, says Benedick 'that
we may lighten our own hearts and our wives' heels'. But an
Elizabethan audience would have discerned wider meanings in it
than this; and even we, as we visualise each actor taking his part
in the graceful, *orderly*, steps, his every movement perfectly allied
to his fellows' movements and the whole governed by music, can
without difficulty appreciate the dance as symbol of order.
(Consider how we still use such words as 'concord' 'harmony'
'attuned', each a dead metaphor from music). Beatrice has
already (II i 68–79) briefly and delightfully parodied Sir John
Davies' *Orchestra; A Poem of Dancing* (1596), a very well known
work which uses the dance as symbol of order, on personal,
political and indeed universal levels. Clearly, an early audience
would have seen the concluding dance as a satisfactory symbol of
the happiness-confirming order with which comedy leaves us. As

marriage itself is a symbol of order, society's divinely-sanctioned means of controlling and directing sexual relations. About this the Elizabethan homilists are explicit. Shakespeare and his audience would have regarded the marriage with which each of his comedies ends as more than a convenient stopping-place or as a 'romantic' (in its modern, debased sense) convenience; they take their place as the fitting resolution of the diverse experience in which each play has dealt.

So the play has moved through gaiety and woe on to confirmed happiness: love begun, love challenged and love triumphant in marriage. For an audience or reader the experience is one of 'pleasurable reassurance'—a demonstration in terms of theatre that good will conquer, that 'all shall be well'. So it is with all Shakespeare's comedies before, say, 1601 (the 'early' and 'mature' but not the 'problem' nor of course 'the last'). All are 'happy' (Dover Wilson's word) in the sense that they deal vivaciously with their subjects, and all display an almost total absence of severe judgements. Exceptions do of course exist: Shylock, for example, and Malvolio are treated with clear disapproval, as is Don John in the present play. And yet *Much Ado* is characteristic in focusing attention at the end elsewhere than on the villain:

MESS. My lord, your brother John is ta'en in flight,
        And brought with armèd men back to Messina.
BENE. Think not on him till tomorrow. I'll devise thee brave
        punishments for him. Strike up, pipers! [v iv 120–3]

The philosophy behind these plays involves, as the final speech suggests, the belief that evil can be excluded and punished, and without having first caused irreparable damage to the society on which it was parasitic.

SOURCE: extract from *Shakespeare: 'Much Ado About Nothing'* (London, 1965), pp. 14–25.

Paul and *Miriam Mueschke*   Illusion and Metamorphosis (1967)

The gaiety of *Much Ado About Nothing* is consistently praised; its somber aspects are either ignored or disparaged. Most critics agree that *Much Ado* is the gayest of Shakespeare's three joyous comedies, that its theme is courtship, and that the main plot centers on the wooing and winning of Hero. These basic assumptions lead to a number of widely accepted conclusions: since the subplot is more original than the main plot, the witty lovers overshadow the troubled lovers; Hero, shadowy and silent, is not a credible heroine since the audience, assuming a vindication of her innocence, takes her plight lightly; Claudio, the titular hero, is a cad who should not be rewarded by marrying the lady he has flagrantly slandered; John, the nominal villain, is unconvincing because he delegates his plotting to Borachio; and finally, the repudiation scene, though theatrically effective, is a blot on an otherwise brilliant comedy.[1]

The interpretation of *Much Ado* developed in this article is, point for point, at variance with the view generally accepted. We hold that the theme of this comedy is honor, that its spirit is less joyous than reflective, and that courtship, a peripheral concern, is presented as an imminent threat to masculine honor. Once the accent on honor is established, interest in the witty lovers becomes subordinated to interest in the troubled lovers; John, the malevolent match-breaker, becomes more than a nominal villain; the main plot focuses less on the birth and growth of love than on the death and rebirth of love. Finally, seen in the light of lost faith restored and sincere atonement for 'unintentional' injury, the recantation scene (v iii) restores the moral equilibrium lost in the repudiation scene (iv i) with the result that Hero becomes more credible and Claudio more admirable. The intermittent gaiety of *Much Ado* is not an end in itself, it serves as a foil to the gravity. This comedy is of mingled yarn, in which the grave and the gay are at times contrasted, at times fused—so artfully that they sometimes temper, sometimes enrich each other.

The structure of *Much Ado*—composed of three hoaxes, four witheld secrets, and three metamorphoses—achieves organic unity through an integration of subplot with main plot. This integration, based on parallel construction, is elaborated by opposing antithetical images, ideas, characters, motives, or scenes. The first four scenes, like the first three scenes in *Othello*, are treated as a prologue to the main action; in both plays the villain's initial attempt to sow dissension is short lived, but his subsequent slander, supported by ocular and auditory proof, is devastating. The Claudio—Hero alliance is the exciting force which precipitates the conflict between the benevolent Prince and his malevolent brother as they play their respective roles of matchmaker and matchbreaker.

The Prince, matchmaker in main plot as well as subplot, devises the amiable hoax which facilitates the marriage between the wary lovers. Aided by members of Leonato's household, Don Pedro creates the illusion which culminates in Benedick's and Beatrice's self-appraisal, followed by their commitment to reciprocal love (II iii; III i). In both main and subplot, marriage is delayed by internal impediments, not by external obstacles; the malicious hoax generates an illusory impediment; the amiable hoax dissolves actual impediments. John's ruse culminates in undeserved suffering; Pedro's ruse creates a love that expands into compassionate sympathy for those who suffer.

John, assisted by Borachio, instigates the malicious hoax, which, by playing on the latent fear of cuckoldry, culminates in Claudio's tearful disillusionment and Hero's symbolic death (IV i). The Bastard's vicious slander generates much ado about nothing, since Hero, who is unequivocally chaste, must be, and finally is vindicated. Through the device of the withheld secret, which heightens suspense, her vindication is deliberately delayed until late in V i. Just as the rising action up to and through the climax in IV i depends on the interplay of the three evolving hoaxes, so does the falling action depend on the interplay of the four withheld secrets that culminate in the three metamorphoses of Hero. The first withheld secret, that Hero is belied, culminates in her metamorphosis from virgin to wanton (IV i); the second, that Hero is alive, culminates in her transfiguration from sinner to martyr (V iii); the third, that Hero 'died . . . but whiles her slander liv'd', culminates in her metamorphosis from martyr to bride (v iv). The fourth, that Benedick and Beatrice have been snared into love, a secret withheld from them until near the close of the fifth act, adds greater depth as well as piquancy to their repartee of courtship at the end of II iii and after III i. Our more detailed interpretation of *Much Ado* (1598–1599) is divided into four interlocking sections, developed in the following sequence:

(I) A nexus of hearsay and ordeal not only infiltrates both plot and subplot but also unites them. Emanating from this nexus are hitherto unnoted overtones of thought and feeling which are implied or expressed by a varied range of rhetorical and technical devices.

(II) The rigid concept of honor which flares up in the crises and climax of *Much Ado* is illuminated by references to Castiglione's *Courtier* (trans. Hoby, 1561) and Peter Beverley's *Ariodanto and Ieneura* (1565–6). Once this courtly ethos is seen as the determining factor in Hero's three transfigurations, a significant number of characters and scenes take on an added dimension.

(III) A re-examination of tone, role, structure, and imagery in key scenes provides a broader perspective, from which *Much Ado* emerges as a masterpiece of Shakespeare's maturing dramaturgy.

(IV) This play, a milestone in Shakespeare's development, is less closely related to the two 'joyous comedies' with which it is generally associated than with the history plays with which it is contemporaneous and the tragedies by which it is followed.

I

In the crises of this far from joyous comedy, hearsay creates illusory dilemmas which seemingly necessitate hasty commitment; ill-advised commitment culminates in serio-comic ordeals. Hearsay in the sense of a reported report—as well as such related forms as noting, reputation, rumor, insinuation, and slander— are freighted with or colored by either accidental or deliberate distortion. Distortion due to ignorance, inattention, fear, pride, or malice motivates impulsive and precipitate action which in turn creates or accentuates apprehension, misunderstanding, dissension, and realignment of the individuals or groups in conflict. The impact of hearsay, or its collateral equivalents, alters existing relationships between two pairs of brothers, two pairs of lovers, a trio of gallants, and a father and daughter, when successive conflicts crystallise in a sequence of ascending crises.[2]

The power of hearsay and the potency of defamation that are topics for jesting in the subplot (III i) become sources of anguish in the main plot (IV i). What was a jocular phrase is transformed into a shocking act; the figurative becomes the literal; the impersonal generalisation fortells a personal catastrophe. Hero, who jests about hearsay, is martyred by hearsay; she, the deviser of the comic trap, is herself caught in a vicious trap. Unlike the 'honest slander' with which she proposes to stain Beatrice, John's furtive slander almost destroys not only Hero but also those who cherish her. She herself discovers 'How much an ill word may empoison liking' (III ii 86), when she is deserted by father and lover, who discredit her truth in favor of the Bastard's perjury (IV i).

The impact of hearsay is singularly pervasive; it not only colors dialogue, motivation, and action, but also gives rise to a cryptic irony which is as characteristic of this remarkable comedy as is the wit of Benedick and Beatrice. Intermittent irony frequently stems from crisply phrased oxymoron—a rhetorical device deftly used to intensify the present, recall the past, and foreshadow the future. The comedy opens with a glowing report of Claudio's valor, followed by the messenger's paradox, 'joy could not show itself modest enough without a badge of bitterness' (ll. 18–19). The tone and tenor of this reflection is underscored by Leonato's prophetic response, 'How much better is it to weep at joy than to joy at weeping!'—(as John invariably does). This remark, early in the play, sets off the enigmatic overtones of the dialogue. These overtones—like those in *Troilus and Cressida* (1601–02) and *Othello* (1604–05)—sometimes contrast, sometimes fuse, joy and sorrow, faith and doubt, emotion and reason, love and hate, honor and shame, and substance and shadow. Viewed as reflections of Shakespeare's concern with the fallibility of the senses and the ravages of mutability, these and similar stressed dichotomies somehow evoke the inexpressible about the riddle of existence and the mystery of the human predicament.

II

Honor, whether the setting be the court of Beverley's Jenevra, the palace of Castiglione's *Courtier*, or the court-oriented house of Leonato, is the primary virtue in a caste-conscious society. Uncrowned by honor, all other gifts of nature, fortune, or culture are debased and worthless. The honorable lady must be modest and chaste; the honorable gentleman, loyal and valorous. At all costs, not only honor, but also the reputation for honor, must be zealously preserved. Man's reputation depends on unsullied valor; woman's, on unstained chastity. Once lost, a reputation for either valor or chastity can never be wholly regained. Castiglione, as translated by Hoby, expresses this idea more colorfully; 'And even as in women honestye once stained dothe never retourne againe to the former astate: so the fame of a gentleman that carieth weapon, yf it once take a foile in any little point through dastardliness or any other reproche, doeth evermore continue shameful' (Bk i, p. 48).[3]

Honor in *Much Ado*, as in *The Courtier*, is a rigid, compulsive force which varies from but retains vestiges of the chivalric code exemplified by *The Historie of Ariondanto and Ieneura*.[4] Whether clad in satin or steel, a 'worthie' gentleman must be ever ready to vindicate a victim of calumny. In Beverley's verse romance, the champion enters the lists to save the perjured Jenevra from an actual death by fire; in *Much Ado*, Leonato, Antonio and Benedick in turn challenge Claudio to a duel, charging that his slander has slain Hero (v i). In the narrative as well as in the drama, suspense is heightened when the belied lady as well as her defender suffers an undeserved ordeal. Beverley's ordeals are spectacular and sensational, those in *Much Ado* are serio-comic. Jenevra faces literal death, Hero suffers figurative death; princess and lady alike almost become martyrs of slander.

In both cases, heedless of the law of church or state, their defenders take justice in their own hands. Theirs is the stock response of their caste—once honor is impugned shame must be dissolved in blood. Their courtly code forbids turning the other cheek, it prescribes vengeance through bloodshed. As Castiglione confirms: 'me thinketh it a meete matter to punish them . . . sharply, that with lyes bring up a sclaunder upon women. And I beleave that everie worthie gentilman is bounde to defend alwaies with weapon . . . when he knoweth any woman falslye reported to be of little honestie' (p. 249).

Courtly honor is the matrix of the ironies and reversals which characterise Hero's two rejections (II i; IV i) and three metamorphoses (IV i; V iii; V iv). Whether Hero acts or fails to act is less significant than what she essentially is; what she is, less important than what she symbolises. Even were one to ignore, as many critics still do, Hero's obediently guarded repartee during the courtship by proxy in II i, her chaste thoughts and language during the snaring of Beatrice in III i, and her virginal forebodings about marriage in III iv, she still remains the embodiment of the courtly concept of ideal daughter and bride. Emblem of the sheltered life—crowned by beauty, modesty, and chastity—she is bred from birth for a noble alliance which will add luster to her lineage.

In the crises, Hero is intentionally portrayed as vulnerably passive. Her passivity as well as her innocence not only intensifies the shock of her martyrdom but also heightens the dramatic effectiveness of her three transfigurations. The centrality of Hero's role must be re-established, emphasis must be shifted from her function as foil to Beatrice, to her function as center of the mores, the imagery, and the irony of the action.

Thematically linked to the direct attack on honor, which separates the hearsay-crossed pair in the climax, is the covert fear of dishonor, which keeps the taunting lovers of the subplot apart in their initial skirmish for ascendancy. Verbally, Benedick flees while Beatrice pursues (I i 99–124). That the maid is far from reticent in her pursuit of the bachelor is as apparent as that he is no less attracted by her than fearful of her wit and disdain. The reason for his fear of Beatrice and matrimony is elaborated later in the scene when Claudio hazards ridicule by admitting an inclination toward marriage.

Comically aghast at the prospect of separation from his brother-in-arms, Benedick inadvertently reveals his own hidden fear of the tender trap. Haunted by phantom horns, the professed misogynist attempts to dissuade his enamored friend from courting cuckoldry: 'Is't come to this? In faith, hath not the world one man but he will wear his cap with suspicion?' (ll. 170–1). When accused of being 'an obstinate heretic in the despite of beauty', Benedick not only reaffirms his mistrust of women and marriage but also again reveals his fear of cuckoldry. So even in the subplot, where courtship is dwelt upon and depicted with inimitable verve, the accent is on honor—not on the raptures of courtship, but on the gnawing fear which discourages marriage: 'That a woman conceived me, I thank her . . . but that I will have a recheat winded in my forehead, or hang my bugle in an invisible baldrick, all women shall pardon me. Because I will not do them the wrong to mistrust any, I will do myself the right to trust none; and the fine is, for the which I may go the finer, I will live a bachelor' (ll. 204–13).

The cuckoldry jest, ubiquitous in Renaissance and Restoration comedy, has lost much of its evocative power for the modern mind. Yet even now, witty allusions to cuckoldry trigger the wry laughter which stems from an awareness of the distrust and antagonism between the sexes; an antagonism which is heightened when women challenge male dominance and upset the *status quo*. Although the timeworn taunts of cuckoldry have lost the full measure of their emotive impact, in context, they still are much more than obsolete obscenity. This antic wit, often offensive as the phallic pun, is still laden with invaluable clues to Renaissance thought and mores. Then as now, a dominant wife implies an inadequate husband; a weak husband led by a wily wife portends dishonor. Then, before marriage, a man's honor is his own responsibility; only real or apparent breach of faith or lack of valor can debase him. After marriage, part of his honor passes into his wife's keeping; her actual or seeming unchastity blots his escutcheon.[5]

Honor is the warp of the three hoaxes, hearsay is the weft, and illusion spins the web. Don Pedro's amiable hoax unites the subplot lovers, Don John's malicious hoax separates the main-plot lovers, and the Friar's benign hoax reunites the hearsay-crossed pair. The purpose of each of the three hoaxes is to reverse existing relationships. Each hoax is designed to create the specific illusion which will secure such a reversal. Dupes of illusion, both pairs of lovers are somewhat plot-ridden; they act less than they are acted upon.

The Prince, blithely unaware that the Claudio-Hero alliance is being undermined, concerns himself solely with the amiable hoax, directed toward the bickering pair, which is intended to create faith by destroying fear and distrust. John's malicious hoax, directed against the Claudio-Hero alliance, is based on the latent fear of cuckoldry; it subverts instinctive love and faith by substituting in their stead doubt, confusion, and shame. The malicious hoax induces Claudio, Pedro, and even Leonato, to credit and support the slander which in IV i culminates in Hero's first metamorphosis from virgin to wanton. To counteract John's hoax, the Friar devises the benign hoax which culminates in Hero's second transfiguration—from wanton to martyr (v iii). Hero's third metamorphosis—from martyr to bride—is reserved for the surprise and discovery in the denouement, where the masked 'niece' of Leonato is discovered to be Claudio's slander-slain betrothed who died 'but whiles her slander liv'd' (v iii. 66).

The malicious hoax, the most complex of the three, is prominent in both the rising and falling action of the main plot. That Borachio, not John, concocted the scheme is relatively unimportant, that John never appears in person after IV i is even less significant. Coleridge was essentially right in observing, 'Don John, the mainspring of the plot, is merely shown then withdrawn'.[6] Modern critics who quote Coleridge usually omit the all important appositive, 'the mainspring of the plot'. Consequently they fail to see that, once injected, the venom of John's slander spreads its infection. Whether he is present or not, evil dominates good, judgement is poisoned, will is perverted, shadow becomes substance, and undeserved ordeals proliferate.

III

John is actually the mainspring of the counterintrigue in the main plot. The force of his villainy is not rooted in a talent for plotting; his power stems from a tenacious will, implemented partly by his familiarity with the peculiarities of the courtly code, and partly by his talent for distortion, hyperbole, and innuendo. Impresario of fantasy, he fashions hydras from latent fear of cuckoldry. The sly treachery with which John drops insinuation into the initially unreceptive ears of Claudio and the Prince recalls Iago, that other dissembling rogue who, posing as a plain-dealer, 'twists suspicion into assurance'. Both villains are qualified by nature and experience to play on the passions of their betters; both know how to sting emotion until reason dissolves, how to arouse a sense of betrayed honor, and how to goad illusory betrayal into rash action.

Spawn of paternal venery, John envies his more fortunate brother's power and prestige; Pedro, the licit heir, inherits honor and authority, the Bastard is born to shame and subjection. The frustrated malcontent is obsessed by a desire to debase others as he himself has been debased, to cause suffering as he himself has suffered, and to dishonor as he himself has been dishonored. Act I, scene iv traces the Bastard's metamorphosis from passive malcontent railing at Fortune into an active villain eager to hamper the very alliance his brother is attempting to assure. At first John's mood is that of a muzzled mastiff unable to lick festering wounds. His ego smarts, he recalls his abortive revolt against his brother and winces at the very mention of Claudio, who had the 'glory of his overthrow'; nothing will soothe his smarting pride except an opportunity to crush the 'start up' Claudio, and to pit wit and will against those of his invulnerable brother. After hearing the report that the Prince intends to woo Hero for Claudio, John invites his cronies to help devise a means of forestalling the anticipated match.

Out of the kaleidoscopic merriment of the masked revelry scene—a perfect setting for a miniature comedy of errors—John emerges as matchbreaker (II i.). Here, the villain pretends he has mistaken the masked Claudio for Benedick; Claudio, in turn, deliberately encourages the seeming error. So the curious youth (like the subplot lovers in II iii, III i) by eavesdropping hears more disturbing gossip than he had anticipated. The villain makes his dupe's ears tingle by confiding, 'my brother . . . is enamour'd on Hero . . . dissuade him . . . she is no equal for his birth' (II i 142–4).

The embittered lover releases pent emotions in a soliloquy: 'Friendship is constant in all other things/Save in the office and affairs of love' (ll. 154–5). These verses condone Pedro's seeming violation of trust, the next lines bemoan beauty's mystic power to ensnare and to betray: 'beauty is a witch/Against whose charms faith melteth into blood . . . . Farewell, therefore, Hero!' (ll. 158–61). Reasoning in metaphorical absolutes, Claudio decides: Friendship shrivels in the flame of desire; his patron has become his rival; Hero who has bewitched the Prince is to blame; she alone is the source of dissension; she must be rooted out of

Claudio's mind and heart.[7] This sudden, short-lived rejection of Hero is a prelude to the longer lasting, more shocking repudiation at the altar.

Claudio's susceptibility to suspicion emanating from hearsay indicates that under stress the immature lover values friendship for the Prince, who appears faithless, above love for Hero, who appears fickle. When finally aware that both Claudio and Benedick assume Pedro has wooed Hero for himself, he assures them that he has not only won her for Claudio but has also gained Leonato's consent to an immediate betrothal. Obviously, John's initial attempt to frustrate his brother by destroying the Claudio-Hero alliance has been a fiasco. At this point, there is a triple irony of situation; on the one hand, John's abortive attempt to sow lasting dissension fails; on the other, neither the Prince nor his favorites suspect John of renewed treachery; and most ironical of all, the mutual faith binding the trio of gallants is strengthened by the very trial to which it was subjected.

In III ii, the Prince and Count, who in the first half of the scene are genial jesters at Benedick's metamorphosis into an avowed lover, are themselves transformed in the second part to dazed dupes of John's calumny. This sort of ironical reversal, which is both typical of and recurrent in *Much Ado*, probes deeper beneath the surface of events than is customary in Shakespeare's earlier comedies. Toward the middle of III ii, the matchbreaker traps the matchmaker and undermines Claudio's certainty that he will wed Hero on the morrow; by whipping up stock responses to illusory dishonor, John impels her admirers to become detractors. After arousing the apprehension of the Prince and Claudio by demanding a private conference on a mysterious matter which deeply concerns both patron and lover, the villain implies that if Claudio knew what John knows, he would shun marriage. The villain obliquely suggests a secret impediment which threatens honor; he implies, then asserts, Hero is unchaste; her unchastity is the impediment which must be faced (ll. 71–108). The entire process of leading up to the slander is calculatingly ambiguous. He deliberately tantalises his victims until their nerves are raw and fear of dishonor is fomented; after their judgement is paralysed by innuendo, he lures men reft of judgement to make an immediate and irrevocable choice between tainted love or undefiled honor.

Mercilessly, John's defamatory taunts dare the beguiled Prince and Count to swear what they would do if the unchastity charge were true, before it has been proved true. Vacillating between faith that the unchastity charge is false and fear that it is true, Claudio resolves his dilemma with the promise, 'If I see anything to-night why I should not marry her, to-morrow in the congregation, where I should wed, there will I shame her' (ll. 110–12). And the Prince adds, 'as I wooed for thee to obtain her, I will join with thee to disgrace her'.

The repudiation scene (IV i), the adroitly delayed climax of the malicious hoax, depicts prescribed response to apparent unchastity. John's hoax, never staged, intermittently reported— part slander, part timing, part mistaken identity, part perjured witness, and part duped witnesses—creates an illusion of dishonor that engenders delusion and revulsion. Convinced that father and daughter have connived to conceal Hero's unchastity at the expense of her bridegroom's honor, Claudio enters the church determined to turn the tables by publicly shaming those who had conspired to dishonour him. On the other hand, Leonato, confident that he is about to witness a union of virtue and valor, is perplexed but not deeply disturbed when Claudio, with the deliberate ruthlessness of a disillusioned idealist, turns the words of the marriage ceremony itself into an inquisitor's catechism (ll. 3–30). Soon, cryptic quibbles about secret impediments turn into outright rejection, as Claudio cries, 'She's but the sign and semblance of her honour . . . Her blush is guiltiness, not modesty' (ll. 32–41).

Vainly, Leonato seeks reassurance from the Prince, who scoffs, 'I stand dishonour'd that have gone about/To link my dear friend to a common stale' (ll, 63–4). After Hero denies guilt, Pedro challenges her denial: 'Upon mine honour,/Myself, my brother, and this grieved count/Did see her, hear her . . . Talk with a ruffian at her chamber-window;/Who hath . . . Confess'd the vile encounters' (ll. 87–92). John, at the height of his Pyrrhic victory, gloats, 'pretty lady,/I am sorry for thy much misgovernment' (ll. 97–9). In riddling oxymoron Claudio laments the loss of love and faith: 'But fare the [sic] well, most foul, most fair! Farewell,/Thou pure impiety, and impious purity!/For thee I'll lock up all the gates of love,/ . . . turn all beauty into thoughts of harm' (ll. 102–6). Again, as in the initial rejection (II i), Claudio fears and denounces the enigmatic power of defiled beauty. Struck by irony, hyperbole, antithesis, and paradox, the thread of laughter vibrates fitfully as deluded father and lover grapple with illusory unchastity.

Leonato, convinced of Hero's infamy, thinks of his dishonor, not of her plight; he demands, 'Hath no man's dagger here a point for me?' (l. 108). Perhaps the audience are not unduly perturbed, since the Watch have overheard Borachio's inadvertent confession (III iii), and even though neither Dogberry nor Verges understands the tenor of the drunkard's babblings, the audience does. Nevertheless, though the audience may be certain that Hero is belied, her father, her bridegroom, and the Prince, convinced of her guilt, play their roles with tragic intensity. Leonato's despair submerges his judgement, he accepts appearance for reality, perjury for proof; love turns to loathing, his cherished daughter dwindles from virgin to wanton (ll. 120–43). Obsessed by illusory dishonor, the Bastard's dupes intensify their own serio-comic ordeals. The malicious hoax has created havoc. There is a realignment of forces, the duped patron, the embittered lover, and the distracted father flee into John's camp to escape contagion! Friendship displaces courtship or fatherhood; male honor withdraws from female defilement. The Lady is a harlot; let her die for shame. Theirs is the stock response of their caste, the rigidity of the courtly code sanctions little compassion for frailty or dishonor.

The repudiation scene, examined with the courtly code of honor in mind, is much more than a *coup de théâtre*. In terms of Renaissance mores, it is a scene of poignant disillusionment and despair. In the conflict between appearance and reality, between emotion and reason, tension increases when lover turns inquisitor and father turns executioner. Here, in a conflict between good and evil, truth clashes with error in a charged atmosphere of contradictory moods and shifting relationships while the outraged moral sense oscillates between absolute praise and absolute blame. Here, when malice triumphs, shame so submerges compassion that slander, mirage, and perjury are accepted as ocular and auditory proof. Incensed by defiled honor, men argue in absolutes shorn from any rational mean, and under the aegis of the courtly code act and react with prescribed cruelty.

The significance of the Friar's role, in and after the climax, has never been recognised; it is his wisdom that casts out the demons of despair; it is his compassion that substitutes symbolic death for literal death. After the exit of the Count and Princes, Hero revives from the swoon that resembles death. Leonato, convinced that Hero is 'mir'd with infamy', believes honor prescribes that she, like Lucrece, should literally die for shame. That is why he cries, 'O Fate! take not away thy heavy hand./Death is the fairest cover for her shame' (ll. 114–15). The Friar, aided by Benedick and Beatrice, gradually leads the distraught father's thoughts from fatalistic acceptance of shame to active vindication of honor. After the Friar argues that 'ocular proof' may be an illusion, and after Benedick suggests that the Bastard belies Hero, Leonato's wrath turns from his daughter's shame to her detractors' slander. Leonato urges vindication through bloodshed. The Friar prefers a ruse designed to change slander to remorse: 'She dying, as it must be so maintain'd,/Upon the instant that she was accus'd,/Shall be lamented, pitied, and excus'd' (ll. 214–16).

What is trite chronological narrative in Bandello and Beverley becomes foreshadowing through prophecy in *Much Ado*, as the Friar foresees and foretells the psychology of Claudio's remorse: 'When he shall hear she died upon his words,/Th'idea of her life shall sweetly creep/Into his study of imagination' (ll. 223–5). Throughout his incisively truncated recantation, Claudio does mourn; throughout his rapt vigil he mourns the martyr slain by slanderous tongues. Hero, glowing with more than mortal glory, does rise before his inner eye. In the penultimate scene, the vision which elevates Hero displaces the illusion which debased her. The intensity of Claudio's remorse atones for the cruelty of the public repudiation at the altar. Staged in retarded tempo, embellished by stylised movement, haunting music, and appropriate lighting, the recantation scene not only ennobles Claudio, who lost stature in the repudiation scene, but also sanctifies his delayed union with Hero. To appreciate the organic unity of *Much Ado* in terms of illusion and metamorphosis—the tense climax (iv i), the evocative recantation (v iii), and the animated denouement (v iv) must be envisioned, though they seldom are, as mutually illuminating.

The recantation scene, a miniature masque, depicts the ritual of expiation performed by Claudio, shortly before his union with Leonato's 'niece'. By torchlight, Claudio, accompanied by his

Prince and several other witnesses, solemnly approaches Hero's ancestral tomb to propitiate her 'bones' and absolve his blood guilt. The tapers flicker on the mourning weeds of the celebrants, as, bowed with contrition, Claudio ascends the seven steps of atonement. The lyric intensity of this requiem masque is heightened by the hour, the setting, and the allusion: (1) The scroll which bears the epitaph is unrolled; (2) the retraction is read aloud before hushed mourners, 'So the life that died with shame/Lives in death with glorious fame'; (3) symbolically, the recantation is eternised by hanging the epitaph-bearing scroll on the tomb, 'Praising her when I am dumb [dead]'; (4) the music is prelude to a dirge burdened with contrition and a plea that the penitents responsible for the virgin's death be forgiven, 'Pardon, goddess of the night,/Those that slew thy virgin knight'; (5) with ritualistic solemnity, the procession circles the tomb; (6) as *coup de grâce*, Claudio, still intent upon perpetuating the bitter-sweet memory of his betrothed, pledges, 'unto thy bones good night!/ Yearly will I do this rite'; (7) finally, with an insight which begets empathy, Claudio, aware that he is no longer Fortune's favorite, begs Hymen to guard Leonato's 'niece' from the woes experienced by his daughter, 'Hymen now with luckier issue speed's/ Than this for whom we rend'red up this woe'.

The power of language to create an illusion which either elevates or debases a relationship has been stressed not only in our comparison of the function of illusion in the subplot with that in the main plot, but also in our integration of the shifting imagery with the ironies and reversals clustering about the three transfigurations. Our integration of imagery with action demonstrates that the precarious equilibrium of the volatile aristocrats is disturbed less by ocular illusion than by verbal delusion; in the crises, not ocular proof but hearsay and insinuation twist suspicion into assurance. The sporadic word-play on 'die for love' which snares the wary couple into both declarations and reaffirmations of reciprocal love is paralleled by the more grim and pervasive word play on 'die for shame' which first separates, then, after literal death is transmuted into symbolic death, finally unites the hearsay-crossed pair.

The tantalising ambiguities in the subplot lovers' repartee of courtship has fascinated critics; but even the most astute commentators have ignored the multifaceted word-play on death which centers on Hero's transfigurations. This intricate pattern of calculated ambiguity sustains suspense throughout the falling action: the climax ends with the Friar's paradox, 'die to live'; the three challenges of Claudio are justified by the iterated refrain, slander slew Hero; Claudio recants by playing variations on the theme, 'done to death by slanderous tongues'; and finally, in the denouement, martyred Hero, who 'died defil'd', is reborn through vindicated fame and becomes the bride of Claudio, who, chastened by remorse and atonement, becomes a more deserving bridegroom.

The contrast between the adroit use and the maladroit abuse of language which distinguishes the speech of Dogberry, Verges, and the Watch from that of the articulate aristocrats is no less self evident than an endless source of delight. The aptly inept word-play of Dogberry and his flunkies has been explored with gusto— not only as an end in itself, as a means of characterisation, and as a comic foil for the subtler wit of Benedick and Beatrice, but also as a technical device for delaying the exposure of John's defamation. Word-play in *Much Ado*, unlike that in the earlier romantic plays, is ever closely integrated with and dependent on action—as it runs the gamut from broad low comedy to sophisticated high comedy. Laughter in *Much Ado* is frequently ironic; pervasively reflective. The symbolism in the much maligned main plot is at least as significant as is the comic potential in the deliberate use and inadvertent abuse of language in the subplots. The enigmatic word-play of John, Hero, Claudio, Leonato, and the Friar, too long overlooked, is at least as important for a balanced appraisal of tone, structure, and values as are the inimitable ineptitudes of Dogberry and Verges, or the widely heralded witticisms of Benedick and Beatrice.

IV

Much Ado (1598–1599), as we interpret it, is closer in spirit to *Henry IV* (1597–8) than to the two joyous comedies (*As You Like It*, 1599–1600; *Twelfth Night*, 1599–1600) with which it is generally associated. Written contemporaneously, the comedy of private conflict and the chronicle of public strife, though seldom compared, are reciprocally illuminating. The accent in both plays is on honor; dishonor in the comedy is illusory, dishonor in the history play is real. Honor, in the one, is viewed in terms of seeming and being; honor, in the other, is discussed in terms of a mean contrasted with two extremes. The conflict in the comedy centers on feminine honor sullied by slander; that in the chronicle, on male honor tainted by cowardice or foolhardiness. The dominant ethos in both plays is rooted in the courtly code that prescribes modesty and chasity for women, valor and loyalty for men. In the comedy all four attributes of honor come into play; in the chronicle where the attributes of feminine honor are less relevant, the interest is centered on the attributes of masculine honor.

The tragicomic ordeals in *Troilus and Cressida* (1602-3) which culminate in disillusionment and the serio-comic ordeals in *Much Ado* which culminate in delusion differ less in tone than in sustained intensity. Both center on violated fidelity; real violation in the former, seeming violation in the latter. Whereas Claudio's delusion can be and is dispelled by exposing its contrived origin, Troilus's disillusionment, battening on mutability, corrodes faith in love and in valor. The implications of the action in the problem play are predominantly cynical largely because the amorous entanglements of Priam's sons are as costly to the walled Trojans as the bickering between the strategists and warriors is to the encamped Greeks. The oath of fealty, the Achilles tendon of the chivalric code, is stretched to the snapping point, no less by the deteriorating military alliances between the Greeks than by the amatory misalliances and political expediencies of the two willful Trojan princes.

Troilus, enmeshed in his own casuistry, is first apostle and later victim of appetite; his own misalliance like his sophistic defence of Paris's stolen love is steeped in bitter irony. The *fine amour* of Troilus, abetted by Pandar, culminates in copulation and is interrupted by the fortunes of war. Separation imminent, Troilus insists upon iterated vows of eternal fidelity which the worldly-wise Cressida reluctantly swears. Later, after his unsuspected rival in turn appropriates Troilus's mistress, his love-tokens, and his charger, his love affair shatters into irrational disillusionment. Betrayed, in varying degrees, by Fortune, by Cressida, by Paris, and by his own rash words and acts, Troilus, seemingly impervious to death, hazards foolhardy valor.

Finally shocked out of the confines of the wish to die into the realm of Trojan survival by the murder of Hector, Troilus belatedly comes of age when he instinctively dons his slain brother's mantle by assuming leadership of a doomed nation. Seen in the light of pagan-humanism, the subsequent repudiation of Pandarus is an additional indication that Troilus, seasoned by ordeal, frees himself from the debilitating influence of Paris and dedicates his valor and his future to Hector's vision of enduring glory. Throughout the martial as well as throughout the extra-marital crises in this controversial play, character, dialogue, and incident fuse in an enigmatic atmosphere of cosmic irony which grows less oppressive in v x, where Troilus's spirit soars above self-indulgence and adversity.

The similarities between *Much Ado* and *Othello* (1604–5) are more numerous than are those between any other comedy and tragedy in the entire Shakespeare canon. The exciting force in both plays is an alliance between virtue and valor which the villain intends to destroy by creating an illusion that the heroine is unchaste. In the comedy the first four scenes—in the tragedy the first three scenes—are treated as a prelude to the main action; a prelude in which the villain's initial attempt to create havoc fails. In both plays a strong-willed villain is substituted for the rival lover of the source. In both, the power of insinuation to engender, heighten, and sustain relatively flimsy ocular proof is stressed.

The process by which the villain dupes the gullible soldier-lover—the illusion by which faith is transformed into doubt, love into loathing, and pride into shame—is fundamentally the same in the two plays. The delusions of both bridegrooms—the recurrent lapses into soul-searing dichotomies, the tensions between emotion and will—are expressed in oxymoron. The heroine's inability to foresee and cope with the hero's change in attitude toward her is similar in kind, though in the tragedy increased in degree. Honor in each case is a compulsive force which incites the warrior-lover in the comedy to cruelty; in the tragedy, to crime. The cultural milieu, the philosophical, and ethical assumptions in *Much Ado, Troilus and Cressida,* and *Othello* are similar. In all three, the fallibility of the senses and the vulnerability of reason contribute to the mutability of fame and glory. Illusion, which shatters into metamorphosis and culminates in ironic disillusionment, characterises the tone of the climax in *Much Ado*, the falling action of *Othello*, and almost the entire action of *Troilus and Cressida*.

SOURCE: 'Illusion and Metamorphosis in *Much Ado About Nothing*', *Shakespeare Quarterly*, XVIII (1967), 53–67.

NOTES

[Modified and renumbered from the original Notes to this essay—Ed.]

1. All these points are covered by Brander Matthews, *Shakespeare as Playwright* (New York, 1913), pp. 152–6. In modified form, and with varying emphasis, they are restated by: Oscar James Campbell, *The Living Shakespeare* . . . (New York, 1949); Hardin Craig, *The Complete Works of Shakespeare* (Chicago, 1951); George Lyman Kittredge, *Sixteen Plays of Shakespeare* . . . (Boston, Mass., 1946); William Allan Neilson and Charles Jarvis Hill, *The Complete Plays* . . . . Cambridge, Mass., 1942); Thomas Marc Parrott, *Shakespeare: Twenty-Three Plays* . . . (New York, 1938).

2. For distinguished comments on the philosophic and aesthetic implications of 'noting-nothing', see Paul A. Jorgensen, 'Much Ado About "Nothing"', *Shakespeare Quarterly*, V (1954), 287–95.

3. Hoby's translation of Castiglione, edited by Walter Raleigh (London, 1900).

4. Charles T. Prouty, *The Sources of 'Much Ado About Nothing'* . . . (New Haven, Conn., 1950). The 'lost' text of Peter Beverley's adaptation from the *Orlando Furioso* is here reprinted for the first time (pp. 76–140).

5. Curtis Brown Watson, *Shakespeare and the Renaissance Concept of Honor* (Princeton, N. J., 1960): 'much modern Shakespeare criticism reveals, on many key points of "interpretation" . . . historical ignorance . . . [and] a basic lack of sympathy with Renaissance pagan-humanist values in general and Shakespeare in particular . . . our critics are often insufficiently aware of their own preconceptions and of the many respects in which our democratic ideals in the 20th century basically contradict the aristocratic assumptions of Elizabethan society' (p. 9, and passim).

6. T. M. Raysor, *Coleridge's Shakespeare Criticism* (Cambridge, Mass., 1931), I, p. 226.

7. See Kittredge on 'image magic' (*Sixteen Plays* . . ., p. 119, l.

187). Combining his suggestion of literal black magic with the more obvious implication of metaphorical witchcraft explains why Claudio momentarily envisages Hero as a Medea, and instinctively rejects her.

Perhaps he recalls that his knowing friend Benedick, wary of Beatrice, compared her with 'the infernal Ate in a good apparel' (II i).

3. *AS YOU LIKE IT*

Helen Gardner   'Let the Forest Judge'
(1959)

As its title declares, *As You Like It* is a play to please all tastes. It is
the last play in the world to be solemn over, and there is more
than a touch of absurdity in delivering a lecture, particularly on a
lovely summer morning, on this radiant blend of fantasy,
romance, wit and humour. The play itself provides its own ironic
comment on anyone who attempts to speak about it: 'You have
said; but whether wisely or no, let the forest judge.'
  For the simple, it provides the stock ingredients of romance: a
handsome, well-mannered young hero, the youngest of three
brothers, two disguised princesses to be wooed and wed, and a
banished, virtuous Duke to be restored to his rightful throne. For
the more sophisticated, it propounds, in the manner of the old
courtly literary form of the *débat*, a question which is left to us to
answer: Is it better to live in the court or the country? 'How like
you this shepherd's life, Master Touchstone?', asks Corin, and
receives a fool's answer: 'Truly, shepherd, in respect of itself, it is
a good life; but in respect that it is a shepherd's life, it is naught.
In respect that it is solitary, I like it very well; but in respect that it
is private, it is a very vile life.' Whose society would you prefer, Le
Beau's or Audrey's? Would you rather be gossiped at in the court
or gawped at in the country? The play has also the age-old appeal
of the pastoral, and in different forms. The pastoral romance of
princesses playing at being a shepherd boy and his sister is
combined with the pastoral love-eclogue in the wooing of
Phoebe, with the burlesque of this in the wooing of Audrey, and
with the tradition of the moral eclogue, in which the shepherd is
the wise man, in Corin. For the learned and literary this is one of
Shakespeare's most allusive plays, uniting old traditions and

playing with them lightly. Then there are the songs—the forest is full of music—and there is spectacle: a wrestling match to delight lovers of sport, the procession with the deer, which goes back to old country rituals and folk plays, and finally the masque of Hymen, to end the whole with courtly grace and dignity. This is an image of civility and true society, for Hymen is a god of cities, as Milton knew:

> There let *Hymen* oft appear
> In Saffron robe, with Taper clear,
> And pomp, and feast, and revelry,
> With mask, and antique Pageantry.

The only thing the play may be said to lack, when compared with Shakespeare's other comedies, is broad humour, the humour of gross clowns. William makes only a brief appearance. The absence of clowning may be due to an historic reason, the loss of Kempe, the company's funny man. But if this was the original reason for the absence of pure clowning, Shakespeare has turned necessity to glorious gain and made a play in which cruder humours would be out of place. *As You Like It* is the most refined and exquisite of the comedies, the one which is most consistently played over by a delighted intelligence. It is Shakespeare's most Mozartian comedy.

The basic story is a folk-tale. The ultimate sources for the plots of Shakespeare's greatest tragedy and his most unflawed comedy are stories of the same kind. The tale of the old king who had three daughters, of whom the elder two were wicked and the youngest was good, belongs to the same primitive world of the imagination as the tale of the knight who had three sons, the eldest of whom was wicked and robbed the youngest, who was gallant and good, of his inheritance. The youngest son triumphed, like Jack the Giant Killer, over a strong man, a wrestler, joined a band of outlaws in the forest, became their king, and with the aid of an old servant of his father, the wily Adam Spencer, in the end had his revenge on his brother and got his rights. Lodge retained some traces of the boisterous elements of this old story; but Shakespeare omitted them. His Orlando is no bully, threatening and blustering and breaking down the doors to feast with his boon companions in his brother's house. He is brave enough and quick-tempered; but he is above all gentle. On this simple story Lodge grafted a pastoral romance in his *Rosalynde.* He made the leader of the outlaws a banished Duke, and gave both exiled Duke and tyrant usurper only daughters, as fast friends as their fathers are sworn enemies. The wrestling match takes place at the tyrant's court and is followed by the banishment of Rosalynde and the flight of the two girls to the forest, disguised as shepherd and shepherdess. There the shepherd boy is wooed by the gallant hero, and arouses a passion of love-sickness in a shepherdess who scorns her faithful lover. The repentance of the wicked brother and his flight to the forest provide the necessary partner for the tyrant's good daughter, and all ends happily with marriages and the restoration of the good Duke.

Shakespeare added virtually nothing to the plot of Lodge's novel. There is no comedy in which, in one sense, he invents so little. He made the two Dukes into brothers. Just as in *King Lear* he put together two stories of good and unkind children, so here he gives us two examples of a brother's unkindness. This adds to the fairy-tale flavour of the plot, because it turns the usurping Duke into a wicked uncle. But if he invents no incidents, he leaves out a good deal. Besides omitting the blusterings of Rosader (Orlando), he leaves out a final battle and the death in battle of the usurping Duke, preferring to have him converted off-stage by a chance meeting with a convenient and persuasive hermit. In the same way he handles very cursorily the repentance of the wicked brother and his good fortune in love. In Lodge's story, the villain is cast into prison by the tyrant who covets his estates. In prison he repents, and it as a penitent that he arrives in the forest. Shakespeare also omits the incident of the attack on Ganymede and Aliena by robbers, in which Rosader is overpowered and wounded and Saladyne (Oliver) comes to the rescue and drives off the assailants. As has often been pointed out, this is both a proof of the genuineness of his repentance and a reason, which many critics of the play have felt the want of, for Celia's falling in love. Maidens naturally fall in love with brave young men who rescue them. But Shakespeare needs to find no 'reasons for loving' in this play in which a dead shepherd's saw is quoted as a word of truth: 'Whoever lov'd that lov'd not at first sight.' He has far too much other business in hand at the centre and heart of his play to find time for mere exciting incidents. He stripped Lodge's plot down to the bare bones, using it as a kind of frame, and created no sub-plot of his own.

But he added four characters. Jaques, the philosopher, bears the same name as the middle son of Sir Rowland de Boys—the one whom Oliver kept at his books—who does not appear in the play until he turns up casually at the end as a messenger. It seems possible that the melancholy Jaques began as this middle son and that his melancholy was in origin a scholar's melancholy. If so, the character changed as it developed, and by the time that Shakespeare had fully conceived his cynical spectator he must have realised that he could not be kin to Oliver and Orlando. The born solitary must have no family: Jaques seems the quintessential only child. To balance Jaques, as another kind of commentator, we are given Touchstone, critic and parodist of love and lovers and of court and courtiers. And, to make up the full consort of pairs to be mated, Shakespeare invented two rustic lovers, William and Audrey, dumb yokel and sluttish goat-girl. These additional characters add nothing at all to the story. If you were to tell it you would leave them out. They show us that story was not Shakespeare's concern in this play; its soul is not to be looked for there. If you were to go to *As You Like It* for the story you would, in Johnson's phrase, 'hang yourself'.

In an essay called 'The Basis of Shakespearian Comedy' (*Essays and Studies*, 1950), Professor Nevill Coghill attempted to 'establish certain things concerning the nature of comic form, as it was understood at Shakespeare's time'. He pointed out that there were two conceptions of comedy current in the sixteenth century, both going back to grammarians of the fourth century, but radically opposed to each other. By the one definition a comedy was a story beginning in sadness and ending in happiness. By the other it was, in Sidney's words, 'an imitation of the common errors of our life' represented 'in the most ridiculous and scornefull sort that may be; so that it is impossible that any beholder can be content to be such a one'. Shakespeare, he declared, accepted the first; Jonson, the second. But although *As You Like It*, like *A Midsummer Night's Dream*, certainly begins in sadness and ends with happiness, I do not feel, when we have said this, that we have gone very far towards defining the play's nature, and I do not think that the plot in either of these two lovely plays, or in the enchanting early comedy *Love's Labour's Lost*, which indeed has hardly any plot at all, can be regarded as the 'soul' or animating force of Shakespeare's most original and characteristic comedies. Professor Coghill's formula fits plays which we feel rather uneasy about, *The Merchant of Venice* and *Measure for Measure*. It is precisely the stress on the plot which makes us think of these as being more properly described as tragicomedies than comedies. Neither of them is a play which we would choose as a norm of Shakespeare's genius in comedy. In *As You Like It* the plot is handled in the most perfunctory way. Shakespeare crams his first act with incident in order to get everyone to the forest as soon as he possibly can and, when he is ready, he ends it all as quickly as possible. A few lines dispose of Duke Frederick, and leave the road back to his throne empty for Duke Senior. As for the other victim of a wicked brother, it is far more important that Orlando should marry Rosalind than that he should be restored to his rights.

Mrs Suzanne Langer, in her brilliant and suggestive book *Feeling and Form* (London, 1953), has called comedy an image of life triumphing over chance. She declares that the essence of comedy is that it embodies in symbolic form our sense of happiness in feeling that we can meet and master the changes and chances of life as it confronts us. This seems to me to provide a good description of what we mean by 'pure comedy', as distinct from the corrective or satirical comedy of Jonson. The great symbol of pure comedy is marriage by which the world is renewed, and its endings are always instinct with a sense of fresh beginnings. Its rhythm is the rhythm of the life of mankind, which goes on and renews itself as the life of nature does. The rhythm of tragedy, on the other hand, is the rhythm of the individual life which comes to a close, and its great symbol is death. The one inescapable fact about every human being is that he must die. No skill in living, no sense of life, no inborn grace or acquired wisdom can avert this individual doom. A tragedy, which is played out under the shadow of an inevitable end, is an image of the life pattern of every one of us. A comedy, which contrives an end which is not implicit in its beginning, and which is, in itself, a fresh beginning, is an image of the flow of human life. The young wed, so that they may become in turn the older generation, whose children will wed, and so on, as long as the

world lasts. Comedy pictures what Rosalind calls 'the full stream
of the world'. At the close of a tragedy we look back over a course
which has been run: 'the rest is silence'. The end of a comedy
declares that life goes on: 'Here we are all over again.' Tragic
plots must have a logic which leads to an inescapable conclusion.
Comic plots are made up of changes, chances and surprises.
Coincidences can destroy tragic feeling: they heighten comic
feeling. It is absurd to complain in poetic comedy of improbable
encounters and characters arriving pat on their cue, of sudden
changes of mind and mood by which an enemy becomes a friend.
Puck, who creates and presides over the central comedy of *A
Midsummer Night's Dream*, speaks for all comic writers and lovers
of true comedy when he says:

> And those things do best please me
> That befall preposterously.

This aspect of life, as continually changing and presenting fresh
opportunities for happiness and laughter, poetic comedy idealises
and presents to us by means of fantasy. Fantasy is the natural
instrument of comedy, in which plot, which is the 'soul' of
tragedy, is of secondary importance, an excuse for something
else. After viewing a tragedy we have an 'acquist of true
experience' from a 'great event'. There are no 'events' in comedy;
there are only 'happenings'. Events are irreversible and comedy
is not concerned with the irreversible, which is why it must
always shun the presentation of death. In adapting Lodge's story
Shakespeare did not allow Charles the wrestler to kill the
Franklin's sons. Although they are expected to die, we may hope
they will recover from their broken ribs. And he rejected also
Lodge's ending in which the wicked Duke was killed in battle,
preferring his improbable conversion by a hermit. But why
should we complain of its improbability? It is only in tragedy that
second chances are not given. Comedy is full of purposes mis-
took, not 'falling on the inventor's head' but luckily misfiring
altogether. In comedy, as often happens in life, people are
mercifully saved from being as wicked as they meant to be.

Generalisation about the essential distinctions between
tragedy and comedy is called in question, when we turn to
Shakespeare, by the inclusiveness of his vision of life. In the great

majority of his plays the elements are mixed. But just as he wrote one masterpiece which is purely tragic, dominated by the conception of Fate, in *Macbeth*, so he wrote some plays which embody a purely comic vision. Within the general formula that 'a comedy is a play with a happy ending', which can, of course, include tragi-comedies, he wrote some plays in which the story is a mere frame and the essence of the play lies in the presentation of an image of human life, not as an arena for heroic endeavour but as a place of encounters.

Tragedy is presided over by time, which urges the hero onwards to fulfil his destiny. In Shakespeare's comedies time goes by fits and starts. It is not so much a movement onwards as a space in which to work things out: a midsummer night, a space too short for us to feel time's movement, or the unmeasured time of *As You Like It* or *Twelfth Night*. The comedies are dominated by a sense of place rather than of time. In Shakespeare's earliest comedy it is not a very romantic place: the city of Ephesus. Still, it is a place where two pairs of twins are accidentally reunited, and their old father, in danger of death at the beginning, is united to his long-lost wife at the close. The substance of the play is the comic plot of mistakings, played out in a single place on a single day. The tragi-comic story of original loss and final restoration provides a frame. In what is probably his second comedy, *The Two Gentlemen of Verona*, Shakespeare tried a quite different method. The play is a dramatisation of a *novella*, and it contains no comic place of encounters where time seems to stand still. The story begins in Verona, passes to Milan, and ends in a forest between the two cities. None of these places exerts any hold upon our imaginations. The story simply moves forward through them. In *Love's Labour's Lost*, by contrast, Shakespeare went as far as possible in the other direction. The whole play is a kind of ballet of lovers and fantastics, danced out in the King of Navarre's park. Nearby is a village where Holofernes is the schoolmaster, Nathaniel the curate, and Dull the constable. In this play we are given, as a foil to the lords and ladies, not comic servants, parasitic on their masters, but a little comic world, society in miniature, going about its daily business while the lovers are engaged in the discovery of theirs. Shakespeare dispensed with the tragi-comic frame altogether here. There is no sorrow at the beginning, only youthful male fatuity; and the 'putting right' at the close lies in the chastening of the lords by the ladies. The picture of the course of life as it appears to the comic vision, with young men falling in love and young women testing their suitors, and other men 'labouring in their vocations' to keep the world turning and to impress their fellows, is the whole matter of the play. Much more magical than the sunlit park of the King of Navarre is the wood near Athens where Puck plays the part of chance. Shakespeare reverted here to the structural pattern of his earliest comedy, beginning with the cruel fury of Egeus against his daughter, the rivalry of Lysander and Demetrius and the unhappiness of the scorned Helena, and ending with Theseus's over-riding of the father's will and the proper pairing of the four lovers. But here he not only set his comic plot of mistakings within a frame of sorrow turning to joy, he also set his comic place of encounters apart from the real world, the palace where the play begins and ends. All the centre of the play takes place in the moonlit wood where lovers immortal and mortal quarrel, change partners, are blinded, and have their eyes purged.

Having created a masterpiece, Shakespeare, who never re-peated a success, went back in his next play to tragi-comedy, allowing the threat of terrible disaster to grow through the play up to a great dramatic fourth act. *The Merchant of Venice* has what *The Two Gentlemen of Verona* lacks, an enchanted place. Belmont, where Bassanio goes to find his bride, and where Lorenzo flees with Jessica, and from which Portia descends like a goddess to solve the troubles of Venice, is a place apart, 'above the smoke and stir'. But it is not, like the wood near Athens, a place where the changes and chances of our mortal life are seen mirrored. It stands too sharply over against Venice, a place of refuge rather than a place of discovery. *Much Ado About Nothing* reverts to the single place of *The Comedy of Errors* and *Love's Labour's Lost*; and its tragi-comic plot, which also comes to a climax in a dramatic scene in the fourth act, is lightened not by a shift of scene but by its interweaving with a brilliant comic plot, and by all kinds of indications that all will soon be well again. The trouble comes in the middle of this play: at the beginning, as at the end, all is revelry and happiness. A sense of holiday, of time off from the world's business, reigns in Messina. The wars are over, peace has broken out, and Don Pedro and the gentlemen have returned to where the ladies are waiting for them to take up again the game of love and wit. In the atmosphere created by the first act Don John's malice is a cloud no bigger than a man's hand. And although it grows as the play proceeds, the crisis of the fourth act is like a heavy summer thunder-shower which darkens the sky for a time but will, we know, soon pass. The brilliant lively city of Messina is a true place of mistakings and discoveries, like the park of the King of Navarre; but, also like the park of the King of Navarre, it lacks enchantment. It is too near the ordinary world to seem more than a partial image of human life. In *As You Like It* Shakespeare returned to the pattern of *A Midsummer Night's Dream*, beginning his play in sorrow and ending it with joy, and making his place of comic encounters a place set apart from the ordinary world.

The Forest of Arden ranks with the wood near Athens and Prospero's island as a place set apart, even though, unlike them, it is not ruled by magic. It is set over against the envious court ruled by a tyrant, and a home which is no home because it harbours hatred, not love. Seen from the court it appears untouched by the discontents of life, a place where 'they fleet the time carelessly, as they did in the golden age', the gay greenwood of Robin Hood. But, of course, it is no such Elysium. It contains some unamiable characters. Corin's master is churlish and Sir Oliver Martext is hardly sweet-natured; William is a dolt and Audrey graceless. Its weather, too, is by no means always sunny. It has a bitter winter. To Orlando, famished with hunger and supporting the fainting Adam, it is 'an uncouth forest' and a desert where the air is bleak. He is astonished to find civility among men who

> in this desert inaccessible,
> Under the shade of melancholy boughs,
> Lose and neglect the creeping hours of time.
> [II vii 110–12]

In fact Arden does not seem very attractive at first sight to the weary escapers from the tyranny of the world. Rosalind's 'Well, this is the forest of Arden' does not suggest any very great enthusiasm; and to Touchstone's 'Ay, now I am in Arden; the more fool I: when I was at home, I was in a better place: but travellers must be content,' she can only reply 'Ay, be so, good Touchstone.' It is as if they all have to wake up after a good night's rest to find what a pleasant place they have come to. Arden is not a place for the young only. Silvius, for ever young and for ever loving, is balanced by Corin, the old shepherd, who reminds us of that other 'penalty of Adam' beside 'the seasons' difference': that man must labour to get himself food and clothing. Still, the labour is pleasant and a source of pride: 'I am a true labourer: I earn that I eat, get that I wear, owe no man hate, envy no man's happiness, glad of other men's good, content with my harm; and the greatest of my pride is to see my ewes graze and my lambs suck.' Arden is not a place where the laws of nature are abrogated and roses are without their thorns. If, in the world, Duke Frederick has usurped on Duke Senior, Duke Senior is aware that he has in his turn usurped upon the deer, the native burghers of the forest. If man does not slay and kill man, he kills the poor beasts. Life preys on life. Jaques, who can suck melancholy out of anything, points to the callousness that runs through nature itself as a mirror of the callousness of men. The herd abandons the wounded deer, as prosperous citizens pass with disdain the poor bankrupt, the failure. The race is to the swift. But this is Jaques's view. Orlando, demanding help for Adam, finds another image from nature:

> Then but forbear your food a little while,
> Whiles, like a doe, I go to find my fawn
> And give it food. There is a poor old man,
> Who after me hath many a weary step
> Limp'd in pure love: till he be first suffic'd,
> Oppress'd with two weak evils, age and hunger,
> I will not touch a bit.   [II vii 127–33]

The fact that they are both derived ultimately from folk-tale is not the only thing that relates *As You Like It* to *King Lear*. Adam's sombre line, 'And unregarded age in corners thrown', which Quiller-Couch said might have come out of one of the greater sonnets, sums up the fate of Lear:

> . . .
> Dear daughter, I confess that I am old;
> Age is unnecessary: on my knees I beg
> That you'll vouchsafe me raiment, bed and food.
>   [*K.L.*, II iv 152–4]

At times Arden seems a place where the same bitter lessons can be
learnt as Lear has to learn in his place of exile, the blasted heath.
Corin's natural philosophy, which includes the knowledge that
'the property of rain is to wet', is something which Lear has
painfully to acquire:

> . . . When the rain came to wet me once and the wind to
> make me chatter, when the thunder would not peace at
> my bidding, there I found 'em, there I smelt 'em out. Go
> to, they are not men o' their words: they told me I was
> everything; 'tis a lie, I am not ague-proof.
> [*K.L.*, IV vi 99–105]

He is echoing Duke Senior, who smiles at the 'icy fang and
churlish chiding of the winter's wind', saying:

> . . .
> This is no flattery: these are counsellors
> That feelingly persuade me what I am. [II i 10–11]
> . . .

Amiens's lovely melancholy song:

> Blow, blow, thou winter wind,
> Thou art not so unkind
>   As man's ingratitude;
> . . .
>
> Freeze, freeze, thou bitter sky,
> That dost not bite so nigh
>   As benefits forgot:
> . . .   [III i 174–6, 184–6]

is terribly echoed in Lear's outburst:

> Blow, winds, and crack your cheeks! rage! blow!
> . . .
> Rumble thy bellyful! Spit, fire! spout, rain!
> Nor rain, wind, thunder, fire, are my daughters:
> I tax not you, you elements, with unkindness;

I never gave you kingdom, call'd you children;
...   [*K.L.*, III ii 1, 11–14]

And Jaques's reflection that 'All the world's a stage' becomes in
Lear's mouth a cry of anguish:

> When we are born, we cry that we are come
> To this great stage of fools . . . [*K.L.*, IV vi 183–4]

It is in Arden that Jaques presents his joyless picture of human
life, passing from futility to futility, and culminating in the
nothingness of senility—'sans everything'; and in Arden also a
bitter judgement on human relations is lightly passed in the twice
repeated 'Most friendship is feigning, most loving mere folly.' But
then one must add that hard on the heels of Jaques's melancholy
conclusion Orlando enters with Adam in his arms, who, although
he may be 'sans teeth' and at the end of his usefulness as a servant,
has, beside his store of virtue and his peace of conscience, the
love of his master. And the play is full of signal instances of
persons who do not forget benefits: Adam, Celia, Touchstone—
not to mention the lords who chose to leave the court and follow
their banished master to the forest. In . . . *Shakespeare Survey* [VIII
(1955)], Professor Harold Jenkins has pointed out how points of
view put forward by one character find contradiction or
correction by another, so that the whole play is a balance of sweet
against sour, of the cynical against the idealistic, and life is shown
as a mingling of hard fortune and good hap. The lords who have
'turned ass', 'leaving their wealth and ease a stubborn will to
please', are happy in their gross folly, as Orlando is in a love-
sickness which he does not wish to be cured of. What Jaques has
left out of his picture of man's strange eventful pilgrimage is love
and companionship, sweet society, the banquet under the boughs
to which Duke Senior welcomes Orlando and Adam. Although
life in Arden is not wholly idyllic, and this place set apart from the
world is yet touched by the world's sorrows and can be mocked at
by the worldly wise, the image of life which the forest presents is
irradiated by the conviction that the gay and the gentle can
endure the rubs of fortune and that this earth is a place where
men can find happiness in themselves and in others.

The Forest of Arden is, as has often been pointed out, a place which all the exiles from the court, except one, are only too ready to leave at the close. As, when the short midsummer night is over, the lovers emerge from the wood, in their right minds and correctly paired, and return to the palace of Theseus; and, when Prospero's magic has worked the cure, the enchanted island is left to Caliban and Ariel, and its human visitors return to Naples and Milan; so the time of holiday comes to an end in Arden. The stately masque of Hymen marks the end of this interlude in the greenwood, and announces the return to a court purged of envy and baseness. Like other comic places, Arden is a place of discovery where the truth becomes clear and where each man finds himself and his true way. This discovery of truth in comedy is made through errors and mistakings. The trial and error by which we come to knowledge of ourselves and of our world is symbolised by the disguisings which are a recurrent element in all comedy, but are particularly common in Shakespeare's. Things have, as it were, to become worse before they become better, more confused and farther from the proper pattern. By misunderstandings men come to understand, and by lies and feignings they discover truth. If Rosalind, the princess, had attempted to 'cure' her lover Orlando, she might have succeeded. As Ganymede, playing Rosalind, she can try him to the limit in perfect safety, and discover that she cannot mock or flout him out of his 'mad humour of love to a living humour of madness', and drive him 'to forswear the full stream of the world, and to live in a nook merely monastic'. By playing with him in the disguise of a boy, she discovers when she can play no more. By love of a shadow, the mere image of a charming youth, Phoebe discovers that it is better to love than to be loved and scorn one's lover. This discovery of truth by feigning, and of what is wisdom and what folly by debate, is the centre of *As You Like It*. It is a play of meetings and encounters, of conversations and sets of wit: Orlando versus Jaques, Touchstone versus Corin, Rosalind versus Jaques, Rosalind versus Phoebe, and above all Rosalind versus Orlando. The truth discovered is, at one level, a very 'earthy truth': Benedick's discovery that 'the world must be peopled'. The honest toil of Corin, the wise man of the forest, is mocked at by Touchstone as 'simple sin'. He brings 'the ewes and the rams together' and gets his living 'by the copulation of cattle'.

The goddess Fortune seems similarly occupied in this play: 'As the ox hath his bow, the horse his curb, and the falcon her bells, so man hath his desires; and as pigeons bill, so wedlock would be nibbling.' Fortune acts the role of a kindly bawd. Touchstone's marriage to Audrey is a mere coupling. Rosalind's advice to Phoebe is brutally frank: 'Sell when you can, you are not for all markets.' The words she uses to describe Oliver and Celia 'in the very wrath of love' are hardly delicate, and after her first meeting with Orlando she confesses to her cousin that her sighs are for her 'child's father'. Against the natural background of the life of the forest there can be no pretence that the love of men and women can 'forget the He and She'. But Rosalind's behaviour is at variance with her bold words. Orlando has to prove that he truly is, as he seems at first sight, the right husband for her, and show himself gentle, courteous, generous and brave, and a match for her in wit, though a poor poet. In this, the great coupling of the play, there is a marriage of true minds. The other couplings run the gamut downwards from it, until we reach Touchstone's image of 'a she-lamb of a twelvemonth' and 'a crooked-pated, old, cuckoldy ram', right at the bottom of the scale. As for the debate as to where happiness is to be found, the conclusion come to is again, like all wisdom, not very startling or original: that 'minds innocent and quiet' can find happiness in court or country:

> Happy is your Grace,
> That can translate the stubbornness of fortune
> Into so quiet and so sweet a style. [II i 18–20]

And, on the contrary, those who wish to can 'suck melancholy' out of anything, 'as a weasel sucks eggs'. [II v 12–3]

In the pairing one figure is left out. 'I am for other than for dancing measures', says Jaques. Leaving the hateful sight of revelling and pastime, he betakes himself to the Duke's abandoned cave, on his way to the house of penitents where Duke Frederick has gone. The two commentators of the play are nicely contrasted. Touchstone is the parodist, Jaques the cynic. The parodist must love what he parodies. We know this from literary parody. All the best parodies are written by those who understand, because they love, the thing they mock. Only poets who love and revere the epic can write mock-heroic and the finest parody of classical tragedy comes from Housman, a great scholar. In everything that Touchstone says and does gusto, high spirits and a zest for life ring out. Essentially comic, he can adapt himself to any situation in which he may find himself. Never at a loss, he is life's master. The essence of clowning is adaptability and improvisation. The clown is never baffled and is marked by his ability to place himself at once *en rapport* with his audience, to be all things to all men, to perform the part which is required at the moment. Touchstone sustains many different roles. After hearing Silvius's lament and Rosalind's echo of it, he becomes the maudlin lover of Jane Smile; with the simple shepherd Corin he becomes the cynical and wordly-wise man of the court; with Jaques he is a melancholy moralist, musing on the power of time and the decay of all things; with the pages he acts the lordly amateur of the arts, patronising his musicians. It is right that he should parody the rest of the cast, and join the procession into Noah's ark with his Audrey. Jaques is his opposite. He is the cynic, the person who prefers the pleasures of superiority, cold-eyed and cold-hearted. The tyrannical Duke Frederick and the cruel Oliver can be converted; but not Jaques. He likes himself as he is. He does not wish to plunge into the stream, but prefers to stand on the bank and 'fish for fancies as they pass'. Sir Thomas Elyot said that dancing was an image of matrimony: 'In every daunse, of a most auncient custome, there daunseth together a man and a woman, holding eche other by the hande or the arme, which betokeneth concorde.' There are some who will not dance, however much they are piped to, any more than they will weep when there is mourning. 'In this theatre of man's life', wrote Bacon, 'it is reserved only for God and angels to be lookers on.' Jaques arrogates to himself the divine role. He has opted out from the human condition.

It is characteristic of Shakespeare's comedies to include an element that is irreconcilable, which strikes a lightly discordant note, casts a slight shadow, and by its presence questions the completeness of the comic vision of life. In *Love's Labour's Lost* he dared to allow the news of a death to cloud the scene of revels at the close, and, through Rosaline's rebuke to Berowne, called up the image of a whole world of pain and weary suffering where

'Mirth cannot move a soul in agony.' In the two comedies whose main action is motivated by hatred and with malice thwarted but not removed, *The Merchant of Venice* and *Much Ado About Nothing*, Shakespeare asks us to accept the fact that the human race includes not only a good many fools and rogues but also some persons who are positively wicked, a fact which comedy usually ignores. They are prevented from doing the harm they wish to do. They are not cured of wishing to do harm. Shylock's baffled exit and Don John's flight to Messina leave the stage clear for lovers and well-wishers. The villains have to be left out of the party at the close. At the end of *Twelfth Night* the person who is left out is present. The impotent misery and fury of the humiliated Malvolio's last words, 'I'll be reveng'd on the whole pack of you', call in question the whole comic scheme by which, through misunderstandings and mistakes, people come to terms with themselves and their fellows. There are some who cannot be 'taught a lesson'. In Malvolio pride is not purged; it is fatally wounded and embittered. It is characteristic of the delicacy of temper of *As You Like It* that its solitary figure, its outsider, Jaques, does nothing whatever to harm anyone, and is perfectly satisfied with himself and happy in his melancholy. Even more, his melancholy is a source of pleasure and amusement to others. The Duke treats him as virtually a court entertainer, and he is a natural butt for Orlando and Rosalind. Anyone in the play can put him down and feel the better for doing so. All the same his presence casts a faint shadow. His criticism of the world has its sting drawn very early by the Duke's rebuke to him as a former libertine, discharging his filth upon the world, and he is to some extent discredited before he opens his mouth by the unpleasant implication of his name. But he cannot be wholly dismissed. A certain sour distaste for life is voided through him, something most of us feel at some time or other. If he were not there to give expression to it, we might be tempted to find the picture of life in the forest too sweet. His only action is to interfere in the marriage of Touchstone and Audrey; and this he merely postpones. His effect, whenever he appears, is to deflate: the effect does not last and cheerfulness soon breaks in again. Yet as there is a scale of love, so there is a scale of sadness in the play. It runs down from the Duke's compassionate words:

> Thou seest we are not all alone unhappy;
> This wide and universal theatre
> Presents more woeful pageants than the scene
> Wherein we play in. [II vii 136–9]

through Rosalind's complaint, 'O, how full of briers is this working-day world' [I iii 10–1], to Jaques's studied refusal to find anything worthy of admiration or love.

One further element in the play I would not wish to stress, because though it is pervasive it is unobtrusive: the constant, natural and easy reference to the Christian ideal of loving-kindness, gentleness, pity and humility and to the sanctions which that ideal finds in the commands and promises of religion. In this fantasy world, in which the world of our experience is imaged, this element in experience finds a place with others, and the world is shown not only as a place where we may find happiness, but as a place where both happiness and sorrow may be hallowed. The number of religious references in *As You Like It* has often been commented on, and it is striking when we consider the play's main theme. Many are of little significance and it would be humourless to enlarge upon the significance of the 'old religious man' who converted Duke Frederick, or of Ganymede's 'old religious uncle'. But some are explicit and have a serious, unforced beauty: Orlando's appeal to outlawed men,

> . . .
> If ever you have look'd on better days,
> If ever been where bells have knoll'd to church,
> . . . [II vii 113–14]

Adam's prayer,

> . . . He that doth the ravens feed,
> Yea, providently caters for the sparrow,
> Be comfort to my age! . . . [II iii 43–5]

and Corin's recognition, from St Paul, that we have to find the way to heaven by doing deeds of hospitality. These are all in character. But the God of Marriage, Hymen, speaks more solemnly than we expect and his opening words with their New

Testament echo are more than conventional:

> Then is there mirth in heaven,
> When earthly things made even
> Atone together.
> . . .
>   [v iv 102–4)

The appearance of the god to present daughter to father and to bless the brides and grooms turns the close into a solemnity, an image of the concord which reigns in Heaven and which Heaven blesses on earth. But this, like much else in the play, may be taken as you like it. There is no need to see any more in the god's appearance with the brides than a piece of pageantry which concludes the action with a graceful spectacle and sends the audience home contented with a very pretty play.

SOURCE: essay (originally delivered as a lecture) in John Garrett (ed.), *More Talking of Shakespeare* (London, 1959), pp. 17–32.

Sylvan Barnet   'Strange Events': Improbability in *As You Like It* (1968)

It must have been as apparent to their first audiences as it is to us that Shakespeare's comedies are filled with improbabilities. Criticism has duly noted them, but it has tended to regard them tolerantly, as unimportant bits that only slightly mar the whole. We are probably most at ease when we do not look at the improbabilities, when we can say with Dr Johnson that Shakespeare's 'persons act and speak by the influence of those general passions and principles by which all minds are agitated, and the whole system of life is continued in motion'; 'his real power is not shewn in the splendour of particular passages, but by the progress of his fable, and the tenour of his dialogue'; he 'exhibited only what he saw before him'; 'his drama is the mirrour of life'. Still, Johnson was no slower than other critics to see the improbabilities, especially those near the ends of the comedies: he attributed them to the dramatist's desire to finish the job now that the end was in view. 'In many of his plays', Johnson says, 'the latter part is evidently neglected. When he found himself near the end of his work, and, in view of his reward, he shortened the labour to snatch the profit.'[1] Although some such explanation is psychologically plausible, it is of course artistically discreditable.

The present century, reacting against earlier critics' emphasis on the importance of plausible characters, fairly early came up with a counter theory: Levin Schücking and E. E. Stoll, for instance, suggested that Shakespeare was chiefly concerned with theatrically effective scenes, and was not overmuch concerned with plausible continuity of character from scene to scene. Here are three critics, talking of episodes in *As You Like It*, who invoke this principle with only minor variations. Michael Jamieson, writing of Celia's and Oliver's swift tumble into mutual love, says that it is 'a speed . . . theatrically necessary'. John Palmer, writing of Oliver, says: 'Shakespeare takes the bad brother for his plot but never takes him seriously as a person and throws him into Celia's arms at the end of the story with . . . nonchalance.' Kittredge, writing of Oliver's conversion, says: 'Sudden conversion of the villain is often an imperative *coup de théâtre*. . . . We sometimes forget that we are just as conventional as the Elizabethans, though with a different set of conventions, and that to Shakespeare, the practical playwright, the conventions of his age were rules of the game.' C. L. Barber amplifies the importance of plot convention, saying that 'it is not the credibility of the event that is decisive, but what can be expressed through it. Thus the shipwreck [in *Twelfth Night*] is made the occasion for Viola to exhibit an undaunted, aristocratic mastery of adversity. . . . What matters is not the event, but what the language says as gesture, the aristocratic, free-and-easy way she settles what she will do and what the captain will do to help her.'[2] But one can ask Jamieson *why* the improbable speed is 'theatrically necessary', and one can point out that it is really no swifter than the speed with which Rosalind and Orlando fall in love; all four experience love at first sight. If exigencies of concluding the

play explain the speediness of the love between Celia and Oliver,
how can we then explain the speediness of the love between
Rosalind and Orlando, which occurs in the first act? One can
reply to Palmer that it is no service to Shakespeare to suggest that
he did not take seriously a character who plays a fairly large role;
furthermore, the 'nonchalance' with which Shakespeare seems to
treat Oliver appears in the treatment of other characters too: for
example, in the uncertain motivation of Jaques's melancholy and
in Frederick's conversion. And Kittredge's explanation minimises Shakespeare's artistry by suggesting that an episode is
acceptable simply because other plays of the period have similar
episodes. Finally, Barber's statement that 'it is not the credibility
of the event that is decisive' minimises what is highly visible and
cannot be minimised. I do not think that the patent improbabilities in the plays are transparent conventions, comparable to,
say, the invisible fourth wall that allows us to see the deeds going
on in a room on the stage. Rather, I will argue, these
improbabilities are an essential part of the meaning—at least of
As You Like It.

It is probably true that most of us cannot quite escape from a
view of literature that in one respect may be called Aristotelian:
we expect to see in literature (as distinct from history) deeds
growing out of motives, and motives growing out of the
conjunction of personality and circumstances: In such-and-such
circumstances, such-and-such a man will probably act in such-
and-such a way. We can recognise the necessity of conventions,
but it will not quite do to suggest that improbable actions are
acceptable merely because similar actions occur in other plays.
We want to know what is achieved through the improbability –
what is achieved through those fairies, those forests, those
coincidental encounters, those shipwrecks. This paper will argue
that Shakespeare goes out of his way to heighten the improbabilities in *As You Like It*, presumably for a purpose, and that it is
therefore an error to dismiss them or to suggest that they are to be
accepted unthinkingly as conventions.

As You Like It, for all of its gentle satire on pastoral life and
literature, is nevertheless set in a world where, despite
Touchstone's dial, there is 'no clock i' th' forest'. That is, this
pastoral world is utterly different from the shepherd world that
King Henry VI calls to mind when, like any of us trying to get

through the working-day world, he enumerates a shepherd's
chores:

> . . .
> So many hours must I tend my flock;
> So many hours must I take my rest;
> So many hours must I contemplate;
> So many hours must I sport myself;
> So many days my ewes have been with young;
> So many weeks ere the poor fools will ean;
> So many years ere I shall shear the fleece.
> . . .
>
> [3 *H.VI*, II v 31–7]

While it would be a mistake to say that nothing happens (as
someone has remarked, dialogue is what characters *do* to one
another), it is true to say that the characters in Arden are in a sort
of suspended animation, waiting for the reformation of Oliver
and of Frederick, and largely free from the need to make choices
and to take effective action. Orlando, for example, defeats a
wrestler and (on Adam's advice) runs away, but once in Arden
he does very little until near the end, when he saves Oliver.
Chance – or Providence – brings him to the good Duke and to
Rosalind, and once there he gets what little direction he needs
from Rosalind, who herself does very little, for she is in 'a holiday
mood', until near the end when she presides over the denouement. It should be noted that although at the end she is the
mistress of ceremonies, in fact she has contrived almost nothing
when compared, say, to Portia or to Helena or to Prospero or to
the Duke in *Measure for Measure*. She does not arrange any of the
meetings; at the end of the fifth act she runs things only because at
the end of the first act she decided to adopt a man's attire. Even
the decision to leave the court was forced upon her by her uncle,
and the decision to adopt a disguise is a modification of Celia's
idea. The characters, that is, live in a wonderful Eden-like world,
and Shakespeare on three occasions calls attention to the
improbability. Of her chance encounter with Orlando, Celia
says, 'O wonderful, wonderful, and most wonderful, and yet
again wonderful, and after that out of all whooping' [III ii 190].
Commenting on Oliver's report of 'Ganymede's' swoon, Orlando

says he has heard of 'greater wonders', referring to the amazing swiftness with which Celia and Oliver fall in love. And near the end of the play, Hymen says:

> . . .
> Whiles a wedlock hymn we sing,
> Feed yourselves with questioning,
> That reason wonder may diminish
> How thus we met, and these things finish. [v iv 131-4]

But reason will not be able to diminish the wonder by explaining 'how thus we met', because there is no explanation, other than, perhaps, guidance by Him

> that doth the ravens feed,
> Yea, providently caters for the sparrow. [II iii 43-4]

Orlando had sought out neither the good Duke nor Rosalind, but he encountered both. The echo of *Luke*, xii 24 and of *Psalms*, cxlvii 9, evoked by the reference to the raven, and of *Luke*, xii 6, evoked by the reference to the sparrow, is underscored by the explicit reference to Providence; and in the final scene Hymen twice speaks of heaven, suggesting that there is 'mirth in heaven/When earthly things made even/Atone together'. Jaques gives us a comic version of the wonder evoked by miracle when, looking at the paired lovers, he says, 'There is, sure, another flood toward, and these are couples coming to the ark' [v iv 35-6]. This sense of wonder, with a concomitant hint of Providence, is of course found elsewhere, not only in the romances, where it has often been noticed, but also in the earlier comedies, for example in *The Merchant of Venice*, where Portia's revelations, like 'manna', leave the characters 'amazed', and where the audience itself cannot but wonder how Portia has news that Antonio's ships are safe. In *As You Like It*, Hymen himself is part of the wonder that concludes the play; he is never explained in the play, and those productions that make him recognisably one of the Duke's men, or a Corin whose Falstaffian girth reveals his identity beneath his sheet, do an injustice to this element in the play. Rosalind, I have said, really does very little, but one of the things she does do is mysteriously produce Hymen.

In keeping with the strangeness of this world, Shakespeare in several places *lessens* the motivation he found in Lodge's *Rosalynde*. It is customary in critical discussions of Shakespeare's use of his sources, to point out how he increases the probability of his actions, as though he were writing *pièces bien faites*, or as though he felt compelled to heed Aristotle's comments on probability. Yet in fact he often lessens the probability. For example, Lodge's Sir John of Bourdeaux bequeathed Rosader (the youngest son, who thus corresponds to Orlando) 'sixteene ploughlands', which was two more than he bequeathed to Saladyne, the oldest son. Saladyne has a long internal debate, weighing his father's moral exhortations against his own envious impulses, concluding with the decision to 'raign . . . sole Lord over al thy Fathers possessions'.[3] Shakespeare might have followed Lodge in having the eldest son envious of his young brother's ample possessions, but instead Shakespeare makes Oliver's conspiracy against Orlando *less* intelligible by giving Orlando only a 'poor thousand crowns', a 'poor allottery' that does not seem to interest Oliver. Near the end of the first scene, after we have witnessed the quarrel between the brothers but have been given no explanation for Oliver's treatment of Orlando, Oliver confesses he can offer no explanation, 'for my soul, yet I know not why, hates nothing more than he'. He indeed goes on to pay tribute to Orlando's virtues, and then suggests that because of them 'I am altogether misprized', but this explanation appears as an afterthought, and although Adam later says that Orlando's virtues 'are sanctified and holy traitors' because they arouse envy, it is clear that Oliver's motivation is thereby only the more mysterious. As Adam says of this wonder, 'O, what a world is this, when what is comely/Envenoms him that bears it' [II iii 14–15]. The fact may be plain, but the motive remains mysterious.

Before proceeding to mention some other important instances where Shakespeare lessens the motivation he found in Lodge's *Rosalynde*, and heightens the implausibility of the action, it may be worth mentioning that Lodge's style itself—a sort of saner euphuism—is well-suited to the presentation of the moral debates that lend plausibility to subsequent deeds. It balances the arguments, giving the characters an internal complexity and allowing the reader to perceive clearly the forces that impel them to one course of action or another. The characters do not, of course, regularly act rationally, but we get a sense of persons subjected to various pressures and responding to these pressures according to their personalities. Indeed, *Rosalynde*, like Lyly's narratives, has a good deal of argument, but where in Lyly the elaborate structure of the speeches commonly obscures any advance in thought and diffuses any sense of personality, in Lodge the euphuistic manner is sufficiently restrained so that a sense of internal debate is conveyed. Here, for example, is the beginning of 'Saladynes Meditation With Himself' on the conflicting impulses of avarice and filial duty:

Saladyne, how art thou disquieted in thy thoughts, & perplexed with a world of restlesse passions, having thy minde troubled with the tenour of thy Fathers testament, and thy heart fiered with the hope of present preferment? by the one, thou art counsaild to content thee with thy fortunes; by the other, perswaded to aspire to higher wealth. Riches *(Saladyne)* is a great royalty, & there is no sweeter phisick than store. *Avicen* like a foole forgot in his Aphorismes to say, that golde was the most precious restorative, and that treasure was the most excellent medecine of the minde. Oh *Saladyne*, what, were thy Fathers precepts breathed into the winde? hast thou so soone forgotten his principles? did he not warne thee from coveting without honor, and climing without vertue? did hee not forbid thee to aime at any action that should not be honourable? and what will bee more prejudiciall to thy credit, than the carelesse ruine of thy brothers welfare? [p. 165]

That Saladyne comes to the wrong conclusion and decides to steal his brother's property is irrelevant; the point is that the monologue suggests a reasoning man. This emphasis on reasoning, again appropriately set forth in a balanced style, appears not only in the monologue but also in the intervening narrative links. For example, Lodge does not merely tell us that the usurper decided to hold a tournament, but that the usurper had a purpose in holding the tournament: 'Thus continued the pad hidden in the strawe, till it chaunced that *Torismond* King of *France* had appoynted for his pleasure a day of Wrastling and of Tournament to busie his Commons heads, least being idle their thoughts should runne upon more serious matters, and call to re-membrance their old banished King' [p. 168]. Moreover, Torismond knows his audience, and calculates his action so that it will have the maximum effect. (In the following passage I add italics to clarify the point, and I omit Lodge's italics from the proper nouns.)

To feede their eyes, *and to* make the beholders pleased with the sight of most rare and glistring objects, he had appoynted his owne daughter Alinda to be there, & the faire Rosalynd daughter unto Gerismond, with all the beautifull damosels that were famous for their features in all France. *Thus* in that place did Love and Warre triumph in a simpathie: *for such* as were Martiall, might use their Launce to bee renowmed for the excellence of their Chevalrie; *and such* as were amorous, might glut themselves with gazing on the beauties of most heavenly creatures. [p. 169]

This is a fair sample of the sort of thinking that is revealed throughout the story; it insistently announces itself and conveys a sense of a reasoning and in some degree reasonable world.

Although in a play there cannot be narrative links precisely like these, unless the dramatist uses a chorus, this sort of information can be conveyed through dialogue, soliloquies and asides if the dramatist cares about it. But Shakespeare does not bother to tell us why a wrestling match is being held; 'Tomorrow, sir, I wrestle for my credit.' Charles tells Oliver. That is as much motive as we get, and while it tells us something about Charles, it tells us nothing at all about Frederick's reason for holding a tournament.

The reasons for Frederick's banishment of Rosalind are similarly less detailed and less plausible than those for Torismond's banishment of Rosalynde. Le Beau has earlier warned Orlando (and us) that Frederick is unpredictable:

. . .
Yet such is now the Duke's condition
That he misconsters all that you have done.
The Duke is humorous. . . . [ɪ ii 254–6]

In the following scene he enters, 'his eyes full of anger', and orders Rosalind to 'get you from our court'. When she asks how she has offended, he calls her a traitor, and when he is pressed for a more detailed explanation he answers: 'Thou art thy father's daughter, there's enough.' Rosalind points out that she was her father's daughter when Frederick first usurped the throne, and to Celia's interruption Frederick answers that he allowed Rosalind to remain for Celia's sake. But now, for some unstated reason, Rosalind is to be banished. When Celia protests further, Frederick at last offers something that can be called an explanation: Rosalind's very excellence is Celia's enemy because it diminishes Celia's excellence. This indeed is a reason, but it is a bad one, and we can only echo Le Beau's earlier conclusion: 'The Duke is humorous.' But that is a conclusion, not an explanation. In contrast, Torismond fears that 'some one of the Peeres will ayme at her love, ende [i.e. consummate] the marriage, and then in his wifes right attempt the kingdome. To prevent therefore had I wist in all these actions, she tarries not about the Court, but shall (as an exile) either wander to her father, or els seeke other fortunes' [p. 176]. This is a tyrant's logic, but it is logic; it allows us to follow Torismond's thought-processes, whereas Frederick's remain mysterious.

Celia's decision to flee with Rosalind marks a departure from Lodge, whose Alinda is banished by her father Torismond. Here we may at first glance feel that Shakespeare's action is more plausible: rather than have a father unnaturally banish his daughter, Shakespeare has the daughter leave the court in order to remain with her devoted friend. And yet again Shakespeare's action is more mysterious, more wonderful, for devotion of such magnitude is inexplicable. This is not to say that it is unreal, only that it cannot be explained in terms of cause and effect. On the other hand, Lodge provides an adequate explanation for Torismond's apparently impossible conduct. Torismond in a long speech attempts to argue with Alinda ('in liking *Rosalynd* thou hatchest up a bird to pecke out thine owne eyes'), then abandons his attempt to 'alleadge policie' and curtly rebukes her, and finally, when Alinda threatens suicide, banishes her. Lodge patiently explains why Torismond banishes his own daughter:

When *Torismond* heard his daughter so resolute, his heart was so hardned against her, that he set downe a definitive and peremptorie sentence that they should both be banished: which presentlie was done. The Tyrant rather choosing to hazard the losse of his only child, than any waies to put in question the state of his kingdome: so suspicious and feareful is the conscience of an usurper. [p. 178]

If for a moment we wonder why Torismond should harden his heart, Lodge quickly explains the psychology of a tyrant: such a man will prefer his kingdom to his kin, 'so suspicious and fearful is the conscience of an usurper'.

In yet another crucial episode Lodge's usurper behaves more plausibly than Shakespeare's. Torismond banishes Saladyne in order to gain possession of all the lands of Sir John of Bourdeaux, Saladyne having enlarged his own holdings by annexing Rosader's. Torismond first imprisons Saladyne on account of 'the wrongs hee proffred to his brother' [p. 198], and then banishes him, explaining 'I spare thy life for thy fathers sake' [p. 199]. Frederick, however, learning that Celia and Rosalind have fled the court, perhaps with Orlando, says [II ii 17–19] that if indeed Orlando is missing he will send Oliver to find him. Five scenes intervene before this subject is returned to, when [in III i] Frederick orders Oliver to find Orlando and confiscates Oliver's property. In this scene nothing is said of the likelihood that Orlando is with the two girls, and nothing at all is said of the girls; without reference to the earlier brief discussion of this likelihood it is unclear why Frederick is concerned about Orlando. Again we get a sense that the Duke is 'humorous', unpredictable, rather than a coherent perverse character.

But of course in *As You Like It* the most unpredictable happenings (from the point of view of psychology, not of literary conventions) are the instantaneous love affairs and the conversions of the villains. Lodge's Rosader falls quickly, but Rosalynde is less precipitous. There is not space here to give in detail the process that Lodge sets forth at length, but a few short quotations will suggest his attempt to explain what happens to Rosalynde when she sees Rosader. She is 'touched' by the 'beautie and valour of *Rosader* . . . but she accounted love a toye, and fancie a momentarie passion, . . . and therefore feared not to dallie in the flame . . .' [p. 172]. She sends Rosader a jewel and in return he sends her a poem. '*Rosalynd* returning home from the triumph, after she waxed solitarie, love presented her with the *Idea* of *Rosaders* perfection, and taking her at discovert, strooke her so deepe, as she felt her selfe grow passing passionate. . . . Sucking in thus the hony of love, by imprinting in her thoughtes his rare qualities, she began to surfit with the contemplation of his vertuous conditions . . .' [p. 174]. There

follows a long internal monologue, 'Rosalynds Passion', full of
doubts and self-rebukes, but concluding with the assertion that if
she loves, it must be Rosader or no one. Shakespeare assumes that
beautiful young people fall in love for no apparent reason. This
assumption is especially evident in the love exchanged between
Celia and the reformed Oliver. In Lodge, Saladyne, repentant
and reunited with Rosader, saves Alinda from 'certaine Rascalls
that lived by prowling in the Forrest'. When Alinda recovers her
composure, she looks upon her rescuer and begins 'to measure
everie part of him with favour, and in her selfe to commend his
personage and his vertue, holding him for a resolute man, that
durst assaile such a troupe of unbridled villaines' [p. 222]. Her
love for him, that is, is partly rooted in her gratitude for his
actions; his love, too, is a little less than instantaneous: '*Saladyne*
hearing this Shepheardesse speake so wisely began more narrowly to prie into her perfection, and to survey all her liniaments
with a curious insight; so long dallying in the flame of her beautie
that to his cost he found her to be most excellent . . .' [p. 222].
Shakespeare, on the other hand, goes out of his way to insist upon
the suddenness and the improbability of the love between Celia
and Oliver. There is no rescue from brigands, nor any other
stated reason for it. (Perhaps it should be mentioned that
Shakespeare's Arden, however green or golden, could have
harbored brigands as well as a lioness and snake.) Rosalind is our
source for what happened between Celia and Oliver:

> . . . There was never anything so sudden but the fight of
> two rams and Caesar's thrasonical brag of 'I came, saw,
> and overcame'; for your brother and my sister no sooner
> met but they looked; no sooner looked but they loved; no
> sooner loved but they sighed; no sooner sighed but they
> asked one another the reason; no sooner knew the reason
> but they sought the remedy: and in these degrees have
> they made a pair of stairs to marriage, which they will
> climb incontinent, or else be incontinent before mar-
> riage. . . . [v ii 27–36]

This insistence on the suddenness and improbability of the
experience suggests not that Shakespeare is winding things up

quickly because (in Johnson's words) he is 'in view of his reward', or that (in Paul V. Kreider's words⁴) Shakespeare is mocking his 'patently inadequate plot', but that suddenness and improbability are part of the meaning of the play. It will not do to take Johnson's or Kreider's positions, or those of the critics mentioned earlier in this paper. Here is one more version, by John Wain, concentrating on the surprising conversions of Oliver and Frederick:

The plot of *As You Like It*, like that of *Twelfth Night*, contains absurdities which, under the influence of the warmth and gaiety of the play, we swallow light-heartedly enough. The double conversion of the two villainous characters, Duke Frederick and Orlando's brother Oliver, is sketched in with a perfunctoriness that saves the play, perhaps, from ridicule; if Shakespeare had not shown us so plainly that he did not care whether we believed in the story or not, if he had made it even a shade more credible, we might have tried to believe in it. And this could only have led to disappointment. We must take the action as a mere charade, and let Shakespeare guide our serious interest into areas where it has something to feed on.⁵

Wain's terms are a little uncertain; one does not quite know what to make out of the shift from not *believing* in the plot to *feeding* on the other 'areas', but apparently the point is that the plot is of no interest or consequence. Now, just as no one believes that the dialogue of a play is a transcript of real talk, or that the *dramatis personae* are real people, so no one believes that the plot is an exact reproduction of a chain of historical events. But plot, like dialogue and character, presumably has some sort of intimate connection with reality. One might say that plot, dialogue, and character are symbolic, standing for realities. In *As You Like It*, presumably the sudden alterations in Rosalind, Orlando, Celia, and Oliver suggest changes in personality of a sort suggested, say, in Ovid's *Metamorphoses*. In those legends, suffering humanity—usually consumed by guilt or fear—is unable to continue its existence, the metamorphosis representing the sort of change that in life is accomplished by suicide, by retreat into a psychotic state, or by religious conversion. Tolstoi's conversion, preceded by enormous anxieties, contradictory actions and suicidal impulses, is a familiar example from life of the sort of thing that much of Ovid implies. And this brings us back to the matter of the

conversion of Oliver, for he not only falls in love with Celia but
first loses the hatred for Orlando that animated him when in the
first act he said, 'for my soul, yet I know not why, hates nothing
more than he'. In Lodge, Saladyne repents while in Torismond's
prison. There is nothing strange here. Whatever our modern
doubts about the value of imprisonment, a stubborn part of our
mind sees such a change as reasonable. A man who is subjected to
punishment, we think, is likely to avoid repeating the sort of
behavior that got him punished. Saladyne, in prison, 'began to
fall into consideration . . . with himselfe' [p. 198], and by the end
of a 'complaint' he has realized that he behaved badly. He vows
to do penance, and to seek Rosader. But, again, Shakespeare
omits such motivation, heightening the abruptness of Oliver's
conversion, making it (like love at first sight) a matter of minutes.
Certainly it is understandable; Orlando nobly has saved Oliver's
life, but Oliver in the first act had clearly perceived Orlando's
nobility and had hated him for it. Now, in an instant, Oliver is a
new man. Asked by Celia if he is the man 'that did so oft contrive
to kill' Orlando, Oliver replies:

'Twas I. But 'tis not I. I do not shame
To tell you what I was, since my conversion
So sweetly tastes, being the thing I am. [IV iii 134–6]

Oliver explicitly speaks of his 'conversion', and the experience he
describes has obvious affinities with religious conversion, which
utterly transforms one's personality, as, for example, on the road
to Damascus Paul's personality was transformed. And as Paul,
who persecuted Christ, finally yielded utterly to him, so Oliver,
who persecuted Orlando, yields to him 'all the revenue that was
old Sir Rowland's' [v ii 9–10]. I want to dwell a moment more on
two other Biblical analogues. First, we might note that Orlando
suspends the *lex talionis*, and requites evil with good. His action is
not the mechanical counteraction evoked by Oliver's actions, but
an act of overflowing love. Second, early in the play Orlando had
introduced a reference to the parable of the prodigal son, quite
rightly denying that he is a prodigal. But the parable in fact deals
with *two* brothers, and Oliver in the earlier part of the play has
the meanness of the second brother, who in the parable stands
apart from the festivities that celebrate the return of the prodigal.

In the last two acts we see that this cold brother is converted and drawn into the festivities; his transformation is confirmed by his experience of falling in love, an experience which similarly involves a surrender of the old self and provides a new perception of all experiences. And Oliver is awarded Celia; though he has labored in the vineyard only very briefly, his reward is full.

Shakespeare, it should be mentioned, did not need to convert Oliver merely to end the play; Oliver could have remained wicked, to be dealt with in an unwritten sixth act, as Don John in *Much Ado* is to be dealt with. Nor is Oliver's conversion necessary merely to provide Celia with a husband; one of Duke Senior's 'loving lords' might have served. Similarly, Frederick might have been captured and pushed offstage. But Shakespeare gives us a different plot, and it is likely that his plot is meaningful rather than slipshod or perfunctory.

Frederick's conversion at the hands of 'an old religious man' is only the last of a series of implausible happenings that suggests the existence of a benevolent Providence. *As You Like It* is not devoid of oblique references to Providence, some of which have already been glanced at. But it is in the strange happenings, rather than in the oblique references in the dialogue, that one perceives most clearly that, to quote from *Cymbeline* [v v 64–5],

> The fingers of the pow'rs above do tune
> The harmony of this peace.

Or, to quote from *The Tempest* [v i 242–4],

> This is as strange a maze as e'er men trod;
> And there is in this business more than nature
> Was ever conduct of.

Like Oliver's conversion, Frederick's is apparently triggered by a sudden experience, and it has 'an element of marvel', to use words that William James in Lecture IX of *The Varieties of Religious Experience* used of conversion. But as James pointed out, conversion is often preceded by a hidden complex psychic state. James writes:

A mental system may be undermined or weakened . . . just as a building is, and yet for a time keep upright by dead habit. But a new perception, a sudden emotional shock, or an occasion which lays bare the organic alteration, will make the whole fabric fall together; and then the centre of gravity sinks into an attitude more stable, for the new ideas that reach the centre in the rearrangement seem now to be locked there, and the new structure remains permanent.

Early in the play, by means of references to Frederick's unpredictability and to Oliver's confession that his hatred was inexplicable, Shakespeare indicates that the villains' personalities were unstable, and therefore that they were open to sudden re-information, or reformation. One might add here that the melancholy Jaques—whose melancholy is inexplicable, for it is not the scholar's or the musician's or the courtier's or the soldier's or the lawyer's, and it does not really seem to be the traveler's either—is a similar figure, puzzling because his principle of behavior is unclear. (There have, of course, been various studies of his melancholy, but the scholarship adduced to prove it is due to one or another cause is not substantiated in the play.) That he will seek out Frederick, because 'Out of these convertites/There is much matter to be heard and learned', is not at all strange; earlier he was faintly associated with the humorous duke by virtue of being said to be 'compact of jars'. Jaques's discords, like Frederick's discordant actions, betoken a personality that has not become integrated, and at the conclusion of the play, after the report of Frederick's conversion, Jaques's intention to visit Frederick reminds us of this sort of anxious personality and it reminds us also of its great potentiality for change. In Jaques's statement that he hopes to learn 'much matter' from the convertite, we may hear, very faintly, a voice like that of the jailer who asked Paul and Silas, 'What must I do to be saved?' Zera Fink says Jaques 'has lost any real faith in life',[6] but the implication of the play is, I think, that his dissatisfaction with things as they are prepares him for the possibility of conversion of the sort experienced by Frederick and Oliver, by the lovers.

These remarks do not, I hope, resemble those on the girlhood of Shakespeare's heroines, the child-bearing of Lady Macbeth, or the heavenly or hellish destinations of the figures in the tragedies. The point is not that the characters have a life before the first act or after the fifth, but that in the play as we have it they engage in strange behavior because strange behavior is what Shakespeare is talking about, not because he is employing meaningless conventions or winding things up quickly. In the romances the working of grace is more prominent, but even as early as *The Comedy of Errors*, when Luciana's words cause Antipholus of Syracuse to say, 'Would you create me new?' [*C.E.*, III ii 39] we find in Shakespeare suggestions of powers that mysteriously transform nature into something higher. Such inexplicable and wonderful transformations are entirely in harmony with another thread that runs through comedy, on which Puck remarked:[7]

> . . . those things do best please me
> That befall prepost'rously. [*M.N.D.*, III ii 120–1]

In comedy we find things absurd to reason. As the etymology indicates, the preposterous is that in which the natural order is broken, the first coming last, and the conversions we have been speaking of involve the unnatural, the implausible. But it should be noted, too, that although in the last act of *As You Like It* some of the chief characters return to the court from which they had been exiled, what we saw at first is not what we now see last. The court society at the end is not identical with the court society of the first act, where a capricious usurper ruled, and where ribs were cracked. As Northrop Frye says, 'The action of a Shakespearean comedy, then, is not simply cyclical but dialectical as well: the renewing power of the final action lifts us into a higher world, and separates that world from the world of the comic action itself.'[8] There is at the end a return to the court, but the court now will house the rightful duke and a Rosalind and an Orlando transformed by love. Moreover, two former court-figures, Frederick and Oliver, who have undergone the greatest transformations, will not be there; though Duke Senior is the ruler of no mean city, these two feel the claim of a higher city, and Jaques also indicates an awareness of it. That is, Shakespeare's pastoral world in *As You Like It* is not only a place where innocence is achieved through retreat, abstinence, and self-sufficiency, as is common in pastoral literature; it is also a place where innocence is achieved through conversion, and, for Frederick and Oliver, through some degree of self-mortification.

Early in the play Jaques describes as a 'strange eventful

history' man's unhappy progress through seven rather uneventful ages; in the last act, when conflicts have been wondrously reconciled through patently unreasonable (but not therefore perfunctory or meaningless) transformations, Hymen justly speaks of 'strange events'. Had Shakespeare wished to write a more plausible play, he needed only to have followed his source more closely. But he apparently took pains to make his play implausible, and we ought not to let our awareness of conventions, or our tolerance for occasional perfunctoriness, mislead us into thinking that the plot of *As You Like It* is negligible, or that the play is about anything less strange than 'strange events'.

SOURCE: essay in *Shakespeare Studies*, IV (1968), 119–31.

NOTES

[Modified and renumbered from the original Notes in the essay—Ed.]

1. Walter Raleigh (ed.), *Johnson on Shakespeare* (London, 1952), pp. 12–21.

2. M. Jamieson, *Shakespeare: As You Like It* (London, 1965), p. 61; J. Palmer, *Comic Characters of Shakespeare* (London, 1946), p. 32; G. L. Kittredge, edition of *As You Like It* (Boston, 1939), pp. x–xi; and C. L. Barber, *Shakespeare's Festive Comedy* (Princeton, N.J., 1959), pp. 241–2.

3. Quoted in G. Bullough (ed.), *Narrative and Dramatic Sources of Shakespeare* (New York, 1957; London, 1963), II, p. 166. All subsequent references to Lodge's *Rosalynde* are to this edition, with the page number in parentheses after the quotation.

4. P. V. Kreider, 'Genial Satire in the Forest of Arden', *Shakespeare Association Bulletin*, x (1935), 227.

5. J. Wain, *The Living World of Shakespeare* (London, 1964), pp. 85–6. Cf. Helen Gardner's comments that Shakespeare 'handles very cursorily the repentance of the wicked brother', and that 'the plot is handled in the most perfunctory way'. [See Helen Gardner's study, reproduced above—Ed.]

6. Z. Fink, 'Jaques and the Malcontent Traveler', *Philological Quarterly*, XIV (1935), 240. Somewhat like Fink, James Smith takes a melancholy view of Jaques in '*As You Like It*', *Scrutiny*, IX (1940), 9–32.

7. On re-reading the major critical discussions I find that in her essay [reproduced above—Ed] Miss Helen Gardner quotes Puck's lines. Although the gist of my essay is very different from hers, I am doubtless

indebted to her here. My essay modifies her view that the plot is of minor importance.

8. N. Frye, *A Natural Perspective* (New York, 1965), p. 133.

D. J. Palmer   As You Like It and the Idea of Play (1971)

Now in myth and ritual the great instinctive forces of civilised life have their origin: law and order, commerce and profit, craft and art, poetry, wisdom and science. All are rooted in the primeval soil of play. (J. Huizinga, *Homo Ludens*, 1949)

Here nowe I recke not much, to passe over untouched, how no matter, acte, or noble deede was ever attempted, nor any arte or science invented other, than of whiche I might fully be holden first author. (Erasmus, *The Praise of Folie*, translated by Sir Thomas Chaloner, 1594)

I

There is only enough story in *As You Like It* to send the main characters to the Forest of Arden and finally to bring most of them out again. Once in the forest, the action virtually dispenses with narrative plot. Rosalind, for instance, no longer requires her disguise when she has found her father, whom she came to seek, and Orlando as well; but she delays the discovery of her identity for as long as she can. Like the other sojourners in Arden, she passes the time (although there seems nothing to wait for) by playing games. The heart of the comedy might be described as a demonstration of man's natural propensity for play.

We first hear of Arden in the opening scene, when Charles the wrestler describes how Duke Senior and his companions live in exile:

They say he is already in the Forest of Arden, and a many
merry men with him; and there they live like the old
Robin Hood of England. They say many young gentlemen flock to him every day, and fleet the time carelessly,
as they did in the golden world. [I i 105–9]

It seems as though life has become a pastime for the Duke and his
followers, as though they have passed out of reality into a story-
book world. A legend of Merry England is merged with the
classical myth of the Golden Age, and even in the word 'flock'
there is a hint of pastoral associations. Yet this is only by report, as
the repetition of 'they say' reminds us. Hearsay distances reality,
and is itself the way in which legends come into being. We are left
uncertain, therefore, whether this idyllic picture of life in Arden is
the creation of the Duke and his followers or of Charles and his
informants.

As a world of make-believe, however, it certainly reflects a
sharp contrast with the stern realities of court life, where instead
of a society of 'merry men' there is the conflict of brother with
brother. As Duke Frederick usurped his brother's throne, Oliver
now plots against Orlando, and immediately after Charles's
description of the pastimes pursued in Arden we hear talk of
another kind of play: 'You wrestle tomorrow before the new
Duke?' Wrestling makes sport out of conflict, yet Oliver has a
sinister design to turn Charles's match with Orlando into a game
to be played in deadly earnest.

The juxtaposition of these two images is followed in the second
scene by Celia's persuasion of her cousin to shake off melancholy
and 'be merry':

> ROS. From henceforth I will, coz, and devise sports. Let
> me see; what do you think of falling in love?
> CEL. Marry, I prithee, do, to make sport withal; but love
> no man in good earnest, nor no further in sport
> neither than with safety of a pure blush thou mayst in
> honour come off again.
> ROS. What shall be our sport, then?
> CEL. Let us sit and mock the good housewife Fortune from
> her wheel, that her gifts may henceforth be bestowed
> equally.
> ROS. I would that we could do so; . . . [I ii 21–31]

Their sport is in devising sport, experimenting with the exhilarating possibilities of play, and casting around for some suitable object for their wit and mockery. At this point Touchstone joins them, and the advent of the professional fool adds another dimension to the treatment of life as a game. The fool's wit is intelligence at play, delighting in its own caprice, and extending by inverting them the contrary values of folly and wisdom.

Before we reach Arden, therefore, we are given some anticipation of the nature of play, and of the equivocal relations between fiction and reality, game and earnest, folly and wisdom. Each of the different kinds of pastimes presented in these first two scenes is a response to a society broken by violent enmities: Duke Senior and his companions turn their exile into a make-believe life of good fellowship; the wrestling match between Charles and Orlando is a projection of the hostility between the two brothers; while the games of wit that Celia and Rosalind play with Touchstone make sport out of adversity ('Nature hath given us wit to flout at Fortune', as Celia says). Play may be seen as a civilising impulse to create a better world, or as a way of releasing energies restrained by civilised life. Significantly, in a world that has been reduced to barbarism, where violence and cruelty are real enough, there is little use for play: the wrestling match turns into a murder-plot, and the fool is put to silence. Wrestling is a fairly primitive form of sport, in any case ('Is there yet another dotes upon rib-breaking?' says Rosalind, determined out of perverse humour to stay and watch a sport not fit for ladies). But while it reflects what has become of courtly tastes and values in the ascendancy of Duke Frederick, it also suggests by analogy the element of ritualised conflict that exists in wit-combats and games of mockery. Similarly, the pastoralism of Duke Senior's way of life in Arden, as Charles describes it, is both primitivist and civilising. If poetry and drama are themselves forms of play, Shakespeare is also playing games with his own art in *As You Like It*. His critical intelligence and creative imagination are held in perfect equilibrium as he sports with style through parody and burlesque, and finding the pastimes of Arden primitive analogues to the spirit of comedy. The forest itself, as we are several times reminded, is both literally and figuratively 'this wide and universal theatre', the wooden circle into which we are drawn,

like fools at the call of 'Ducdame', and the 'abandoned cave' that
we leave when the comedy is over.

II

After Charles's picture of the exiled Duke and his 'merry men'
fleeting the time carelessly, it comes as something of a surprise
when we first encounter the Duke in Arden to find him indulging
a vein of serious philosophising:

> Now, my co-mates and brothers in exile,
> Hath not old custom made this life more sweet
> Than that of painted pomp? Are not these woods
> More free from peril than the envious court?
> Here feel we not the penalty of Adam,
> The seasons' difference? – as the icy fang
> And churlish chiding of the winter's wind,
> Which when it bites and blows upon my body,
> Even till I shrink with cold, I smile and say
> 'This is no flattery; these are counsellors
> That feelingly persuade me what I am'.
> Sweet are the uses of adversity;
>   . . .   [II i 1–12]

The climate, too, is apparently less hospitable than Charles's
comparison with the golden world led us to anticipate. But it is
only the nature of the game that is different: this is just as much an
exercise in make–believe as playing at Robin Hood. The Duke is
using imagination to convert the harshness of existence in Arden
into a blessing in disguise; the struggle for survival in a hostile
world becomes a benevolent schooling in self-knowledge. It is not
the philosophical truth of the Duke's propositions that require
assent, but his willingness to look on the bright side. So Amiens
responds, not with 'How wise, how true, how noble', but with

>   Happy is your Grace,
>   That can translate the stubbornness of fortune
>   Into so quiet and so sweet a style. [II i 18–20]

The only moralist in evidence is the winter's wind, whose

'churlish chiding' is in marked contrast to the 'sweet' style of the Duke.

But discarding this role for another, the Duke abruptly changes his tune by proposing another pastime, and one that matches the cruelty of nature which has just been his theme:

> Come, shall we go and kill us venison?

The victim of adversity would now reverse roles; but he recollects himself immediately and returns to his vein of fanciful reflection:

> And yet it irks me the poor dappled fools,
> Being native burghers of this desert city,
> Should, in their own confines, with forkèd heads
> Have their round haunches gor'd. [II i 22–5]

By attributing rights of prior occupation to the deer, and conflating their 'forkèd heads' with those of the huntsmen's arrows, the Duke puts man and beast on the same level, and relates bloodsport to the barbarism of the world that has expelled him.

This is the attendant lord's cue to report Jaques's meditation on the 'poor sequester'd stag'. It echoes the Duke's own sentimentalising of misfortune so well that we can recognise Jaques and the Duke as complementary figures, even though the Duke's 'sweet' style and his love of fellowship are antithetical to Jaques's bitter raillery and solitariness. The wounded deer was a commonplace emblem of affliction and melancholy retirement, and the familiar Elizabethan pun of hart/heart, which lies just below the threshold of this image, enables it to be extended to conceits about amorous suffering, as we shall see. For his part, by identifying with the forlorn beast Jaques disassociates himself from his comrades-in-exile:

> . . .
> Thus most invectively he pierceth through
> The body of the country, city, court,
> Yea, and of this our life; swearing that we
> Are mere usurpers, tyrants, and what's worse,
> To fright the animals, and kill them up
> In their assign'd and native dwelling-place. [II i 58–63]

Hunting now provides the metaphor for another pastime played between Jaques and the ducal party. His invective 'pierceth through/The body . . . of this our life' like a wounding arrow, but it causes amusement instead of pain, for the Duke and company treat Jaques as fair game for their mockery. The scene ends as the Duke goes to seek Jaques like a sportsman stalking his quarry:

> Show me the place;
> I love to cope him in these sullen fits,
> For then he's full of matter.

Again, in introducing Jaques through the attendant lord's account, the technique of report has been used to arouse anticipation and to present action at an ironic distance.

The first scene in Arden reflects the equivocal nature of play as a series of reversible roles: the victim of misfortune is also its agent, man and beast change places, the usurped become the usurpers, the hunters hunted, the critic a butt of his adversaries. Men are feelingly persuaded what they are, not by 'churlish chiding', but by the contrary parts they play in their games. And these games are a bitter-sweet mixture of whimsical sentiment and wanton cruelty.

III

Play in Arden takes the form of a series of encounters, seemingly at random, for the suspension of narrative progression produces a sense of timelessness. Scenes must follow each other in linear succession, but the effect created is also that of simultaneity as we are taken from 'one part of the forest' to 'another part of the forest', in the words that eighteenth-century editors used for their scene-headings. Indeed, within Arden there is no constant impression of different locations; although logically we must suppose that the Duke's encampment, Rosalind's cottage, and the trysting-place of Touchstone and Audrey lie at a distance from each other, the play as conceived for the Elizabethan stage calls only for a forest setting. The sense of meandering through the forest, of paths that cross by chance, and of a corresponding dislocation in the time scheme, is essential to the feeling of liberation in the free activity of play.

It is curious, therefore, that time occupies so much attention in Arden. In the original golden world of pastoralism, there was no time; spring was eternal. Arden, however, is subject to 'the penalty of Adam,/The seasons' difference', and characters are aware of the passing of time. But since 'there's no clock in the forest', as Orlando says, the sense of time is relative, and Rosalind replies, 'Time travels in divers paces with divers persons'. Despite Orlando's assertion, Touchstone has brought a timepiece with him, for Jaques describes the fool drawing 'a dial from his poke':

> . . .
> And, looking on it with lack-lustre eye,
> Says very wisely 'It is ten o'clock;
> Thus we may see' quoth he 'how the world wags;
> 'Tis but an hour ago since it was nine;
> And after one more hour 'twill be eleven;
> And so, from hour to hour, we ripe and ripe,
> And then, from hour to hour, we rot and rot;
> And thereby hangs a tale'. . . . [II vii 21–8]

If this melancholy rumination is an antecedent of Macbeth's despairing reflections on the 'petty pace' that creeps through 'tomorrow and tomorrow and tomorrow', it is also a tale told by an idiot. Touchstone is mocking the sense of futility produced, not by time itself, but by the way time is spent, in fruitless moralising. 'Pastime', on the other hand, is the way in which those who devise sports 'lose and neglect the creeping hours of time'. Rosalind, for instance, is well aware that love is subject to time: 'men are April when they woo, December when they wed; maids are May when they are maids, but the sky changes when they are wives'. But the purpose of play is to '*fleet* the time carelessly', to make time pass quickly, as in Marvell's response to 'Time's wingèd chariot':

> Thus, though we cannot make our sun
> Stand still, yet we will make him run.

Since 'life is but a flower', in the words of the song, sweet lovers

must 'therefore take the present time'. There is nothing leisurely
about Rosalind's life in Arden: 'woman's thoughts run before her
actions'; and, in addition to her impatience and restlessness, the
headlong dash of the prose she speaks is that of a wit moving so
fast that the tongue and breath can scarcely keep up with it:

> Good my complexion! dost thou think, though I am
> comparison'd like a man, I have a doublet and hose in my
> disposition? One inch of delay more is a South Sea of
> discovery. I prithee tell me who is it quickly, and speak
> apace. I would thou could'st stammer, that thou might'st
> pour this conceal'd man out of thy mouth, as wine comes
> out of a narrow-mouth'd bottle—either too much at once
> or none at all. I prithee take the cork out of thy mouth
> that I may drink thy tidings. [III ii 181–9]

IV

The mating game is of course the comedy's principal pastime,
and, like the other encounters in Arden, those between the lovers
have a certain combative quality which recalls the wrestling at
the beginning of the play. Indeed, Orlando and Rosalind fall in
love in wrestling terms. The conqueror of Charles confesses that
'my better parts are all thrown down' at his first meeting with
Rosalind, and she acknowledges a similar defeat:

> . . .
> Sir, you have wrestled well, and overthrown
> More than your enemies. [I ii 233–4]

It is only one of the many perversities in love that losers are also
winners (as in Juliet's paradox, 'learn me how to lose a winning
match'.)

After this preliminary but decisive bout between Rosalind and
Orlando, their mock-courtship in the forest is like a further series
of rounds in which roles are again reversed. As Orlando was the
unknown youth who overthrew Charles, he now finds himself
outplayed by 'Ganymede'. Rosalind exploits the advantage of
her disguise not only to take the initiative in wooing but to floor

her partner in the lists of love (until she is herself literally floored by the sight of Orlando's bloody napkin). The analogy between love and fighting is continued in Rosalind's comparison of the encounter between Celia and Oliver with 'the fight of two rams and Caesar's thrasonical brag of "I came, saw, and overcame" '. The wrestling match was a game played in deadly earnest, and the treatment of love as a contest between adversaries is a means of using play to explore the cruelties and antagonisms inherent in sexual relationships. Similarly the bawdiness of the comedy confronts aspects of sexuality denied by romantic or Petrarchan attitudes; as the hunting song puts it,

> . . .
> The horn, the horn, the lusty horn,
> Is not a thing to laugh to scorn. [IV ii 17–18]

but we do laugh at the old jest about cuckoldry, because we are inclined to joke about what is otherwise embarrassing. So Touchstone's impromptu jingle parodying Orlando's bad verses reflects in its indecent wordplay the use of game to release repressed realities:

> If a hart do lack a hind,
> Let him seek out Rosalinde,
> If the cat will after kind,
> So be sure will Rosalinde.
> . . .
> He that sweetest rose will find
> Must find love's prick and Rosalinde. [III ii 91–4, 101–2]

The point of 'love's prick' is felt by Silvius as 'the wounds invisible/That love's keen arrows make', as he sublimates the pain of unrequited passion into extravagant conceits. Through Silvius the fictions of the Elizabethan sonneteers are taken to their furthest extremes and reduced to absurdity, in Shakespeare's own game with contemporary poetic fashions. But Silvius himself is not disabled by the wounds of mockery, embracing his folly and wallowing in Phebe's scorn. Their 'pageant truly play'd' is a sado-masochistic farce, another variation of that sexual conflict called love. Yet at the point of

Phebe's greatest cruelty, when she would employ Silvius thank-
lessly in her own suit to 'Ganymede', the game ceases to be quite
so funny, and Silvius's devotion becomes for one brief glorious
moment entirely moving instead of merely silly:

> So holy and so perfect is my love,
> And I in such a poverty of grace,
> That I shall think it a most plenteous crop
> To glean the broken ears after the man
> That the main harvest reaps. . . .

But the poignancy topples over into absurdity again:

> Loose now and then
> A scatter'd smile, and that I'll live upon. [III v 98–103]

Such a moment illustrates the precarious poise between playful
and serious values in this comedy, and Shakespeare's ability to
turn artifice inside out. 'The truest poetry is the most feigning.'
    Of all the love-games played in the forest, Rosalind's counter-
feiting with Orlando is the most sophisticated and double-edged.
It is essentially equivocal because Rosalind has three *personae*: as
herself, as 'Ganymede', and as 'Ganymede-playing-Rosalind';
and we often cannot tell with which voice she is speaking.
'Ganymede' is an inversion of Rosalind's true identity both
sexually and as an enemy of love:

> Love is merely a madness; and, I tell you, deserves as well
> a dark house and a whip as madmen do; and the reason
> why they are not so punish'd and cured is that the lunacy
> is so ordinary that the whippers are in love too. Yet I
> profess curing it by counsel. [III ii 368–72]

As the free play of a sportive disposition, assuming attitudes for
their amusing possibilities rather than their truth, Rosalind's wit
has something in common with the teasing disinterestedness of
Touchstone's mockery, and her disguise is another version of the
fool's motley. But at the same time, since we know 'how many
fathom deep in love' she is, the constant scepticism directed
towards love's young dream verges on the melancholy disillusion

of Jaques. The distinguishing feature of her wit is that, unlike Jaques who is always in earnest and Touchstone who never is, Rosalind/Ganymede is poised in ambivalence:

> . . . The poor world is almost six thousand years old, and in all this time there was not any man died in his own person, videlicet, in a love-cause. Troilus had his brains dash'd out with a Grecian club; yet he did what he could to die before, and he is one of the patterns of love. Leander, he would have liv'd many a fair year, though Hero had turn'd nun, if it had not been for a hot midsummer-night; for, good youth, he went but forth to wash him in the Hellespont, and, being taken with the cramp, was drown'd; and the foolish chroniclers of that age found it was—Hero of Sestos. But these are all lies: men have died from time to time, and worms have eaten them, but not for love. [IV i 83–95]

This is the literary game again, turning artifice against itself in mockery of poetic fictions. But if there is a joyful exuberance in the demolition of the 'foolish chroniclers', felt through the running-on of the clauses, the last sentence invites a pause and a slight change of tone. One can almost detect a certain wistfulness in the dying fall of the conclusion, 'but not for love', as though Rosalind sighs behind 'Ganymede's' back. Her enthusiasm for play reflects both security and insecurity in love:

> ROS. Now tell me how long you would have her, after you have possess'd her.
> ORL. For ever and a day.
> ROS. Say 'a day' without the 'ever'. No, no, Orlando; men are April when they woo, December when they wed; maids are May when they are maids, but the sky changes when they are wives. . . . [IV i 127–33]

At such moments as these, there is a precarious balance between wit and feeling, between the delightful make-believe and the uncomfortable reality.

As for Orlando, for most of the time in these scenes he is little more than Rosalind's 'feed' and the butt of her wit. Her treatment of her lover, whose charm hardly lies in his mental agility, betrays a latent sexual aggression which sometimes rises to the surface:

> ROS. . . . Make fast the doors upon a woman's wit, and it will out at the casement; shut that, and 'twill out at the keyhole; stop that, 'twill fly with the smoke out at the chimney.
> ORL. A man that had a wife with such a wit, he might say 'Wit, whither wilt?'
> ROS. Nay, you might keep that check for it, till you met your wife's wit going to your neighbour's bed.
> ORL. And what wit could wit have to excuse that?
> ROS. Marry, to say she came to seek you there. You shall never take her without her answer, unless you take her without her tongue. O, that woman that cannot make her fault her husband's occasion, let her never nurse her child herself, for she will breed it like a fool!
> [IV i 144–57]

In those unenlightened days, before Women's Lib was afoot, such an attitude was accounted shrewishness. Rosalind was sufficiently peremptory when she encountered it in Phebe:

> . . .   Down on your knees,
> And thank heaven, fasting, for a good man's love.
> [III v 57–8]

But her own treatment of Orlando bears a close resemblance to the belligerence she falsely attributes to Phebe's style:

> Why 'tis a boisterous and a cruel style;
> A style for challengers. Why, she defies me,
> Like Turk to Christian: . . . [IV iii 31–3]

If Rosalind's wit frequently leaves us guessing how far she believes what she says, it also seems at times to run away with her: 'The wiser, the waywarder.' 'We that have good wits', says Touchstone, 'have much to answer for: we shall be flouting, we cannot hold.' Her disguise is not merely the assumption of another personality; it serves as a liberation and extension of her true self, licensing what feminine modesty and a sense of decorum would else inhibit. Her game with Orlando is a lesson in awareness for each of them, a rehearsal for encountering with resilience the adversities that lie ahead. Yet, if she is being cruel only to be kind, there is no doubt that she also enjoys the sport, and that she proves herself as capricious as 'that same wicked bastard of Venus, that was begot of thought, conceived in spleen, and born of madness; that blind rascally boy' [IV i 190–2]. The truths that are spoken in jest flout not only at semantic illusions but at the painful realities as well. Nevertheless, if love has its limitations, so does the play-world of Rosalind's wit. She seems willing to prolong the game for ever, but when Orlando learns that his brother and Celia are betrothed without fussing about such preliminaries as courtship, he loses interest in make-believe, knowing 'how bitter a thing it is to look into happiness through another man's eyes'. The game must come to an end when he 'can no longer live by thinking'.

v

As commentators on the world of play around them, Jaques and Touchstone are complementary figures, the one transparently foolish in his wisdom, the other opaquely wise in his fooling. In a comedy composed of mutually balancing elements, where the qualities of correspondence and antithesis are as evident in the encounters between the characters as in the disposition of scenes or the characteristics of the prose style, Jaques and Touchstone are symmetrically related. Jaques himself recognises this kinship of opposites in his ambition for motley, though his description of his meeting with the fool is another example of the dramatic use of report to give ironic distance:

> . . .   When I did hear
> The motley fool thus moral on the time,
> My lungs began to crow like chanticleer
> That fools should be so deep-contemplative;
> . . .   [II vii 28–31]

The encounter might have been staged but instead the joke is enriched at Jaques's expense by having him relate what is patently a parody of his own 'deep-contemplative' moralising, while he himself remains oblivious to the irony: 'O that I were a fool!'

Jaques might be described as the one character in Arden who lacks the capacity for play, since he refuses to join any of the pastimes around him. In another sense, however, to this detached observer of the passing scene life has indeed become no more than a play, as he declares in his speech on the Seven Ages of Man. 'All the world's a stage', and he is its spectator. Yet nobody takes him at his own valuation, because there is a self-conscious *préciosité* about his melancholy that smacks of affectation:

> . . . It is a melancholy of mine own, compounded of many simples, extracted from many objects, and, indeed, the sundry contemplation of my travels; in which my often rumination wraps me in a most humorous sadness.
> [IV i 14–18]

Jaques is suspected by his fellow-exiles of playing a game, and especially he is made a subject for their sport; even Orlando gets the better of him. But Jaques comes into his own at the end of the comedy, by sustaining his part after they have abandoned theirs. He will remain in Arden while they return to court, and his consistency lends a certain authority to his wry benedictions. As he awaits the next party of 'convertites', Jaques the spectator is the only character who refuses to believe that the comedy is over.

If Jaques is paradoxically at home in exile, Touchstone is out of his element in Arden, wasting his sharpness on the desert air and the rustics, 'like Ovid among the Goths'. True to his name, his wit serves to bring out the nature of those he encounters, particularly through parody. He seems only to exist as a witty echo of those around him, turning all experience into a disinterested love of wordplay. His encounter with Corin is typical:

> COR. And how like you this shepherd's life, Master Touchstone?
> TOU. Truly, shepherd, in respect of itself, it is a good life; but in respect that it is a shepherd's life, it is nought.

In respect that it is solitary, I like it very well; but in respect that it is private, it is a very vile life. Now in respect that it is in the fields, it pleaseth me well, but in respect that it is not in the court, it is tedious. As it is a spare life, look you, it fits my humour well; but as there is no more plenty in it, it goes much against my stomach. . . . [III ii 11-20]

Touchstone's wit is evasive. He remains perfectly uncommitted, sceptical of every point of view. His motley is so impenetrable that we wonder whether there is any identity at all beneath it. And his relationship with Audrey especially brings out this opaqueness: it is impossible to be certain whether he is happy or cynical, infatuated or merely contemptuous in his intentions towards her:

. . . I press in here, sir, amongst the rest of the country copulatives, to swear and to forswear, according as marriage binds and blood breaks. A poor virgin, sir, is an ill-favour'd thing, sir, but mine own; a poor humour of mine, sir, to take that that no man else will: . . . [v iv 53-7]

One can understand Jaques's concern for Touchstone, and bafflement at intelligence seemingly wasting itself in this way: 'O knowledge ill-inhabited, worse than Jove in a thatched house!' Perhaps his function is no more than that of the professional fool, to expose others but not himself. Yet delightful as it is there remains a sense of limitation in Touchstone's inability to do anything except in play, forever hedging his bets.

Before the lovers are united in Hymen's bands (the ceremonials of the theatre doing service for those of the church), it is Touchstone who rounds off this comedy of pastimes with his account of how a quarrel may be translated into a courtly game:

O, sir, we quarrel, in print by the book, as you have books for good manners. I will name you the degrees. The first, the Retort Courteous; the second, the Quip Modest; the third, the Reply Churlish; the fourth, the Reproof Valiant; the fifth, the Countercheck Quarrelsome; the sixth, the Lie with Circumstance; the seventh, the Lie

Direct. All these you may avoid but the Lie Direct; and
you may avoid that too with an If. I knew when seven
justices could not take up a quarrel; but when the parties
were met themselves, one of them thought but of an If, as:
'If you said so, then I said so'. And they shook hands, and
swore brothers. Your If is the only peace-maker; much
virtue in If. [v iv 85–97]

Like the Lie Direct, the confusions of make-believe are finally
resolved with an If, as Rosalind reveals herself:

> D. SEN. If there be truth in sight, you are my daughter.
> ORL.   If there be truth in sight, you are my Rosalind.
> PHE.   If sight and shape be true,
>   Why then, my love, adieu!
> ROS.   I'll have no father, if you be not he;
>   I'll have no husband, if you be not he;
>   Nor ne'er wed woman, if you be not she.
>   [v iv 112–18]

And Hymen unites the lovers in similar style:

> HYM. Peace, ho! I bar confusion;
>   'Tis I must make conclusion
>   Of these most strange events.
>   Here's eight that must take hands
>   To join in Hymen's bands,
>   If truth holds true contents.
>   . . .   [v iv 119–24]

In the world that now lies before them, subject to time and the
stubbornness of fortune, there is indeed much virtue in vows
made with an If. 'If' is the provisional assent that play requires of
us.

SOURCE: essay in *Critical Quarterly*, XIII (1971), 234–45.

David Young   'Pastoral Poetry and
Drama' (1972)

... The rapid spread of [the] pastoral [literary convention],
from Italy to Spain, France, England and the rest of Europe in
the sixteenth century, made its influence felt in all the literary
modes, but its marked successes were always non-dramatic to
begin with; it was only after the fashion for pastoral had been
established in poetry and narrative romance that dramatists took
it up, although they were by no means slow to do so. The reason
for this pattern had surely to do in part with the existing classical
models, which were poetic—the idylls and eclogues of Theocritus
and Virgil—and narrative—the *Daphnis and Chloe* of Longus.
When it came to ancient precedents in the drama, theorists were
reduced to speculation. No one was sure what a satyr play ought
to be, but conjecture linked it to tragi–comedy and a pastoral
setting.[1] Beyond that dramatists had to be content to adapt
pastoral for the stage from other literary forms and to imitate
each other.

Two aspects of Renaissance pastoral have traditionally been
identified as containing the seeds of its eventual growth in drama:
the conversational and dialectical form of the eclogue and the
popularity of pastoral as a framework for court entertainment.
Both, however, can be said to have had their drawbacks, if only
because they suggested drama where it did not in fact exist. The
implied dramatic relationships of the eclogue—the overheard
complaint, the singing contest, the disputation about court and
country—become both artificial and static when transferred
directly to the stage. The problems inherent in stretching the
eclogue's features for stage presentation can be seen in the
operatic tendency of much Italian pastoral drama, which was
characteristically built around set pieces, lyrics and choruses, and
often lacked forward movement and genuine tension.

Nor was the static quality of pastoral drama discouraged by its
other root in court entertainment, where a discursive, pres-
entational style was the order of the day. The additional danger
of court entertainment was its relatively narrow perspective. It

was aimed, inevitably, at a small, select audience, and since its
chief aim was flattery (of a special kind, in the case of pastoral,
based on the allegation of simplicity and humility), it could
hardly be said to have much dramatic range. It is one thing to
please a king or queen with shepherds who dance, sing, and turn
compliments to the royal patron; it is quite another thing to
please an audience of diverse tastes expecting to see a play.

With these two slippery footholds in the pastoral, then, the
dramatist had a good deal to overcome. The eclogue proved that
shepherds conversed, sang, gossiped, suffered and mourned; but
it hardly provided useful dramatic models. And the popularity of
pastoral in court entertainments offered the possibility that the
dramatist who could combine it with elements that had a wider
appeal might simultaneously capture a larger audience and
attain to literary respectability; but whoever used it ran the risk of
falling victim to a specialised genre, more lyric than dramatic,
reflecting court needs and values alone. The solution, which
came gradually, proved to be a combination of the features of the
narrative romance and the pastoral: an amalgam which could be
traced back to *Daphnis and Chloe* [a Greek pastoral romance of the
second century AD—Ed.]—surely a respectable and promising
ancestry—and which had achieved both popular and critical
success in three romances combining prose and verse,
Sannazaro's *Arcadia* (1504), Montemayor's *Diana* (1545) and
Sidney's *Arcadia* (1590), as well as in two great narrative poems,
Tasso's *Gerusalemme Liberata* (1576, 1581) and Spenser's *The
Faerie Queene* (1590, 1596).[2] It is the manifestation of pastoral
represented by these works, I would maintain, that, with the
exception of some individual songs and eclogues, produced the
most significant and lasting achievements of Renaissance pastoral; and if I am right, then it is plays like *The Winter's Tale*
which belong to the main line of development rather than plays
like *Aminta* [Tasso] and *Il Pastor Fido* [Guarini], so long thought to
represent the central accomplishment of pastoral drama. . . .

Four of Shakespeare's plays—*As You Like It, King Lear, The
Winter's Tale* and *The Tempest*—have precisely in common a story
concerned with the exile of some of its central characters into a
natural setting, their sojourn in that setting, and their eventual

return. All four exhibit, moreover, the themes which had become attached to this structural pattern in earlier pastoral writings. In addition, certain external features, mainly stylistic, which had become part of the pastoral tradition can be found in each of the four.

The fundamental appeal of pastoral to an artist like Shakespeare is difficult to isolate, given the variety of possibilities open to writers who chose to work with it. The relation between subject and audience, however, provides an important clue. Pastoral was about rustic life, but it was not for rustics. The man who wrote it might pose as a shepherd, but everyone knew he was not. Arcadia, or its equivalent, was always elsewhere—often in time as well as space. Pastoral offered an *alternative* to the complex, hectic, urban present, but it was an imaginary alternative. For if pastoral writers sometimes appealed to a historical Golden Age, or praised the life in a known, accessible region, there was generally a shared understanding that the pastoral novel, poem, or play was to be held to fictive standards only. Our own attitude to science fiction is perhaps analogous; most of us suspect or believe that there is life on other planets, but we do not expect science fiction writers to document it. They must rear their imaginative structures, we understand, out of the here and now.

If pastoral was an alternative, it could not help but be, in one way or another, a criticism of life. As a member of the family of myths based on 'human resentment at the conditions and struggles of life',[3] it tended to branch off toward idealism on the one hand and satire on the other. But its idealism was of a special sort, based not so much on perfection and abundance as on retrenchment, renunciation and retreat. Take less, the pastoral writer seemed to suggest, and you will have more; reduce your needs to the only legitimate one, harmony with nature, and you will experience fulfillment. William Empson puts the general point this way:

The feeling that life is essentially inadequate to the human spirit, and yet that a good life must avoid saying so, is naturally at home with most versions of pastoral; in pastoral you take a limited life and pretend it is the full and normal one, and a suggestion that one must do this with all life, because the normal is itself limited, is easily put into the trick though not necessary to its power.[4]

As Empson suggests, and as the experience of sojourn in plays as different as *As You Like It* and *Lear* confirms, the degree of pretense is variable. He goes on to point out that the sense of life's inadequacy may itself be felt as a pretense, 'intended to hold all our attention and sympathy for some limited life'. Despite these shifts of attitude, pastoral's function as an alternative, born of dissatisfaction, remains constant.

Renato Poggioli identifies the 'psychological root of the pastoral' as 'a double longing after innocence and happiness'.[5] The literary shepherd, he says, is a 'witness', who bears testimony to the superiority of a solitary life, in communion with nature. One thinks of the affectionate treatment of innocence in *Daphnis and Chloe*, the hymn of praise to a Golden Age of unfettered pleasure in the opening chorus of the *Aminta*, and the entire second half of *The Winter's Tale*. Poggioli invokes the insights of Freud: 'the task of the pastoral imagination is to overcome the conflict between passion and remorse, to reconcile innocence and happiness, to exalt the pleasure principle at the expense of the reality principle.'[6] The reality principle suggests that 'erotic happiness cannot be fully attained in our civilisation',[7] and the pastoral imagination accordingly constructs its alternatives.

The dual concern with innocence and happiness helps to explain why love stories again and again form the central subject of pastoral literature, why it tends to value chastity on the one hand and sexual fulfillment on the other, and why it generally equates unhappiness with unrequited love. Critics have balked over the curious mixture in Fletcher's *Faithful Shepherdess* [a pastoral drama, 1610] of exalted chastity and downright lasciviousness in the female characters; but Fletcher was at least in that respect working squarely in the tradition by providing a spectrum, comically observed, of pastoral alternatives of innocence and fulfillment. The same sort of spectrum is provided in *As You Like It*, and both Shakespeare and Fletcher find much of the comic potential of pastoral in the clash of reality and pleasure principles in a setting where they are supposed to be resolved.

Another dream behind the pastoral—or rather another version of the same dream—is the desire for spiritual peace and personal fulfillment through a contemplative existence in communion with nature. A hermit could hardly be expected to achieve sexual fulfillment, but he might hope to arrive at an ideal of the good life nonetheless, 'the state of content and mental self-sufficiency which had been known in classical antiquity as *otium*'.[8] The self-contained and isolated life of the shepherd and the pastoral community was a kind of symbol for an equivalent state of mind, and Renaissance pastorals customarily contain an old man, hermit or shepherd, who is a spokesman for this insight. Corin is such a figure, and Prospero and Lear may be seen as significant variations. Meliboe, in the Sixth Book of *The Faerie Queene*, draws on his years as a courtier for comparison in constructing his apology for the simple life:

'Surely, my sonne,' (then answer'd he againe)
If happie, then it is in this intent,
That having small yet doe I not complaine
Of want, ne wish for more it to augment,
But doe my selfe with that I have content;
So taught of nature, which doth little need
Of forreine helpes to lifes due nourishment:
The fields my food, my flocke my rayment breed;
No better doe I weare, no better doe I feed.

Therefore I do not any one envy,
Nor am envyde of anyone therefore:
They, that have much, feare much to loose thereby,
And store of cares doth follow riches store.
The little that I have grows dayly more
Without my care, but onely to attend it;
My lambs do every year increase their score,
And my flockes father daily doth amend it.
What have I, but to praise th'Almighty that doth send it?
                [*Faerie Queene*, VI 9 20 & 21]

At the basis of such passages lies the assumption that interior peace and harmony are inextricably bound up with exterior peace and harmony; that man in society fails to come to terms with himself and his world because he imposes on himself order and rhythms different from those of the natural world to which he inevitably belongs. This is the point at which the concerns of pastoral and the concerns of lyric poetry tend to merge. Both are concerned to relate human experience to the great rhythms of the natural world. Hence their binding together of such elements as human love, weather, seasons, fertility, sex, and birth and death. The territory of the lyric cuts across the forests, heaths, pastures and islands of Shakespeare's pastorals. And the vision of human experience as an expression of the rhythm of events in nature gives rise to a concern with the nature of time that is especially evident in *As You Like It* and *The Winter's Tale*.

Another consequence of the special link between the inner and outer worlds in pastoral is its subjectivity; its landscapes are as often as not landscapes of the spirit, recording mental events and psychological states. Whether this takes the form of 'sermons in stones', of Lear in the storm, or of Prospero's masque hardly matters; the point is that the pastoral had from the start an expressionistic tendency, and that, of course, helps to explain why writers of pastoral were not held to realistic, objective criteria; subjectivity, artificiality and mannerism were their stock in trade. Nature was a glass that, rightly held, gave access to the regions of the mind.

No wonder, then, in light of its subjective features and its relation to the lyric vision, that Arcadia became a kind of poets' country, a realm of the imagination where the composing of verses and songs was a natural activity, and where poetic values were taken for granted. Arcadia harbored many other ideals as well, of course; as something that predated or avoided human degeneration it could be linked to the legend of Eden on the one hand and the classical Golden Age on the other. But it was natural for poets to assume that poetry had an ideal status in such times and places too. Orpheus, the first poet, was thus depicted as a shepherd. Nature and art were represented as in complete harmony, and art became a leading subject of the pastoral. For someone like Spenser, this art about art implied poems about poetry; he turned to pastoral when he wanted to treat the problems and ideals of his profession. Shakespeare, likewise, makes his pastoral dramas examinations of their medium, exploring the implications of fiction, artifice, convention, genre, and of the impulses that give rise to art. His work reveals to the fullest Renaissance pastoral's tendency toward self-consciousness, toward a stressing of the connections between aesthetic values and the dreams of contentment and fulfillment. If the pastoral could not be true to life, it could be true to the imagination, and that in turn enhanced the meaning and value of art.

To be a credit to art, however, pastoral had to avoid the limited accomplishments of escape and wish-fulfillment, and had to face the issues it raised. In its function as an alternative it was to be dialectical, a kind of discourse between reality and the imagination. This process quite naturally called for continual recourse to antithesis, a favorite stylistic device, and it should be obvious, even to the most casual reader of pastoral, that it is founded on a series of tensions and oppositions.

The social antitheses are perhaps the most obvious: urban versus rural, court versus country. They could deal variously with manners (polished versus rustic), with class divisions (aristocrat versus commoner), and with economic differences (rich versus poor). Disguise a prince as a shepherd and set him among real shepherds, and these contrasts begin to make themselves felt.

Psychological tensions rose from an associated topic, the active life versus the contemplative, a Renaissance favorite that seemed almost designed to fit the pastoral pattern. Worldliness and innocence were another standard pair, and they were related, as were most of the contrasts between complicated and simple forms of existence, to the great antithesis of nurture and nature, which raised moral and educational issues as well: was a man better for the training and refinements of his civilisation—his 'nurture'—or did he come naturally by his goodness, even if he were a 'salvage' or a wild man? This had a historical dimension, as we have seen, in its relation to the issue of human degeneration, a problem that could be posed as an opposition of present and past, or, when pastoral grew Utopian or, as in *Lear*, contemplated the end of the world, present and future.

Perhaps the most pervasive and important of all the pastoral contrasts, however, is the famous Art-Nature opposition. It could be narrowly conceived to deal with aesthetic issues, but it could also be posed so comprehensively (the two terms having so many meanings) as to take in any or all of the above contrasts. For that reason it probably deserves to be described, as Kermode suggests, as the philosophical basis of the pastoral.[9] But Nature has another dichotomous relation in pastoral as well, through its pairing with Fortune. This contrast raises metaphysical questions, and it seems to have formalised the wedding of pastoral and romance. . . . Shakespeare had a deep and abiding interest in both antitheses, Art and Nature and Nature and Fortune . . . . May we not suppose that it was the pastoral's habit of employing such antitheses—and my list is by no means exhaustive—rather than the use of speakers in the eclogue or the fashion for shepherds in court pageants, that attracted the real interest of the dramatist? Conflict and opposition are the stuff of drama, and those of the pastoral simultaneously provided intellectual interest as well. To an artist like Shakespeare, who was fond of organising his plays in terms of polarities and contrasts, they were a natural area for exploitation. The romance plot, with its introduction of outsiders into the pastoral world and its taste for dramatic events, had already accomplished the initial step of embodying contrasts which had been implicit or oblique in the eclogue. The playwright's opportunities were clear. . . .

SOURCE: extracts from *The Heart's Forest: A Study of Shakespeare's Pastoral Plays* (New Haven, Conn., and London, 1972), pp. 11–13, 27–33.

NOTES

[Modified and renumbered from the original Notes to this study—Ed.]

1. For an account of this and of Giambattista Giraldi Cinthio's *Egle* (1545), see Marvin T. Herrick, *Tragicomedy* (Urbana, 1955), pp. 10–14.

2. The dates cited here are of publication. In many cases the work in question was begin much earlier (e.g., Sidney's first *Arcadia*, 1580), and circulated in manuscript before publication.

3. Frank Kermode, *English Pastoral Poetry* (London, 1953), p. 15. He uses the phrase to describe the 'primary impulse' of the Golden Age myth.

4. William Empson, *Some Versions of Pastoral* (London, 1935), pp. 114–15.

5. Renato Poggioli, 'The Oaten Flute', *Harvard Library Bulletin*, XI (1957).

6. Ibid, 159.

7. Ibid, 160.

8. Hallett Smith, *Elizabethan Poetry* (Cambridge, Mass., 1952),
p. 2.

9. Kermode, p. 37.

Agnes Latham   'Satirists, Fools and
Clowns' (1975)

Jaques

. . . It is more profitable to trace in Jaques the generic traits of
the melancholy man than to suppose him a caricature of a
particular person.towards the end of the sixteenth century
temperamental hypersensitivity and thoughtfulness, often a
genuine response to the stresses of an age of transition, was high
fashion.[1] It marked one off from the coarse-fibred, mindless
crowd. 'Oh, it's your only fine humour, sir, your true melancholy
breeds your perfect fine wit, sir. . . . Have you a stoole there, to
be melancholy upon?' (*Every Man in his Humour*: III i 89–100). It
ranked as a 'humour' because its medical origin was long thought
to lie in an excess of melancholy among the four humours of the
blood. Only when these were in perfect equilibrium were body
and mind in perfect health. 'Melancholy', says Bridget Lyons,
'was classified as a disease, condemned as a vice, or exalted as the
condition and symptom of genius. But all these diverse traditions
about melancholy expressed, implicitly, the idea of its social
importance—it was a physical and psychological condition that
expressed an orientation towards the world and society—and this
made it particularly susceptible to literary treatment.'[2] Such
undoubtedly is the use Shakespeare makes of the melancholy of
Jaques, treasured by its professor, mocked by Orlando and
Rosalind, and censured, not too seriously, by the Duke. It is one
more attitude to life among the many of which the plays is
composed. There is never any suggestion that it is a pathological
condition, though it is perhaps something more than an affec-

tation. The play does not support the further contention that the name Jaques is associated with 'melancholy dregs and excrement' and that he is antisocial, 'fleeing the companionship even of the forest exiles who have themselves been outcast from society'.[3] He likes to be alone sometimes, and he likes others to miss him and 'to woo his company'. We meet him first (at II v) as a member of a group, 'merry, hearing of a song'. Then (at II vii) he is joining in a 'banquet'; and later (at IV ii) he is in robust company, encouraging them to rowdy singing. Previously (at III iii) he has joined a wedding ceremony; he breaks it up because it is a ramshackle, beggarly business, not sufficiently ceremonious. The only social act he objects to is dancing, which bores him. He prefers to talk, if only to a herd of deer (II i) or listen, if only to a fool's soliloquy (II vii). He would be much at a loss without society. When he takes himself off at the end of the play, it is to converse with the repentant Duke Frederick. He has a kind of sub-acid geniality and a deep curiosity about people.

The melancholy man, says Sir Thomas Overbury, is

. . . a strayer from the drove. . . . His imagination is never idle, it keeps his mind in a continuall motion, as the poise of a clock; he winds up his thoughts often, and as often unwinds them. . . . He'le seldome be found without the shade of some grove, in whose bottome a river dwels. . . . He thinkes businesse, but never does any: he is all contemplation, no action. He hewes and fashions his thoughts, as if he meant them to some purpose; but they prove unprofitable, as a piece of wrought timber to no use. . . .[4]

This is true to the contemplative nature of Jaques and the constant activity of his mind, but Shakespeare does not exert himself to present the thinking as abortive and inhibiting to action. Neither the Duke nor his retinue is engaged in any major actions in the forest. Were they more perfectly pastoral they would do even less, for they would not even hunt. Contemplation was possible in their circumstances and was esteemed. It is one of the great pastoral values. That Jaques enjoys his melancholy is made abundantly clear. It is not, says Harold Jenkins, 'the fatigue of spirits of the man who has found the world too much for him, but an active principle manifesting itself in tireless and exuberant antics'.[5] We never see him in a mood approaching depression, and he is entirely free of the malcontent's sense of personal injury. He never suggests that the world has treated him more unfairly than anyone else. He proposes to 'cleanse' it, but not to pay scores. His banishment seems to have been voluntarily undertaken, and he certainly elects to prolong it voluntarily. Jonson's *Every Man in his Humour* was played by the Chamberlain's Company in 1598. It introduced the 'humorous' character to the stage: the man with a dominant passion carried to the point of absurdity. There is something of this in Jaques, who treats himself, and is treated by others, as someone who can be depended upon to respond to any situation in a unique and characteristic way.

Scholars who are convinced that Shakespeare drew Jaques from life have come up with the names of three contemporaries. A. H. Gray, seeking a character in a play around the turn of the century to explain a reference in the second *Return from Parnassus*, in which Shakespeare is said to have given a 'purge' to Jonson, selects Jaques as the only possibility.[6] B. H. Newdigate favours Sir John Harington, 'the unlicensed fool of Elizabeth's Court', author of *The Metamorphosis of Ajax*, a book title which puns on jakes, meaning a privy.[7] If Jaques is a caricature of anybody it is an affectionate tribute rather than a purge, and there does not seem to be much foundation for the idea that his name stank in Elizabethan nostrils. . . . The claims of John Marston are more impressive, though they do not in the end perhaps amount to more than that satire, like melancholy, was high fashion. In 1925, G. B. Harrison, editing Marston's *Scourge of Villanie* (1598) compared the author's address 'To him that hath perused mee' with the way in which Jaques defends himself (at II vii 70ff.) against the charge, not actually brought by anybody in the play, of indulging in personal slander.[8] 'If anyone', says Marston, '(faced with his owne guilt) will turne it home and say *Tis I*, I cannot hinder him. Neyther doe I injure him.' Apart from this telling version of the proverbial 'If the cap fits, wear it', the rest reads like the common exculpatory Elizabethan epilogue, protecting the writer against the 'constructions' which he feared might be put on his work and which he probably knew he deserved. There is no fresh note for which Shakespeare could be indebted to Marston and nobody else.

In 1934 Theodore Spencer argued from 'Proemium in librum tertium' of *The Scourge of Villanie* that Shakespeare may well have had Marston in mind when Jaques declares that, given a motley coat, he will 'through and through/Cleanse the foul body of the infected world'.[9] What in Jaques is high spirits, in Marston in near-hysteria:

> Faire *Detestation* of foule odious sinne,
> In which our swinish times lye wallowing,
> Be thou my conduct . . .
> . . .
> O that a Satyres hand had force to pluck
> Some fludgate up, to purge the world from muck;
> Would God I could turne *Alpheus* river in
> To purge this *Augean* oxstaule from foule sin.
>
> [ll. 13–15, 17–20][10]

Arnold Davenport, editing Marston's satires, is reminded less of Jaques than of the Duke rebuking him for the 'foul sin' of disgorging on the world 'th'embossed sores and headed evils' which he has contracted through keeping evil company. The Duke, he claims, like Marston, is 'exploring the powerful effects obtainable by the use of grossly physical words in serious contexts'.[11] But would Elizabethans, only too familiar with minor infections, be particularly squeamish about the words which describe them? Davenport sees something of Jaques in an earlier work of Marston, *Certaine Satyres* (1598), in which a character called 'Bruto the travailer' roams the streets of Westminster with 'a discontented grace', railing at the 'corrupted age' and the scant respect people show for his experience of a wider world.[12] Marston strips his pretensions with the comment that all he ever did was go to Venice, 'to buy a Lute and use a Curtezan'. He is a lightweight, his nausea an affectation and his experience valueless. This is not Jaques, whom the Duke takes seriously, who never considers himself underrated, and who exchanges easy banter with anyone he meets, showing no resentment when the optimists have the last word. He knows in advance that it will be hard to make the world take his medicine, and he plans to shoot his wit under cover of his motley: a strategy beyond the reach of Bruto's limited imagination. There are, however, points of contact. Jaques himself imputes his melancholy to 'the sundry contemplation of my travels', and Rosalind's mocking of the returned traveller, though he may have done nothing to deserve it, is pinned on him. The Duke reminds him 'thou hast been a libertine'. . . .

Touchstone

Jaques is a type and also a personality. Touchstone never fully develops a character and tends to remain a theatrical convenience, though a very delightful one, to whom a skilled actor can give an illusion of life. He puzzles commentators because his occasional shrewdness and his professional skills, which consist largely in putting up a dazzling façade of pseudo-scholarship, seem to contradict his simplicity. He is ignorant of what marriage is, but he knows about Ovid's exile among the Goths. His satire on duelling delights Jaques by its aptness and provokes the Duke to observe that he uses his folly as a stalking-horse and under cover of it shoots his wit. This, however, as James Smith has noted, is 'just what the real Touchstone never does, in spite of what the critics say'.[13] His successes are 'the squandering glances of the fool', or, as Rosalind puts it, he speaks wiser than he is ware of. It is because the audience wants to see him, contrary to all likelihood, score a gold that Shakespeare arranges he shall do so; and the audience wants it because it is a delicious instance of the world turned upside down, of the little man winning. It reassures us that the fool, which in our less confident moments we suspect we are, can put down the wise man. Were he in fact a wise man, only pretending to be a fool, there could be no such reassurance.

His creator's intelligence, not his own, is always putting Touchstone in an advantageous position. In addition, his mastery of the conventions of nonsense, his stock-in-trade, may give an appearance of a cleverness and even of a critical acumen which would make him a real touchstone of values. But his learned allusions, mock logic and fancy words are simply a folk idiom. There is no profundity in them and it is difficult, on investigation, to find him with anything important to say. He does not mock because he encounters anything intrinsically mockable: his business is mocking. He is an allowed fool. Until he came to write *As You Like It*, Shakespeare had created fools only dimly aware of their folly, if at all. Dogberry has no idea that he is comical. Touchstone intends to be.

This change in the kind of fooling was at least in part a response to fashion. Audiences were beginning to hold Hamlet's opinion of a clown who interrupted the course of the play and spoke more than was set down for him. In *The Pilgrimage to Parnassus*, a university skit on the world of literature, played at Cambridge in 1599, a clown is literally dragged in by a rope (v 662–9). For Shakespeare there was a double problem, since in 1599 the company lost their old comedian, who had been with them from their inception, and acquired a new one.

Will Kempe, the leading clown of the Chamberlian's Men, left them some time early in 1599, just as they were moving into the Globe Theatre. His name is printed in the cast of Jonson's *Every Man in his Humour* (1598) but not in that of *Every Man out of his Humour* (1599). Thinking of the Globe, Kempe says in his autobiographical *Nine Daies Wonder* (1600): 'I have daunst my selfe out of the world.' He does not say why. He was replaced eventually by Robert Armin, a comedian with different gifts, including a good singing voice.[14] For Armin, Shakespeare created jester's parts, such as the Fool in *Lear*, Levache in *All's Well*, Feste in *Twelfth Night* and Trinculo in *The Tempest*. Armin, however, was quite capable of taking over Kempe's parts, and there is evidence that he played Dogberry in a revival of *Much Ado*. He was brought up to be a goldsmith, and describes himself so in his will. He was an educated and intelligent man, who wrote plays and pamphlets. He had acted in his own play, *Two Maids of More-clacke*, before he joined the Chamberlain's Men. A sentence in *The Second Part of Tarlton's Jests* places him 'at the Globe on the Bank side' some time before 4 August 1600, when the play was entered in the Stationers' Register. In two of his pamphlets— *Quips upon Questions* and *Foole upon Foole*, printed in that year—he describes himself as 'Clunnyco de Curtanio Snuffe' (Snuffe the Clown of the Curtain). Not until the 1605 edition of *Foole upon Foole* does he appear as 'Clonnico del mondo' (clown of the Globe). His biographer, C. S. Felver, assigns the composition of *Quips upon Questions* to 1599, explaining the date clue on the title– page ('clapt up by a Clown of the towne in this last restraint') as a reference to some special and otherwise unrecorded restraint on

the theatres in that year, perhaps in consequence of the war with
Spain. T. W. Baldwin, who was the first to assign the pamphlet
correctly to Armin, takes it to refer to the usual closing of the
theatres for Lent, in this instance Lent 1600. With the principal
clown engaged at the Curtain, he cannot see how *As You Like It*
could have been played before the summer of 1600, the year in
which it is entered in the Stationers' Register, under 4 August.[15]
If, however, the company acting at the Curtain were in fact the
Chamberlain's Men, Armin can be confidently assigned to them
as their clown. E. K. Chambers, using Armin's title-pages as part
of his evidence, locates them at the Curtain from October 1597
until the autumn of 1599, when it is generally agreed they opened
at the Globe.[16] Had Armin's pamphlets been entered in the
Stationers' Register, there would be further evidence as to the
date of composition, as distinct from that of printing, but they
were not.

To the question whether Touchstone was Shakespeare's first
attempt at a part to suit Armin, or whether he wrote some or all of
it while Kempe was still available, it is impossible to give a
definite answer. Kempe could have played Touchstone. There is
much that suggests his style: the conversation with himself about
horns, for instance (III iii 42–54), which is reminiscent of the self-
colloquies of Launce in *The Two Gentlemen of Verona* and of
Launcelot Gobbo in *The Merchant of Venice*. On the other hand,
Muriel Bradbrook finds his catechisms typical of Armin, notably
the scene with Corin (III ii). She also notes that Armin's fools
attended on ladies rather than lords, which fits Touchstone. In
Two Maids of More-clacke, Tutch the fool is turned out of service for
fidelity to his young mistress. The early descriptions of Touchstone
as 'the clownish fool' and 'the roynish clown' introduce him as a
rather uncouth character, and not at all as a sophisticated jester,
such as Feste is. Rosalind calls him a natural, but Douce argues
that this is merely for the sake of a play on nature and natural
wits.[17] He does not, however, live up to this description. He is
undoubtedly a trained court jester with an excellent repertoire. He
never falls back on the clown's trick of 'mistaking his words',
common in Kempe characters and at its best in Dogberry. An
uncertainty on Shakespeare's part as to what actor he was writing
for may go some way towards explaining inconsistencies.

It is surprising that in a play which is filled with songs none is

given to the jester. It is doubtful whether Touchstone sings when
he mocks Martext with a ballad-snatch (III iii 86), and he almost
certainly does not join the two pages in what seems to have been
an unaccompanied canzonet for two voices (v iii 14). Felver
thinks that Armin may have doubled the parts of Touchstone and
Amiens: a situation in which it would have been unwise to endow
them both with the same, instantly recognisable singing voice.[18]
Armin had done some spectacular doubling in his own *Two
Maids of More-clacke*, playing a half-wit called Blue John, a jester
called Tutch, Tutch disguised as Blue John, and Tutch as a
Welshman. Doubling was, in any case, something that was
expected of a competent actor. Touchstone's long coat, the livery
of the acknowledged fool, would make changes of costume easy.
Amiens and Touchstone are never on the stage at the same time,
except in the last scene of the play, when Amiens is given an
entrance by name but has nothing to say. It is conceivable that
Armin joined the company as a singer and not, at first, as a clown,
in which case he and Kempe may have played side by side, before
Kempe danced himself out of the world. The resemblance
between the names Armin and Amiens would not have been
obvious in the sixteenth century because of the rolled *r* in Armin.

Touchstone wears the common garment of the fool which,
whether he was a court jester or just the weak intellect in the
family, was a child's long coat. His immaturity kept him in this
for life. It was gathered at the waist and fell in voluminous folds
below the knee. There was a certain practicality about the dress,
which was made of a coarse woollen material, warm and hard-
wearing. An indulgent affection added such things as would
please a child: a bauble, bells on the sleeve, a cap with a
cockscomb or feather. Wherever he wandered, the fool was
known for what he was: mocked, perhaps, but also protected. If
he was an allowed fool, kept to entertain a court or noble
household, this was his livery. It was imaginatively designed, as
can be seen in the portraits of court fools, but it was not, as the
stage has so long believed, a short tunic divided in colour down
the middle and worn with stockings of different colours. The
particolour of the fool's motley was in the weave of the material,
and not in the cut of the coat.[19] Favourite colours for a fool were
green and yellow, emblematic of his unripe intellect, and
doubtless cheap, fast dyes. It appears from an article by E. W.

Ives that Leslie Hotson was mistaken in supposing that the colours were mingled in the subtle and unemphatic style of modern tweeds, which require advanced manufacturing techniques.[20] They were arranged in stripes or checks or any other simple pattern that can be produced with yarns of two colours on a hand-loom. Thus a fool's costume—often described as pied, patched, or particoloured—could be very fantastic. It seems likely that Touchstone at court cut a startling figure. In Arden he may have been more sober. He was well enough dressed to be treated as a gentleman: an irony used by Armin in *Foole upon Foole*, when he related how Henry VIII's famous fool was saluted by the poor people, 'taking him for a worthy personage, which pleased him'.[21]

The Country Clowns

William and Audrey are true clowns, awkward and ignorant, though indulgently treated by their creator. Geoffrey Bullough suggests that they may derive from an old play called *The Historie of Sir Clyomon and . . . Clamydes*, which was belatedly published in 1599.[22] In it, a princess, escaping in disguise from an undesired suitor, serves a shepherd called Corin, as his boy, and all the maids fall in love with her. Corin speaks in a broad dialect and the matter of his rambling talk is equally unrefined:

But tis as world to zee what mery lives we shepheards lead,
Why were Gentlemen and we get once a thorne bush over our
                                            head,
We may sleep with our vaces against the zone, and were hogs
Bath ourselves, stretch our legs ant were a cennell of dogs:
And then at night when maides come to milkin, the games begin,
But I may zay to you, my nabor *Hodges* maid had a clap, wel let
                                        them laugh that win.
Chave but one daughter, but could not vor vorty pence she were
                        20 sped. [xv 1293ff.][23]

This is far removed from Shakespeare's serious, decent Corin. Nor is it like William and Audrey. Audrey is an obsessively moral girl. 'I do not know what poetical is. Is it honest in deed and word? It is a true thing?' It was surely she who insisted on a wedding. William, in terror of his life, still clings desperately to his manners and his forelock: 'God rest you merry, sir.' The town has always tended to see the country as comical. Actually, Shakespeare spares his Corin even the mild fun that Lodge extorts from Corydon's awkwardness in fine company. Corin has a natural dignity. The awkwardness is concentrated in William and Audrey. If he had needed precedent for bringing comically bucolic characters into a pastoral, Shakespeare could have found it in the shepherd Dametas and his uncouth wife and daughter in Sidney's *Arcadia*. Indeed, he had models in his own Costard and Jaquenetta, who are such a contrast to the elegance of the courtly characters in *Love's Labour's Lost*. . . .

SOURCE: extracts from the Introduction to the Arden edition of *As You Like It* (London, 1975), pp. xlvi–l, li–lvi.

NOTES

[Modified and renumbered from the original Notes—Ed.]
1. On melancholy, see G. B. Harrison's essay in his edition of Breton's *Melancholike Humours* (1929); J. Babb, *The Elizabethan Malady* (1951); and B. G. Lyons, *Voices of Melancholy* (1971).
2. Lyons, p. 1.
3. Ibid, pp. 12–13. See also O. J. Campbell, 'Jaques', *Huntington Library Bulletin*, VIII (Oct. 1935), 71–102.
4. E. E. Rimbault (ed.), *The Miscellaneous Works of Sir Thomas Overbury* (1890), pp. 73–4.
5. H. Jenkins, '*As You Like It*', *Shakespeare Survey*, 8 (1955), p. 45.
6. A. H. Gray, *How Shakespeare 'Purged' Ben Jonson* (1928).
7. B. H. Newdigate, in *Times Literary Supplement* (3 Jan. 1929).
8. G. B. Harrison (ed.), Marston's *The Scourge of Villanie* (1925).
9. T. Spencer, 'John Marston', *The Criterion*, XIII (1934), 581–99.
10. A. Davenport (ed.), Marston's *Satires* (1961), p. 149.
11. Ibid, Intro., p. 27.
12. Ibid, Intro, pp. 12–13. See also O. J. Campbell, 'Jaques'.
13. J. Smith, '*As You Like It*', *Scrutiny*, IX (1940), 9–32. It is a pity that the duelling speech, Touchstone's *chef d'oeuvre*, can raise little spontaneous laughter these days.

14. On Armin, see T. W. Baldwin, 'Shakespeare's Jester', *Modern Language Notes*, xxxix (1924), 447–55; L. Hotson, *Shakespeare's Motley* (1952), ch. 7; C. S. Felver, 'Robert Armin: Shakespeare's Source for Touchstone', *Shakespeare Quarterly*, vii (1956), 135–71, and *Robert Armin, Shakespeare's Fool: A Biographical Essay*, Kent State University Research Series No. 5 (1961); and M. C. Bradbrook, *Shakespeare the Craftsman* (1969), ch. 4, pp. 49–74.

15. Baldwin, 'Shakespeare's Jester'.

16. E. K. Chambers, *The Elizabethan Stage* (1923), ii, pp. 402, 405.

17. F. Douce, *Illustrations of Shakespeare* (1807), i, p. 292.

18. Felver (1961), *Robert Armin . . .*, p. 45.

19. Hotson, *Shakespeare's Motley* ch. 1.

20. E. W. Ives, 'Tom Skelton: A Seventeenth-Century Jester', *Shakespeare Survey*, 13 (1960), pp. 90–105.

21. Hotson, *Shakespeare's Motley*.

22. G. Bullough, *Narrative and Dramatic Sources of Shakespeare* (1958), ii, pp. 155–7.

23. B. J. Littleton (ed.), *The Historie of Sir Clyomon and . . . Clamydes* (1968).

PART THREE

The Comedies on the Stage

1. *MUCH ADO ABOUT NOTHING*

Westland Marston (1888)

Macready as Benedick (1843)

... [William Charles Macready's] Benedick differed widely from that of other well-known actors. Whether it was the truest rendering of the part may be doubted, but I have seen none more effective. In the various conflicts with Beatrice there was not that eagerness of repartee, that animated enjoyment of the wit combat, nor quite that polished address (though Macready was both the soldier and the gentleman) ascribed to Charles Kemble. Macready had rather a provokingly indulgent and half-careless air towards his fair enemy. He wore a somewhat *blasé* manner to her, as of one versed in the serious business of life, and a little cynical through experience, who, nevertheless, good-naturedly consented to trifle and *badiner* with a lady for her amusement, who sometimes forgets his light *rôle* in serious thought, and then, rousing himself, returns apologetically to his recreation. In the celebrated soliloquy in the second act, after he has overheard in the arbour that Beatrice loves him, the complex expression of his face as he advanced drew roars from the house before he uttered a word. One might read there the sense of amazement, of gratification, and of perplexity as to the way of reconciling his newly-revealed passion for Beatrice with his late raillery at her and all women. His amazement was less, even, that Beatrice loved him, than that (his suspicion deepening to conviction as the soliloquy went on) he responded to her love. He evidently remembered his own recent vaunt, 'I do much wonder that one man, seeing how much another is a fool when he dedicates his behaviours to love, will, after he hath laughed at such shallow follies in others, become the argument of his own scorn by falling

in love'. Accordingly, Macready, with great humour, made
Benedick, in his first wish to be consistent, put his response to
Beatrice rather upon the ground of pity and courtesy than of his
own strong inclining: 'Love me! why it must be requited. I hear
how I am censured'—a shallow sophism to disguise his passion,
which again called forth the heartiest mirth. His next step in
reasoning, where he makes a moral aphorism the pretext for
yielding to his inclinations, 'Happy are they that hear their
detractions, and can put them to mending', was not a whit less
effective. In fact, the humour of the position, from his first
surprise and timid regard for his consistency to the defiant scorn
of ridicule at the close, was splendidly brought out. The most
specious argument acquired with him the force of reason, or, if
not, his will dispensed with it. It was an unopposed match, in
which the victor gains audacity as he takes outwork upon
outwork, until he hoists his flag from the citadel. . . .

> SOURCE: extract from Westland Marston, *Our Recent
> Actors* (1888), recalling performances dating from
> Macready's first playing of the part in 1843.

Frederick Wedmore (1882)

Henry Irving as Benedick and Ellen Terry as Beatrice

. . . Mr Irving has never done anything more complete than his
Benedick. He plays it with the keenest sense of enjoyment and
appreciation, and with that authority of interpretation which
comes most readily when a man possesses the agreeable consciousness that the authority will be recognised and accepted.
The element of satire in the part—the conception of a robust
humanity boasting its own strength, and swayed, even while it
boasts, by the lightest of feminine charms—is much in his own
humour. The chivalry of the character suits him, and so does the
graciousness of the character, and so does its quiet and self-

analytical wit. He is excellent in speech, and as excellent in by-play. If Beatrice 'speaks poniards', this newest Benedick can look them. . . .

Nearly all that Miss Ellen Terry can do quite perfectly she can do in Beatrice . . . . Beatrice's seriousness is permitted to be half a jest. The sorrows she deals with are the sorrows of comedy, and she is beset by no perplexities which may not be easily removed. Hero's character she requires to have vindicated, and a vindication is promptly forthcoming. At other times due leisure is allowed her to form a whimsical attachment, and to say defiant things brilliantly, and with the utmost good-nature. So it is that Mr Irving and Miss Terry succeed in their parts entirely. Not one point of importance is lost by either of them, and in both the transitions of mood are rapid and strongly marked. It is this that helps give vivacity to Comedy—the action of comedy is often mental action, taking the place of a drama's development of intrigue. . . .

> SOURCE: extracts from a review in *The Academy* (21 Oct. 1882).

James Agate (1931)

Much Ado at the Old Vic

For some reason *Much Ado About Nothing* has never had the highest place in popular affection. Can this be because the author is more concerned with Beatrice's wit, which is an intellectual virtue, than with Hero's chastity, which is an accomplishment in the moral order? Is the old Puritan instinct offended at this inversion, and do we feel in our subconscious bones, though the conscious mind would reject the idea, that the play would have made for more of edification if not Beatrice but Hero had been its real heroine? Is it that some vestige of the old notion about

masculine superiority makes us a little scared of Beatrice, too near
a sister to those Meredithean young women whom even today we
embrace somewhat gingerly? It takes a very good actress to
disarm as well as fulfil Beatrice, and perhaps none but Ellen Terry
has ever achieved this.

Or does the fault lie with the men? Is Claudio too doltish,
Leonato too advanced in dotage, Don John too woeful–splenetic
and with too much of the motivelessness of Iago, Don Pedro a
little too prodigal of the airs of a *deus ex machina* without being
anything of the sort? Is it because there are rather too many
people to be 'carried', in the Bridge sense, by Beatrice and
Benedick that this play is deemed by playgoers not to be in the
first flight of Shakespearean comedies? Success in its presentation
is always a matter of stalking, and it may be said that the Old Vic
company rounds up its quarry before the end.

The present beautifully-balanced performance should do
something to restore the play to favour. Beatrice is Miss Green's
best part, and she gives it all the grace, glamour, dazzle, wit,
verve and polish that these latter days afford. Mr Gielgud's
Benedick is a little wanting in swagger in the early scenes, in
which he should be more of a Terry. But this actor does well later
on, and I suggest that a professional matinée should be given, so
that our young players may hear from his delivery of the
'behaviour in love' soliloquy how to speak English prose with
beauty, point and audibility. There is, perhaps, good and
sufficient reason why Mr George Howe should not discover much
in Leonato, but Mr Ralph Richardson, made up to look like a
baby lion or a goodtempered plate from Buffon's Natural
History, makes an exceedingly winning Prince of Aragon. Mr
Richard Riddle's Claudio answers very graciously, Mr Henry
Wolston makes a good Warwickshire constable, and Mr Leslie
French, after tunefully bidding the ladies sigh no more, decorates
Verges with all the quaintness proper to senility. Hero can never
be this play's bright spot, and Miss Ethel Glendinning can
doubtless find justification for making that character sad in the
pastry sense and conjecturally like Mrs Gummidge before she
encountered the 'old 'un'. The production is modest, but 'all
right with me', as another world has it!

SOURCE: review in the *Sunday Times* (21 March 1933).

Ruth Ellis (1949)

Gielgud's Production at the Shakespeare Memorial Theatre

Much Ado About Nothing, John Gielgud's first Stratford production, came to the Memorial Theatre on Tuesday as joyously as the holiday sunshine and with something of the serene gaiety of the first apple-blossom. All the beauty of this happy play seemed to come 'as naturally as leaves to a tree', an event rare enough among poets, for all Keats's saying, and far less common on the stage.

But here the producer, instead of presenting us with a series of disconnected scenes, gives the play the buoyant, unchecked rhythm of melody, so that it flows in harmony like a piece of music. Surely this is nearer to Shakespeare's own method of production than anything seen on the stage for a very long time. It is done with no sacrifice of scenic effect, for the exquisite designs of Mariano Andreu play a notable part in the success of the performance; but the necessary scene-changing, done in full view of the audience by skilful, costumed attendants, maintains the movement of the play; and other very beautiful links are the processional entrances and exits, all tuned to be part of the scene, as well as a delight to the eye.

In this arrangement the players have an air of ease and spontaneity, like children in a well-conducted nursery, able to give themselves to the game without anxiety.

Anthony Quayle and Diana Wynyard, as Benedick and Beatrice, lead the cast with distinction. Their comedy has an unforced mirth that seems to be an emanation of natural gaiety, and the love between them is as inevitable as April. Mr Quayle's Benedick is a soldier who has obviously been followed with devotion through many campaigns, and Miss Wynyard's Beatrice is as warm-hearted a girl as ever kept the home fires burning with uncomplaining courage. There is a simple sincerity about their playing which is far more appealing and amusing than any attempt to teach Shakespeare his business.

Then there is the really lovely Leonato of Leon Quartermaine, accompanied by the more than faintly comic Antonio of Michael

Gwynn. Harry Andrews is a pleasing and genial Don Pedro, blessed with an innate dignity that needs no stressing of princely office, and the sombre Don John (Clement McCallin) is a thwarted caricature of the legitimate brother. John Slater makes Borachio a vivid and forceful character, well contrasted with the arrogant villainy of Paul Harwicke's Conrade.

George Rose as an endearing West Country Dogberry appears to make no effort to be funny: he simply is. There is no suggestion that this is a part in which the comedian has to work like a black to get a laugh. Here again there is a naturalness in absurdity, and William Squire's admiring little Verges, maintaining dogged devotion to his neighbour under the most crushing snubs, contributes to it considerably. So do members of the Watch.

Pat Sandys is a very young, very pretty and entirely guileless Hero, playing like a child among trusted relations and stunned by the sudden loss of security. . . .

> SOURCE: extract from review in the *Stratford-upon-Avon Herald* (22 April 1949).

B. A. *Young* (1965)

The National Theatre's Italianate *Much Ado*

For many people I suspect that there may be a pretty thick crust of prejudice to be broken through before they can take Zeffirelli's new production. Whatever its merits or its shortcomings, no one will have seen *Much Ado* played this way before.

In the first place, Zeffirelli has set it in Sicily in, I suppose, the first decade of the present century. Shakespeare set it in Sicily too, of course, or at any rate he began with Leonato saying 'I learn that Don Pedro of Arragon comes this night to Messina'; but he peopled his Sicily with English lords and ladies. Zeffirelli has filled it with Sicilians, wearing tatty uniforms if they are in the military or ghastly double-breasted suits and ridiculous hats and sun-glasses if they are civilians. True, they speak Shakespeare's lines in English (with such alterations as Robert Graves has deemed suitable in the cause of better understanding); but they move and behave in a thoroughly Mediterranean fashion, and Dogberry and his crew have exchanged their conventional Loamshire dialect for comic Italian accents.

Don Pedro and Don John, being Spanish and therefore foreigners, also have accents. To be specific, they also have Italian accents, but this hardly matters. It is only necessary to indicate that they are not Sicilians, and Johannesburg accents would have done just as well.

For there's no attempt to play anything realistically. The piece is done as the broadest kind of farce. Zeffirelli has played the comedy for all its worth, and has grafted a sprig of comedy on to the characters who generally have to get along without one. Don John, for example (Derek Jacobi in a red wig), has become a petulant young man who stirs up trouble with the same elegant pointlessness as Lord Alfred Douglas; and Claudio (Ian McKellen in a blonde wig) has been fitted out with such a store of priggishness that even when he hopes to be dignified we see the moral banana-skin ever-present beneath his feet.

Occasionally the farce goes too far. It was a good idea to hide Beatrice behind a line of washing when Hero and the girls praise Benedick for her advantage: but not to hang a plaster Cupid on it. I was sorry to hear Frank Finlay's Italianate Dogberry leading the watch in a chorus by Verdi, and sorrier still to see him fall off a table. On the whole, however, I found the endless comic invention welcome, ingenious, and never adverse to the text. I loved Verges's old bike and Don Pedro's permanent cigar, and the living statuary that, motionless, helped furnish the scenes but occasionally came to life to add an extra point. (There was a stone soldier resting on his sword in the square where Conrade and Borachio fought with the watch. Before the fight was over he was carrying an umbrella and the sword was being put to its proper use.)

The evening is full of superb comic acting. I am no longer able to write with restraint about Maggie Smith: I can only say that the part of Beatrice might have been written for her. Robert Stephens makes Benedick a provincial Italian wide boy, who soon exchanges his uniform for a variety of sharp suits; he plays the part with sensitivity and wit, and speaks his lines most musically. Albert Finney's Don Pedro, undoubtedly a lineal descendant of the Duke of Plaza Toro, is a gorgeous comic creation.

Hero, usually rather a boring girl, is given a mercurial personality by Caroline John that explains Claudio's otherwise inexplicable *faiblesse* for her. And there are a number of minor heroes—the diminutive clarinetist (John Foley) who competes with Balthasar for the honours in the Rossiniesque setting of 'Sigh no more'; Tom Kempinski's Borachio, straight from the Mafia; Edward Petherbridge's stuttering Conrade; and Lynn Redgrave's bucolic and oddly Anglo-Saxon Margaret.

In the events of the marriage scene there is no room for knockabout, and it takes on all the more unpleasantness in contrast with what has gone before. It also gives an opportunity for some fine serious acting, notably from Gerald James and Harry Lomax as Leonato and Antonio, who, silly old pantaloons as they are, suddenly acquire a pathetic dignity that I found most moving.

This ability to move almost imperceptibly from farce to tragedy and back is a mark of Zeffirelli's tight control as a director. The National Theatre's *Much Ado* is bound to be controversial. I can only say that it made me laugh very much and very contentedly, and you can't ask more of a comedy than that.

SOURCE: review in the *Financial Times* (17 Feb. 1965).

John Barber (1968)

A Young Company at the Royal Shakespeare Theatre

The problem in producing *Much Ado About Nothing*, whose revival by the Royal Shakespeare Company at Stratford-on-Avon last night added the last play to this season's repertory, is no less than the problem of getting on to the stage the hard glitter and tumultuous variety of the High Renaissance.

The protagonists are young and tough and not particularly poetic. Of them, Beatrice and Benedick are dazzlingly quick-witted and they must put across the vitality of good talk even when their quips have been staled by time.

Speed is essential, with giddy transitions from lurid melo-drama to low music hall. Don John—a bastard, so to say, for no other reason than that he is a bastard—must make us believe that his slander against Hero will break up her marriage to the noble Claudio. We must be swept headlong from bridegroom denouncing swooning bride in crowded church to the back street huff-and-puff of the comic-cop Dogberry.

A difficult play, in fact, and Trevor Nunn's production shows signs of over-anxiety. Never was there such a hurry-scurry of damsels, such rustling of ruffs, such frizzing of hair and bouncing on hobby-horses. So the speed suffers.

The young players choose a homely English rather than a brilliantly courtly style of behaviour. Alan Howard's Benedick is tousled and charmingly gauche, while Janet Suzman makes a bubbling, almost a boisterous, Beatrice. It follows that their word-war is spirited rather than witty; they are at their best when suddenly called upon to be serious and declare their love. It follows, equally, that the famous 'Kill Claudio!'—Beatrice's agonised cry to her lover to avenge her maligned friend—provokes unwanted laughter in the audience. The ardour of the characters is all here, but not yet either their subtlety or their sophistication.

David Waller is skilful enough to make Dogberry a sheep-witted, likeable ass instead of the usual bumbling oaf. Equally, Bernard Lloyd gives Claudio dignity instead of the usual priggishness. Helen Mirren is most touching as Hero.

For the rest, eight separate plots and counterplots are clearly expounded, and the whole thing looks sumptuous in Christopher Morley's costumes even though—or perhaps because—it all appears to take place in a glass-roofed basement rather than in the vivid streets of Messina.

SOURCE: review in the *Daily Telegraph* (15 Oct. 1968).

Michael Billington (1977)

John Barton's Production at the Aldwych Theatre

Because it is set in nineteenth-century India, some pursed-lipped critics have accused John Barton's *Much Ado About Nothing* of wanton irreverence. But seeing this production again on its transfer from Stratford to the Aldwych, it strikes me as one of the truest and most touching accounts of this play I can remember. It provokes genuine tears and heartfelt laughter. What more can one ask?

I think the secret of Barton's success is that he endows the characters with a past as well as a present. You see this most conspicuously in Beatrice and Benedick, who are not a couple of cut-price Congrevian smart-asses but a marriage-obsessed pair who have some bruising past liaison. Judi Dench's overwhelming Beatrice says of her heart that 'once before he won it of me with false dice', and you feel her wit is a defence against further breakages. Equally, one notices how Cherie Lunghi's spritely Hero reacts instantly to the mention of Claudio as if she has had her eye on this young blade for a long time, and how Borachio and Margaret are in the throes of a big affaire that explains their blindness to their own duplicity.

On top of this the Indian setting is so completely realised that it gives a binding unity to this notoriously broken-backed play. We are in the midst of an Indian summer of languorous waltzes, amateur theatricals, cricket matches, lime drinks and muslin-shrouded siestas. In this atmosphere of sublime colonial torpor one can begin to accept the play's premise, which is that everyone believes everything that they are told without question. And even the traditionally unfunny Dogberry fits into the scheme played, as he is by John Woodvine, as an aphoristic climber with a subtle mis-command of the English language.

It's the old Shakespearean rule: a closely-imagined society gives the characters roots and purpose. Thus, Donald Sinden's Benedick is a dogmatic Victorian diarist who suddenly finds himself confronted by his emotions; and what is astonishing is the way Sinden keeps inside the character while also 'playing' the house (notice those frozen stares and sudden sharp turns) exactly like a stand-up comic. But one's final plaudits must be for Judi Dench who makes Beatrice a girl of such emotional directness that even her 'Kill Claudio' silences laughter, and who can barely hold back her tears when she sees Hero getting a husband. . . .

SOURCE: review in the *Guardian* (1 July 1977).

2. *AS YOU LIKE IT*

Anonymous (1919)

Nigel Playfair's Production at the Shakespeare Memorial
Theatre

The 'Shakespearean tradition', or rather the manner of acting
that has come to be known by that name—the over-emphasis of
sound rather than of sense, declamation instead of speech, pauses
and periods in place of natural continuity in the dialogue—all
such things would be wildly out of place in so light and amusing a
piece as this, and *As You Like It* gains point and even delicacy
from being taken quickly, like any modern comedy. The absence
of cuts is another of Mr Playfair's chief ideas, and by the brisk
pace of the whole performance the play in full is enabled to be
given.

The young Rosalind is quite frankly a chatterbox—the poet's
creation of an ideal and almost inhumanly verbose chatterbox.
The amount she has to speak is only equalled by the high opinion
she holds of her own wit. With the exception of those moments
when the growth of her love drives her to sincerity, her mouth
opens only to talk voluminously for the delight she takes in her
own voice. Read again through the play and see how often
Orlando and Celia have but half a dozen words to utter, while
Rosalind always replies with half a page or so. Having so much to
say, what could she do but speak at a gallop, like all copious
talkers?

Miss Athene Seyler takes the part at a tremendous rate, but the
delicacy and perfection of her technique wonderfully bring out
the invincible gaiety and tenderness which lie in Rosalind. For all
that it is her first appearance in Shakespeare, her performance,
from her opening lines to the epilogue, is superb, and one is left
with the conviction that there is nothing in the range of her art

which this young actress cannot do to perfection.

The Orlando of Mr Geoffrey Kerr does not come up to this standard, but is successful nevertheless. If a trifle inexperienced, his performance is both great and charming. Miss Marjorie Holman, a youthful Celia, says her lines clearly and delightfully, and is a so very much younger cousin of whom Rosalind might well be fond.

Mr Nigel Playfair has cast himself for Touchstone, and his choice is well justified. Only a born comedian and finished actor could make the part so great a delight as he does. . . .

A special word of praise must go to the scenery and costumes of Mr Lovat Fraser. The period chosen is the fifteenth century, carried out with meticulous care and producing gorgeous colour. There is a scene, the cool and dim interior of a loggia, looking out between high columns on to the sunlit roofs of a town, which will live long in the memory by the completeness of its beauty. . . .

> SOURCE: extracts from a review by 'H.G.' in the *Manchester Guardian* (23 April 1919).

Anonymous (1936, 1937)

Two Views of Edith Evans as Rosalind

At the Old Vic, 1936

. . . The Rosalind of Edith Evans ranks with the finest acting ever seen in a theatre. It is a piece of divine comedy, every note of which should be recorded on the gramophone for the enlightenment of poor posterity.

The first thing about this Rosalind is that she is really witty. We have seen many jolly Rosalinds—charming hoydens romping through the Forest of Arden with lots of glamour, but saying

things they couldn't possibly think of because they hadn't got it in
them. The Rosalind of Edith Evans is the only one I have ever
seen who *could* think of the things Shakespeare makes her say. She
is equal to her wit instead of being nonplussed by it. She might, in
short, have written the part.

The next thing about this Rosalind is that she is in love. Does
she make you fall in love with her? That is not her business. It is
her business to make you fall in love with Orlando, and Miss
Evans triumphantly makes you experience her emotions. What
art there is in every fling of the head, in every luxuriating stretch
of the arm. I know of no one who can act physical beauty as Miss
Evans can act it. . . .

At the New Theatre, 1937

. . . Miss Evans's appearance does not naturally cast her for
Rosalind; she has to make, to create imaginatively, a boyish—or
a girlish—lightness and impudence that another might bring to
the stage with her, or, in Shakespeare's day, with him; and she
does create the impudence and lightness; she can move like an
arrow, she can roll over the ground in a delight of comedy, she
can mock and glitter and play the fool with a marvellous ease and
grace; and if the boyishness—or girlishness—is not there, it is
because she has decided to reject it in favour of a feminine guile
that is her own edge to the part—her deliberately implied and
original criticism of it. And there lies the key to criticism of her
performance. Upon one who feels of Rosalind that, within all the
dazzle of her pretence, there was a girl in love, Miss Evans's recreation of her may produce such an effect as might be made by a
translation of a Shakespearean lyric into the verse of Corneille.
But even this criticism must itself be qualified at one point. When
Miss Evans was at the Old Vic she missed (in the view of one who
will not exclude passion from Rosalind) the vital transition after
Orlando's exit in Act IV, Scene i. Rosalind, disguised as a boy, has
been pulling Orlando's leg. When he is gone, she cries: 'O coz,
coz, coz, my pretty little coz, that thou didst know how many
fathoms deep I am in love!' At the Old Vic Miss Evans spoke even
that lightly, mockingly—consistently, that is, with her whole
sharply ironic and anti-romantic interpretation of the part.
Suddenly, last night, she said it with passionate feeling—

brilliantly and splendidly right—but, for those who see a lyric in Rosalind, too late!

But for a summary of her whole brilliance, see that leg-pulling of Orlando. If ever the scene is to be better played, may we live to see it! The flash, the tenderness, and the exalted spirit of it are astonishing, and are to be discovered not here only but wherever the authenticity of Rosalind's love is not deeply challenged. Much of this is made possible by Mr Redgrave's Orlando, which is more romantic than Miss Evans's Rosalind, but fully responsive to her wit; by Miss Marie Ney's enchantingly precise Celia; by Mr Quartermaine's Jaques, as light as good wine; and by a *décor* and production which—if again one is to welcome eighteenth-century formalism into Arden—have a rare decorative charm. But everything stands or falls by the view one takes of Rosalind, for Miss Evans is the centre about which all things move. The audience was delighted, and with reason: the thing is aflame with invention. If only, through all the surface comedy, the fathoms beneath were always kept within the reach of imagination!

SOURCES: extracts from unsigned reviews in the *Sunday Pictorial* (15 Nov. 1936), and in *The Times* (12 Feb. 1937).

Rosemary Anne Sisson (1957)

Glen Byam Shaw's Production with Peggy Ashcroft's Rosalind

. . . Peggy Ashcroft's Rosalind is gentle and affectionate rather than high–spirited, as befits a girl first in sorrow for her father's banishment and later altogether overcome by love. This results, perhaps, in the loss of some of the spring-tide gaiety of the play, but in compensation many moments rise to new and natural life—the first meeting between Rosalind and Orlando, in the forest, the plighting of troth, with Rosalind sincere, Orlando ignorant, and Celia half-dismayed at this sudden seriousness, or the beautifully judged mixture of pathos and humour in the fainting scene.

This is, above all, a Rosalind whom we know and feel for, and Jane Wenham's charming little Celia contributes to this effect. Her part is not to play second-fiddle to Rosalind, but rather to counterpoint her music; and, at every moment, this pretty, laughing little Celia is directing our attention to Rosalind, silently commenting on events, and emerging, as though out of invisibility, to tease or comfort her much-tried cousin.

Richard Johnson's Orlando, though very much the country boy, has a natural strength and dignity. He is never made a fool of and he has the essential quality for Orlando of being likeable. Mark Dignam is a tremendously effective Duke Frederick and one remembers with joy the moment when he turns upon the unfortunate Oliver, busy protesting that he never loved his brother, and roars in true Henry VIII style, 'More villain thou!' In the banished Duke, Cyril Luckham finds a genuine goodness which shines out and produces in the feasting scene a moment of deep and almost religious emotion.

To the part of Touchstone Patrick Wymark brings a zest and inventiveness which electrifies every scene in which he appears, whether he is indulging in carefully prepared but scantily performed morning ablutions, wooing his willing, if wayward, Audrey (shrewdly and realistically played by Stephanie Bidmead) or preposterously displaying his Court manners to a placidly uncomprehending William (well played by Tony Robertson). This is a Touchstone in the George Robey tradition, gaining laughter by what he is as well as by what he does and says. . . .

The most difficult part in the play is that of Jaques, and one whose nature, I confess, has never been entirely clear to me, either in reading or seeing the play. Do we laugh with or at Jaques? Does he reveal follies in the world, or is he, like Malvolio, perversely out of step with approved merriment? Robert Harris does not paint a clear picture, either of cynical commentator or misguided melancholic, and somehow, as though perhaps he does not yet himself see Jaques clearly, he fails to bring to his speech or movements that grace and authority which we know he owns, while constant carrying of a Prospero–like staff hampers his gestures. His performance comes to life only briefly in the feasting scene—but perhaps before the season ends he will find Jaques for himself and so teach him to us.

Doreen Aris and Robert Arnold prettily play out the pastoral love of Phebe and Silvius. Donald Eccles's Corin manages to emerge from an accent the effect of which is, at first, somewhat strangling; and Robin Lloyd as Oliver, contrives a quite remarkable transformation from ill-favour to handsomeness, making his conversion credible and his love for Celia and hers for him delightfully appropriate. . . .

As Hymen, brought in, half-magic, half-country-festival, on a flower-decked cart, Gordon Wright does not achieve the necessary grace and resonance. Perhaps special lighting might have helped to throw some mystery upon him, but more poetry is needed, too, in his speaking of the lines, if this rarely-played masque is to achieve the climax it merits.

Clifton Parker's music creates throughout a pleasantly romantic frame, and the songs are beautifully sung by Rex Robinson, as Amiens. The performance of 'A lover and his lass' by the two pages, Peter Whitmarsh and Michael Saunders, assisted by Touchstone and his penny-whistle, can only be described as 'a show-stopper'!

The forest settings by Motley are clear and fresh, their only fault a tendency to monotone. (This effect is perhaps heightened by the rich colour of Frederick's Court and that magnificent procession.) But there are moments of great beauty, too, as when the cold morning light slowly gives way to gold and green as the sun strikes upon the shivering, slender trees. (But should not the eye be more precisely drawn to the mysterious silvery depths of the forest behind the clearing?)

Glen Byam Shaw's production has a flowing ease and gracefulness which, with an artistry which conceals art, draws together this play of pretty fragments and turns it into one firm, swift-moving whole, full of poetic touches and revealing moments. This is an *As You Like It* of more gentleness than gaiety, of more feeling than mirth, and, resting as it does upon heart and not cleverness, it has in it a quality of truth and imaginative freshness which is likely still to increase as time goes by.

Source: extracts from a review in the *Stratford-upon-Avon Herald* (5 April 1957).

J. W. Lambert (1961)

Vanessa Redgrave's Rosalind at the Royal Shakespeare Theatre

I should have liked to ranble for a couple of columns or so about this sweet production: first in an attempt to convey its quality of pure delight; then to brood a little on some interesting shadows cast in Arcadia by an admirable team of players under Michael Elliott's straightforward yet subtle direction; and finally to return and linger with one of those players, Vanessa Redgrave.

When the curtain first rose I thought for a startled moment, observing a watery sun above a bleak horizon, and a big bare tree crowning a knoll on the steeply raked stage, that we were to be given instead of the advertised play an outsize production of *Waiting for Godot*. But as Richard Pilboow's lighting played over Richard Negri's designs, and the play flowed smoothly on, the scenery was, as it should be, forgotten. . . .

In Arden Eric Flynn's Amiens sings gently to the idling exiles some of the bitterest songs in Shakespeare, wooing our ears without ever blunting the edge of the sense ('Most friendship is feigning, most loving mere folly.') And here too Colin Blakeley's baggy, peasant Touchstone, marvellously easy—who shall say now that this is an unrewarding part?—stands sturdily up to Max Adrian's Jaques: which I can hardly praise too highly for its restraint, its cankered pathos, its exquisite timing. Here too is an Audrey (Patsy Byrne) whose floppy affection bears not the smallest trace of comic condescension.

And here too Mr Elliott exercises his sole touch of director's licence—fully justified, for Shakespeare must have written that strange little scene of the foresters, the slaughtered deer and the brooding Jaques, with something more in mind than filling another five minutes. By staging the stalking of the prey, its killing amid bestial cries from men momentarily turned wolves, Mr Elliott gives point to Jaques's wincing—and suggests a reason for his melancholy: the old nightmare of the horns.

But when the sun shines, it shines full—most of all in those fleeting moments when Miss Redgrave escapes from her boy's disguise, snatches off her cap so that her hair tumbles like a flock of goldfinches into sunshine. The complicated relationships involved between Celia (given by Rosalind Knight a devoted shrewishness), Rosalind-Ganymede and Orlando are not perhaps helped by encouraging, or allowing, Mr Bannen's love-lorn wanderer—strangely haunted, like all Mr Bannen's heroes—to respond much more eagerly to the apparent boy than to the dream of the lost girl.

Never mind: Miss Redgrave, whose earlier girls have all managed to be sad-spirited without being woe-begone, smiles away all problems, striking a silver note unheard on our stage for years: a note which sings of radiance without effort, of an unstrained charity. This quality, it is true, has not been much in demand in contemporary drama; perhaps Miss Redgrave's gifts may tempt some lowering dramaturge to explore an Arden of the spirit too long neglected.

SOURCE: extracts from a review in the *Sunday Times* (9 July 1961)

Anonymous (1967)

An All-Male *As You Like It*

Clifford Williams's production of *As You Like It* at the National Theatre . . . has an all-male cast. And each of the four female roles is played with varying degrees of womanliness.

Ronald Pickup's Rosalind, willowy and breastless, is the one most clinically drained of sensuality This Duke's daughter radiates the lanky, coltish androgynous sweetness of a young Garbo, sex without gender, a platonic readiness to accept love as an emotion not yet awoken into physical passion. Curiously enough, with darkly widened eyes and a generously pinked mouth setting off a cheeky beak of a nose, Mr Pickup looks more feminine in the white simulated-leather of his Ganymede disguise than in his floor-length knitted dress at court.

At times, he catches an astonishing, glancing resemblance to a Vanessa Redgrave hovering on the verge of puberty. The device of substituting a man (and not the boy whom Shakespeare would have used) in a part which has provided such rich rewarding opportunities in modern times for women, does not produce any extraordinary revelations. The courting games retain their playful ambiguity and adolescent gaiety whatever the real sex of the participants.

Rosalind's cousinly confident, Celia, becomes a much older lady, when played by Charles Kay as a rather waspish, plain spinster in a mini-skirt and intellectual spectacles. Unlike Janet Suzman in the recent Stratford version, she is no twin rival in beauty to her friend but rather a frumpish wallflower chosen, with unconscious cattiness, by Rosalind to set off her own charms.

The two lesser women's roles demonstrate the extremes to which male actors can go in travestying their own masculinity. Anthony Hopkins's Audrey is completely butch: a beefy, bass-voiced rugger captain in drag parodying almost any muscular sixthformer dragooned into a dress for the school play. Richard Kay, on the other leg, is the complete female personator as Phebe, curvaceous, pretty, husky-voiced and flirtatious, far more of the randy rustic nympho than any actress I can remember.

The sexual reversal dominates and transforms the play less radically than one might imagine partly because Ralph Koltai's psychedelic settings and costumes place the action in some science-fiction dream world of the indeterminate future. The trees of Arden become glass tubes and plastic roofings in punched-out patterns like computer tapes. The clothes are pastel uniforms tricked out with gold and silver PVC capes and boots. Visually, it is a cross between a Pierre Cardin shopwindow and 'The Shape of Things to Come'.

This affectionate alienation of the familiar naturalistic wood-land scenery distances the impact of the transvestism, dampening down the eroticism and heightening the artificiality of the sexual pantomime. No spectator is likely to feel either unduly em-barrassed or improperly excited, but simply entertained as at an abstract ballet.

The other reason that the audience swiftly forgets that men are making love to men is that the production contains two splendidly inventive and comical performances in male roles, one running wittily with, one pushing humorously against, the grain of the text.

Robert Stephens's Jaques is a scholarly eccentric from some, probably Germanic, university: a lean and slippered pantaloon with a withered arm, a bookish stoop and a sour line in pedantic sarcasm which alternately irritates and delights his hearty companions in exile. 'All the world's a stage' comes out a pessimistic lecture, ending with a burst of self-pitying near-hysteria on 'sans everything'.

Derek Jacobi as Touchstone is a defensive, campy, professional comedian in the Frankie Howerd vein who takes all the hoaxes and traps of fortune with a Jewish shrug and a Cockney smack of the lips. It is a perverse but triumphant interpretation which embodies the only moments of music-hall effeminacy in the entire evening.

SOURCE: unsigned review in the *Sunday Telegraph* (8 Oct. 1967).

Peter Thompson (1973)

A Modern-Dress Production at the Royal Shakespeare Theatre

. . . The relationship of Rosalind and Celia was a close and strong one. Maureen Lipman's Celia could match Rosalind passion for passion. It was a pity she was so tall—taller, in fact, than Eileen Atkins's Rosalind. Not only was it in conflict with the text, but it seemed to unsettle Eileen Atkins in the early scenes. Why, after all, should it have been she who put on the denim suit? Where was her 'pretty little coz'? It was a strangely modest performance, almost as if Celia had been strengthened at Rosalind's expense. Derek Smith's Touchstone was . . . eager . . . to explain his jokes. His dialogue with Corin

(Jeffrey Dench's beautifully observed old countryman) was a
fine example of the simultaneous acting of text and footnotes. Is
Touchstone's modern equivalent a rather brash seaside comic,
likely to make a song-and-dance act out of his Rosalind rhymes?
The suggestion didn't offend me, and I enjoyed the magnificent
pattern of his 'quarrel on the seventh cause' set-piece as much as
any of the other people who applauded it. Finally there was
Richard Pasco's Jaques, speaking for an older generation of
theatre-goers in his dislike of what was going on around him. It
was an interpretation built round the 'libertine' and the 'scholar'.
His white suit and hat had seen better days. He smoked without
evident pleasure, wore glasses with cheap frames, and walked
with his knees bent in a strange, small-stepping slouch. He had
the air of a man faced with the alternative of alcoholism or
indigestion. Not only did he know that his breath smelt vile, but
also that no one would dare tell him. Graham Greene would have
understood some of his motives, knowing that every smile can
accompany an unpleasant memory. It was a complete enough
performance to justify, even to demand, this kind of description. . . . [It was clear] how carefully each entrance and exit had
been planned and executed. I was much impressed by the
reticence with which a tensely loving relationship between
Jaques and Duke Senior was indicated. Whilst liking to hear
Jaques talk, the Duke was always nervous of his tongue. The
party was never complete when he wasn't there, and never at
ease when he was. Talking, it was implied, was Jaques's social
art. A man confident enough to conclude a scene as Jaques
concludes II v, knows that his effects depend partly on what he
says, and partly on the fact that it is he who says it: 'I'll go sleep if
I can; if I cannot, I'll rail against all the first-born of Egypt.' I
found myself honestly looking forward to 'All the world's a stage',
and honestly enjoying it. 'Muling and puking' became funny
through Pasco's disgust. Left alone at the dining-table, Jaques
wheezed his way into a long belly-laugh—at the Duke, at life, at
us—which became, in effect, the beginning of the interval. At the
end of the play, having watched the modern frenzy of the
wedding from off the raised stage, he spat out 'so, to your
pleasures' disconcertingly. It was only with some difficulty that
Duke Senior recovered sufficient poise to restart the dance:

Proceed, proceed: we will begin these rites,
As we do trust they'll end, in true delights. [v iv 191–2]

Against the strength of Pasco's Jaques, the Duke seemed dangerously sentimental. . . .

> SOURCE: extracts from 'Shakespeare Straight and Crooked: A Review of the 1973 Season at Stratford', *Shakespeare Survey*, XXVII (1974), 149–50

B. A. Young (1977)

Trevor Nunn's Musical Production at the Royal Shakespeare Theatre

. . . You could not ask for a more charming Orlando and Rosalind than Peter McEnery and Kate Nelligan. This Orlando is still young enough to have no beard, to rush off spontaneously after new ideas like a chicken after corn, and to play silly games with the teenage kid Ganymede that he meets in the forest. Denied his due education, he speaks with a little country burr; but he is well aware of his good birth. His reaction to the Good Duke's revelation—'I am the Duke that loved your father'—is fine: a halt in his chat, a swing round to have a closer look, then a dutiful bending of the knee.

Miss Nelligan's Rosalind isn't funny enough in her earlier exchanges with Celia (Judith Paris), but once she is out of Mr Napier's wintry forest she lets herself go. Rightly her Ganymede looks like nothing but Rosalind in boy's gear, but she uses a grainy voice that suggests a boy in the process of puberty. There is none of the embarrassment that sometimes emerges from her insistence on being wooed by another boy. They're just mucking about together. The burgeoning friendship between them as

Rosalind does her show-off bit about time is most beautifully suggested by both of them.

Alan David works hard as Touchstone, but it would take Keaton himself to persuade me that Touchstone is funny. Nor do I get much joy from Jaques, though Emrys James, uncommonly tidy in a black velvet suit and lace collar, does all he can for him. Graham Crowden's Le Beau (who mysteriously turns up in all the pink ribbons of his court suit for the multiple wedding) is a more engaging fellow.

Ian Gelder and Lynsey Baxter as Silvius and Phebe do not try to get more out of their rustic parts than Shakespeare put into them, but they make up some remarkably pretty scenes with their courtship, and Trevor Nunn hasn't slowed them down with intrusive music, as he has with Touchstone and Audrey at their miscarried nuptials. Music really needs rationing; the little band, visible in the wings, stage left, makes pleasing sounds, but we are used to Shakespearean comedy that goes a little faster than this. Why, the interval has come before the real romance has begun.

SOURCE: review in the *Financial Times* (8 Sept. 1977).

SELECT BIBLIOGRAPHY

TEXTS AND SOURCE-STUDIES

Much Ado About Nothing and *As You Like It* are available in the New Penguin Shakespeare and in the Signet Shakespeare editions. *As You Like It* is also available in the new Arden Shakespeare. The sources of the two comedies are considered in Kenneth Muir, *The Sources of Shakespeare's Plays* (London, 1977) and in Geoffrey Bullough, *Narrative and Dramatic Sources of Shakespeare*, vol. II (London, 1958). The latter reprints some of the texts that Shakespeare used.

BOOKS AND ARTICLES

Besides studies on the comedies represented in this Casebook, the following are recommended for further reading:

(a) *General Books*

C. L. Barber, *Shakespeare's Festive Comedy: A Study of Dramatic Form and Its Relation to Social Custom* (Princeton, N.J., 1959).
Ralph Berry, *Shakespeare's Comedies: Explorations in Form* (Princeton, N.J., 1972).
M. C. Bradbrook, *Shakespeare and Elizabethan Poetry* (London, 1951).
Malcolm Bradbury and David Palmer (eds), *Shakespearian Comedy*: No. 14 of *Stratford-upon-Avon Studies* (London, 1972).
John Russell Brown, *Shakespeare and His Comedies* (London, 1957).
H. B. Charlton, *Shakespearian Comedy* (London, 1938).
Bertrand Evans, *Shakespeare's Comedies* (Oxford, 1960).
Northrop Frye, *A Natural Perspective: The Development of the Shakespearean Comedy and Romance* (London and New York, 1965).
Alexander Leggatt, *Shakespeare's Comedy of Love* (London, 1974).
John Palmer, *Comic Characters of Shakespeare* (London, 1946).
H. M. Richmond, *Shakespeare's Sexual Comedy* (New York, 1971).
Leo Salingar, *Shakespeare and the Traditions of Comedy* (London, 1974).
D. L. Stevenson, *The Love-Game Comedy* (New York, 1946).

(b) *Shorter Studies on 'Much Ado About Nothing'*

Shorter studies on this play include articles in *Scrutiny* by James Smith (13, 1945–46) and T. W. Craik (19, 1952–53); a chapter in A. P. Rossiter's *Angel With Horns* (London, 1961); K. Neill's article 'Much Ado About Claudio: An Acquittal for the Slandered Groom', in *Shakespeare Quarterly*, 3 (1952); and two accounts of the style of the play: by Jonas Barrish, in *Rice University Studies*, 60 (1974), and by Brian Vickers, in his *The Artistry of Shakespeare's Prose* (London, 1968).

(c) *Shorter Studies on 'As You Like It'*

Shorter studies on this play include an article by James Smith in *Scrutiny*, 9 (1940), and by Harold Jenkins in *Shakespeare Survey*, 8 (1955); J. L. Halio's 'No Clock in the Forest', in *Studies in English Literature*, 2 (1962); John Shaw's 'Fortune and Nature in *As You Like It*', in *Shakespeare Quarterly*, 6 (1955); Madeleine Doran's 'Yet am I inland bred', in James G. McManaway (ed.), *Shakespeare 400* (New York and London, 1964); and Michael Jamieson's short book on the play in Arnold's *Studies in English Literature* (London, 1965). The style of the play is considered by Brian Vickers (see previous section), and by John Russell Brown in a chapter of his *Shakespeare's Dramatic Style* (London, 1970).

NOTES ON CONTRIBUTORS

JAMES AGATE (1877–1947): Drama critic, especially for the *Sunday Times*, 1923–47.

DAVID ERSKINE BAKER (1730–67): Writer on the theatre, author of a drama, *The Muse of Ossian* (1763) and translator (1763) of the Italian comedy, *La Serva Padrona*.

JOHN BARBER: Theatre critic of the *Daily Telegraph*.

SYLVAN BARNET: Professor of English at Tufts University, Massachusetts, and General Editor of the Signet Shakespeare.

GEORG BRANDES (1842–1927): Danish literary critic, with an international reputation during his lifetime.

MICHAEL BILLINGTON: Deputy drama critic of *The Times* from 1965 to 1971 and currently drama critic of *The Guardian* and film critic of the *London Illustrated News* and the *Birmingham Post*.

JOHN RUSSELL BROWN: Professor of English in the University of Sussex and, since 1973, an Associate Director of the National Theatre. He was previously head of the department of Drama and Theatre Arts in the University of Birmingham. He has published books on the twentieth-century theatre and on Shakespeare, and has edited the new Arden *Merchant of Venice* and the Casebook on *Antony and Cleopatra*.

LEONARD DIGGES (1588–1635): poet, translator and classical scholar.

EDWARD DOWDEN (1843–1913): Professor of English Literature at

Trinity College, Dublin; a noted Shakespearean scholar and literary critic, his publications include *Shakspere: His Mind and Art* (1875) and *Shakspere Primer* (1877).

RUTH ELLIS: In her life-time she reviewed many plays, especially for the *Stratford-upon-Avon Herald*.

BARBARA EVERETT: Formerly Fellow of Somerville College, Oxford, her publications include studies of John Donne and W. H. Auden, and she has edited *All's Well That Ends Well* in the New Penguin Shakespeare.

DAME HELEN GARDNER: Emeritus Professor of English Literature in the University of Oxford. Her publications include studies of T. S. Eliot and Milton, *The Business of Criticism* (1960) and *Religion and Literature* (1971), and she has edited the poems and prose of John Donne, and the new version of the *Oxford Book of English Verse*.

SHERMAN HAWKINS: Professor of English in the University of Rochester, New York State.

WILLIAM HAZLITT (1778–1830): Essayist and literary critic. His articles and reviews were collected in *A View of the English Stage* (1818); and his essays in literary criticism—especially *The Characters of Shakspeare's Plays* (1817–18)—had a powerful influence on popular appreciation of Shakespeare.

SAMUEL JOHNSON (1709–84): Poet, novelist, critic, lexicographer, dramatist and editor of Shakespeare's works (eight volumes), with the famous Preface (1765).

BEN JONSON (1572–1637): Poet and dramatist, and friend of Shakespeare.

J. W. LAMBERT: Arts Editor, until his recent retirement, of the *Sunday Times*.

AGNES LATHAM: Her publications include the new Arden *As You Like It* and she has edited the poems of Sir Walter Ralegh.

WESTLAND MARSTON (1819–90): Drama critic and author of poetic dramas.

MIRIAM and PAUL MUESCHKE teach at the University of Michigan.

J. R. MULRYNE: Professor of English in the University of Warwick and a general editor of the Revels Plays, in which series he has edited Middleton's *Women Beware Women*.

D. J. PALMER: Professor of English in the University of Manchester and a general editor of *Stratford-upon-Avon Studies*. His publications include *The Rise of English Studies* (1965) and the Casebooks on *Twelfth Night* and *The Tempest*.

WILLIAM RICHARDSON (1743–1814): A Professor of Humanity in the University of Glasgow, his publications included *Shakespeare's Dramatic characters* (1774).

ROSEMARY ANNE SISSON: Playwright, novelist and theatre critic.

DONALD A. STAUFFER: Formerly Professor of English at Princeton University. In addition to his study of Shakespeare, he has published books on Yeats, on American poetry and on the art of biography before 1800.

A. C. SWINBURNE (1837–1909): Poet and critic; his writings on Elizabethan literature include *A Study of Shakespeare* (1880) and *The Age of Shakespeare* (1909).

PETER THOMSON: Professor of Drama in the University of Exeter.

SIR FREDERICK WEDMORE (1844–1921): Writer on art, drama and literature, and author of short stories and belles-lettres.

B. A. YOUNG: Theatre critic of the *Financial Times*

DAVID YOUNG: Professor of English at Oberlin College, Ohio. In addition to his study of Shakespeare's pastoral plays, his publications include *Something of Great Constancy* (a book on *A Midsummer Night's Dream*).

INDEX

Page numbers in bold type denote essays or extracts in this Casebook; entries in small capitals denote characters in plays.